Joseph Smith
and the Book of Enoch

Joseph Smith and the Book of Enoch
The Influence on Mormon Theology

MARK LINES

McFarland & Company, Inc., Publishers
Jefferson, North Carolina

ISBN (print) 978-1-4766-9015-5
ISBN (ebook) 978-1-4766-4780-7

Library of Congress and British Library
cataloguing data are available

Library of Congress Control Number 2023013924

© 2023 Mark Lines. All rights reserved

No part of this book may be reproduced or transmitted in any form or by any means, electronic or mechanical, including photocopying or recording, or by any information storage and retrieval system, without permission in writing from the publisher.

On the cover: "Enoch" by William Blake, Medium: Modified lithograph printed in relief from a stone; one state, 21.6 × 30.9 cm (Purchase, Joseph Pulitzer and Brooke Russell Astor Bequests and 2005 Benefit Fund, 2013, The Met); *background:* © Shutterstock

Printed in the United States of America

*McFarland & Company, Inc., Publishers
Box 611, Jefferson, North Carolina 28640
www.mcfarlandpub.com*

Table of Contents

Preface 1

Introduction: Patterns and Parallels in Scripture Scholarship ... 7
- Stories and Patterns 7
- Motifs 10
- Borrowed Traditions and Cultural Influence 11
- Studying Joseph Smith and Early Mormon Scripture .. 15
- The Patternist-Historian Approach 16

Chapter One. An American Farm Boy 23

Chapter Two. Who Is Enoch? 33
- Enoch in the Old Testament 33
- Enoch in the New Testament 36
- Enoch in the Apocrypha 37
- Enoch in the Book of Jasher 37
- Enoch in the Book of Jubilees 43
- Enoch in Mormon Doctrine 46

Chapter Three. The Book of Enoch (1 Enoch) 47

Chapter Four. Ground Rules for This Historical Question ... 54

Chapter Five. Joseph Smith's Access to the Book of Enoch .. 59

Chapter Six. Substantial (and Important) Similarities 63
- Joseph's First Visions 63
- Another Vision with Another Angel: The Angel Moroni .. 69

Chapter Seven. The Book of Moses 72
- Moses 1: The Prologue to Genesis 74
    - 1. Similar Openings and Settings 75
    - 2. Moses Atop a Mountain, Speaks with God and Sees His Glory .. 76
    - 3. Moses Is Shown All Things of the Past and Things Yet to Come .. 76

Table of Contents

- 4. Moses Is Commanded to Write — 77
- 5. Revelations for His Followers — 77
  1. Similar Openings and Settings — 79
  2. Taken Atop a Mountain to Speak with God and Sees His Glory — 79
  3. Moses and Enoch Are Shown All Things Past and Things Yet to Come — 80
  4. Moses and Enoch Are Both Commanded to Write Books — 80
  5. Both Are to Write Books for Their Followers "Who Believe" — 81
- 6. Transfiguration to Speak with God Face to Face — 82
- 7. Falling to the Ground — 82
- 8. Satan Is Rebuked, He Fears and Departs — 83
- 9. Beholding the Numberless on the Earth, from the Beginning and Without End — 86
- 10. Moses and Enoch Both Ask What Is This World? And Why Creation? — 86
- 11. The Purpose: Eternal Life and Everlasting Glory of Mankind — 87
- 12. A Warning That the Children of Men Will Turn Against God's Books — 88
- Moses 2–5 (Genesis 1–4) — 88
- Secret Combinations and Death Penalty Oaths — 92

Chapter Eight. Joseph Smith's Enoch — 93
- Mahujah, Mahijah and Mehujael — 95
- Joseph's Enoch Found in Translation — 98
- Joseph's Enoch as Another Elias — 101
- Enoch's Patriarchal Lineage — 103
- The Wild Man Out of the Wilderness — 104
- Literary Parallels Between Moses and Enoch — 109
  - Bowing or Falling to the Earth — 109
  - Waters in Their Course and Turning Their Ways — 109
  - A "Spirit Prison" — 110
  - God's "Earth Is His Footstool" — 111
  - Men Are Carnal and Devilish — 111
- A Scribe of Righteousness — 111
- Joseph and Sidney Rigdon's Enoch Emerges — 114
  - Again, Speaking with God and Seeing All Generations of the World — 114
  - Angels Declaring Wo! Wo! to the Inhabitants of the Earth — 115

Table of Contents

- Heavenly Weeping on Account of the Earth ... 116
- Enoch's Son Methuselah Prophesies in Moses and the Book of Enoch ... 117
- Enoch Foretells of Noah Building an Ark, and His Family Saved from the Flood ... 117
- Corruption of "Sons of Men," "Giants" and Choosing Wives Among Daughters of Men ... 118
- Enoch Foresees the Coming of the Son of Man ... 119

Chapter Nine. Zion—A New Jerusalem ... 124

Chapter Ten. The Mormon Temple Endowment ... 132
- A Temple-Building People with a Promised Endowment ... 133
- Mormon Temple Allusions and Book of Enoch Parallels ... 140
  - Latter-day Saints, Given Secret Names, Clothed in Garments and Anointed as Kings, Queens, Priests and Priestesses ... 141
  - Kings, Princes and Priests ... 142
  - Queens and Priestesses ... 142
  - Clothed in Garments ... 143
  - Secret Names ... 144
  - Latter-day Saints ... 145
- The Archangel Michael/Adam Creator Doctrine ... 145
- ACT I: The Cosmos and Creation ... 149
- Earth: A Footstool of God, for the Dominion of the Sons of Man ... 150
- ACT II: The Garden ... 152
  - A "New World" and Renewed Awakening ... 153
  - "The tree of knowledge also was there" ... 154
  - Adam and Enoch Are Ashamed, Naked and Wear Veils ... 154
  - Casting Out and Condemning Lucifer ... 155
  - Defeated, Satan Departs ... 157
- ACT III: Knock and It Shall Be Opened Unto You ... 157
  - Seeking Light and Divine Knowledge ... 158
  - Secret Names and Swearing Oaths ... 159
  - The Celestial Room; the Throne Room ... 161

Chapter Eleven. Mormon Cosmology: The Book of Abraham and 1 Enoch ... 163
- "An existence previous to the formation of the luminaries of heaven" ... 164
  - The War in Heaven ... 164
  - A Star Fell from Heaven ... 165

Table of Contents

- ○ Other Stars Also Cast Out from Heaven with the First — 166
- ○ He Shall Dwell Among His Elect — 166
- ○ The Judgment Throne — 166
- ○ The Judged Are Cast into a Lake of Fire and Brimstone — 167
- ○ Tens of Thousands of Angels Surrounding God's Throne — 167
- ○ A New Heaven and Earth — 167
- The First Estate — 168
- The Second Estate — 170
- The Preexistence — 172
- A Spirit Prison — 173
- Multiple Heavens and Celestial and Terrestrial Kingdoms — 175
- Echoes of Enoch in the Book of Abraham — 179
  - ○ Keeping Records for the Benefit of Future Generations — 179
  - ○ A Vision of the Celestial Stars, and the Names of the Great Ones — 180
  - ○ Observing the Times and Seasons and Heavenly Operations — 181
  - ○ A Reckoning of a Day on Earth in the Lord's Time — 181
  - ○ A Book of the Revolutions of the Luminaries — 182
  - ○ Inferior and Superior Luminaries of the Night and Day — 182

Chapter Twelve. Gods of Our Own Worlds — 184
- "The holy, *holy*, Lord of spirits fills the whole world of spirits" — 186
- Counsels of Gods in the Heavens — 189
- Infinite Intelligences — 190
- Light of the World — 191

Chapter Notes — 195
Bibliography — 205
Index — 211

Preface

> "And I, Enoch, alone saw the vision, the ends of all things: and no man shall see as I have seen."
> —1 Enoch 19:3[1]

The year before his martyrdom, in 1843, Joseph Smith wrote a poetical rendering of a vision he first recorded in February 1832, found today in Section 76 of the Doctrine and Covenants ("D&C") (a book of modern-day Mormon scripture). Joseph's 1843 poem was titled "The Vision," written to his dear friend (and ghostwriter) W.W. Phelps, who published it upon receipt in the church-owned periodical the *Times and Seasons* in Nauvoo, Illinois.[2] Rare among most of the historical records of the Church of Jesus Christ of Latter-day Saints (LDS Church), this poetry is actually written by Joseph Smith, the uneducated farm boy himself—a fact that is revealing as one reads through it entirely. In a few of its many verses it reads,

> I, Joseph, the prophet, in spirit beheld, And the eyes of the inner man truly did see Eternity sketch'd in a vision from God, Of what was, and now is, and yet is to be.
> ... To the church of old Enoch, and of the first born: And gen'ral assembly of ancient renown'd, Whose names are all kept in the archives of heav'n, As chosen and faithful, and fit to be crown'd.

Joseph Smith recorded seeing in his 1832 vision the inhabitants of many worlds (D&C 76:18–24), a fallen "angel of God" who was "thrust down from the presence of God" (76:25–27), the coming of a "Son of Man" (76:16), a spirit prison (76:73), the great judgment and destruction of the world when sinners shall "go away into the lake of fire and brimstone, with the devil and his angels" (76:30–36), and "celestial" and "terrestrial" kingdoms of heavenly glory for the elect saints (76:70–71). He refers directly to the mysterious biblical prophet Enoch by name. All of

Preface

these are also found in the apocryphal Book of Enoch (1 Enoch), first published in English in 1821, almost a decade before Joseph Smith published his Book of Mormon (1830), his own "visions of Enoch" (Book of Moses, 1831), and before he recorded his first "First Vision" account (1832). It's a natural question to ask whether Joseph Smith's revelations and writings bear any similarities with the 1821 Book of Enoch given its publication prior to Smith's writings.

Indeed, Joseph's literary works and recorded visions are replete with similar apocalyptic-type visions, in which prophets ascend into clouds, or personages descend in pillars of fire or clouds of light to speak face to face. Mormon beginnings are founded on such splendor.

The Book of Enoch opens with the prophet Enoch being taken in a vision to a high mountaintop, where he speaks face to face with the "Mighty One." Enoch is shown the repositories of the "superior and inferior kingdom," and sees all inhabitants of the earth throughout all time. He is warned that the earth will be destroyed because of the corruption of mankind. The Book of Enoch tells tales of wars and rumors of war, both in a "preexistence" and on Earth. God's fallen children (the "Nephilum") are corrupted by carnal desires, and taught to make swords, shields, and breastplates to wage great battles against one another. The book describes the fine workmanship of their ornate metal tools and jewelry and how, having been corrupted, they became divided as a cursed race. It describes their body paint, makeup, expensive clothing, and how they use stones to deceive. The Book of Enoch also warns of secret combinations, sealed books and secret names, seemingly echoing passages in the Book of Mormon.

Like other ancient Jewish writings, the Book of Enoch includes Enoch's prophecy of a Tree of Knowledge, and a vision of a Tree of Life with its beautiful and fragrant fruit wafting in the midst of dark valleys and streams, deep abysses and buildings without foundations. It describes how Enoch asks those angels accompanying him to explain the meaning of what he has seen. The angels oblige and explain that the fruit of the Tree of Life is an endowment to be given to his elect saints who partake and rejoice with one another as they move toward the path leading to the gates of eternal celestial kingdoms of God.

Remarkably, the Book of Enoch, like the Book of Mormon, foretells of the coming of the Son of man—even the Messiah—*before* Jesus of Nazareth was born. It describes how this "Son of man" would descend from heaven with the voice of God announcing the descension and inviting those who see him to hear him. It describes Enoch, in another

Preface

vision, taken up to God's heavenly temple, where Enoch sees God seated on his throne with glory beyond description. These are interesting parallels we find throughout early Mormon tradition and scripture.

It might even be said that the prophet Enoch can be likened to the Book of Mormon prophet Lehi. Both were apocalyptic dreamers and recorded their visions. Both prophets were commanded to call the people to repentance before an imminent day of destruction (Lehi, Jerusalem; Enoch, the flood). Enoch was a dreamer, recording multiple visions. Lehi's children jeered him as "a visionary man" (Nephi 2:11). Even his wife, Sariah, "complained against my father, telling him that he was a visionary man" (1 Nephi 5:2). Lehi called himself "a visionary man; for if I had not seen the things of God in a vision I should not have known" (1 Nephi 1:4).

Unfortunately, the extent of Lehi's visionary dreams we'll never know. They were lost. In the opening chapter of the Book of Mormon, Nephi explains, "I, Nephi, do not make a full account of the things which my father hath written, for he has written many things which he saw in visions and in dreams ... of which I shall not make a full account" (1 Nephi 1:16). The full written account of Lehi's visions (the acclaimed lost "Book of Lehi") is believed to have been recorded in the first 116 pages of the original Book of Mormon manuscript—the same "lost 116 pages" that were lost in 1828, after Joseph entrusted them to his scribe (and Book of Mormon financier) Martin Harris. So, we don't know exactly what Lehi dreamed or wrote of—at least not 116 pages' worth of dreams and visions.

But we know *some* of them, including the brief description recorded by his son, Nephi, in his opening chapter. As Lehi prayed, he had a vision in which appeared a "pillar of fire" that descended before him and dwelt before him (1 Nephi 1:6). As this vision unfurled, Lehi "cast himself upon his bed, being overcome with the Spirit and the things which he had seen" (1 Nephi 1:7). He "saw and heard much; and because of the things which he saw and heard he did quake and tremble exceedingly" (1 Nephi 1:6). Then, still while on his bed, Lehi was "carried away in a vision, even that he saw the heavens open, and he thought he saw God sitting upon his throne surrounded with numberless concourses of angels in the attitude of singing and praising their God" (1 Nephi 1:8).

The Book of Enoch includes remarkably similar phrases and records visionary experiences like Lehi's. Consider, for example, Enoch's visions:

Preface

> And after this I saw another dream, and explained it all to thee, my son. Enoch arose and said to his son Mathusala; To thee, my son, will I speak. Hear my word; and *incline thine ear to the visionary dream of thy father.* Before I married thy mother Edna, *I saw a vision on my bed;*
>
> ...
>
> I lay down in the midst of them: I awoke and saw the whole. This is the vision which I saw lying down and waking.
>
> While I was looking on, they flowed on account of what *I saw; for all was come and gone by; every individual circumstance respecting the conduct of mankind was seen by me.*
>
> In that night I remembered my former dream; and therefore wept and was troubled, because I had seen that vision
>
> [Enoch LXXXIV. SECT. XVII:1 and XXXXIX:48–50, emphasis added].

And, like Lehi, Enoch also was lifted up in a vision of God seated on his throne in the heavens, which caused him to fall on his face, quaking and trembling:

> I saw that the heaven of heavens shook; that it shook violently; and that the powers of the Most High, and the angels, thousands of thousands, and myriads of myriads, were agitated with great agitation. And when I looked, the Ancient of days was sitting on the throne of his glory, while the angels and saints were standing around him. A great trembling came upon me, and terror seized me
>
> [LIX. SECT. X:1–2].

Such tightly corresponding literary parallels are intriguing.

Joseph Smith's views of cosmology and theology unique to early Mormonism—specifically that man's ultimate celestial glory is to become the King of kings, even a God of his own world—have indicia of influence from extrabiblical sources. Apocalyptic visions, visiting angels and a gathering of the "saints" in the last days are just a few of the LDS-specific-sounding refrains found in the Book of Enoch, an ancient book of Jewish scripture that was believed to be lost to the Western world until a copy was found in the 16th century, buried in the dust among other neglected religious works in a dilapidated Ethiopian monastery, then brought forth and translated from the obscure characters on its pages into English in 1821.[3] Ancient lost scripture, found.

The similarity of one thing—any symbol, theme, metaphor or message—to another is measured in the listener's or reader's mind. Parallels and similarities are in the eyes or ears of a listener or reader when comparing two familiar things. This book offers a comparison sampling between Smith's recorded history and revealed visions and similar

Preface

motifs and story lines found in the Book of Enoch. We also consider aspects of early Mormon doctrine, particularly Joseph Smith's revealed temple endowment and his evolving cosmological ideas, which appear to be influenced by the ancient Enoch writings and traditions. Beyond questions of stylistic influence and textual parallels that Smith's writings share with the Book of Enoch, Smith's literary works should perhaps be more widely praised as restorations of Enochic traditions that were lost or excluded from early canonized scripture.

Introduction: Patterns and Parallels in Scripture Scholarship

> "For a book of remembrance we have written among us, according to the pattern given by the finger of God."
> —Book of Moses 6:46

Stories and Patterns

We are storytellers. We share stories that mean something to us and that we want to share with others. We always have and always will. When we share a story, we relate it to other stories with similar meanings or morals. The problem with language is that it's beautifully imperfect. It can be, as Joseph Smith described it, a "prison, almost as it were, of paper, pen and ink, and of a crooked, broken, scattered and imperfect language."[1] In the process of sharing any story, new stories eventually spread, and others are lost or forgotten.

What was the first story ever? How and where did it start? What was it about? Our Bible tells us it began with light.[2] *Light's on!* That's a short story. Or a singularly endless one. It depends on how you read it. Either way, it's a start. And whether it's true or not, at least the Bible tells us it started "in the beginning." But don't all stories start there?

Not necessarily. Not if there is *another* story behind the story. A source.

How or whenever our first folklore began, our most primitive stories must have been told to pass long nights under the darkest of skies.

Introduction

They may have been told through a warm touch, pantomimed by the light of a fire, scratched in stone or seen only once a year through megaliths aligned with a winter morning's sunrise. It was the heavens that offered our forerunners the warmth of the day and lights in the dark of night.

LDS astrophysicist R. Grant Athay wrote in his 1968 essay "Worlds Without Number: The Astronomy of Enoch, Abraham, and Moses,"

> The history of civilization is filled with folklore of the moon, sun, and stars. The farmer is alerted for frost when the moon is full. He plants by the moon and harvests by the Harvest Moon. A month later he harvests game by the Hunter's Moon under the constellation of Orion the Hunter. In the spring we celebrate Easter on a date set in accordance with the full moon following the spring equinox, a practice stemming from ancient tradition identifying the spring moon with the rejuvenation of earth life following the winter's death-like sleep. These and other traditions have carried over into our day.[3]

Our first stories were told to explain the patterns of the sun, moon and seasons. We shared stories of the stars and about the figures they formed, and to explain why some wander and others fall. We still tell these same stories. Before there was any Genesis, Exodus and ultimate revelations, our stories were about our beginnings, the journey and something to be learned and shared with others along the way. So, I guess "let there be light" sounds about right for the beginning of any story. And, not surprisingly, the light motif is a popular and repeat device on the stage of biblical stories.

We shed light with others through language, allegories, poems, songs and symbols, through familiar patterns. We rely on patterns. We share stories, art and music based on what we know. All stories, songs, science, literature, art and cultures—our own beliefs—are based and built on something else. We stand on each other's shoulders, learning "line upon line, precept upon precept, here a little and there a little," just as the Book of Mormon prophet Nephi prophesied in 2 Nephi 28:30. Or was it Isaiah who first taught us that? (See Isaiah 28:10: "For precept must be upon precept, precept upon precept; line upon line, line upon line, here a little and there a little.") Regardless of who wrote it first, it was apparently worth repeating. And that's the point. Someone was obviously influenced by the other, borrowing the other's language because it is meaningful and memorable. We quote and borrow words that make sense, and repeating them makes a pattern. Attention is captured by familiarity.

Stories about our beginnings are stories about *creation* because we want to know how something came out of chaos. Our favorite stories get

Introduction: Patterns and Parallels in Scripture Scholarship

repeated. They always will be repeated, adapted, enlarged and aggrandized because we want to experience and relive them meaningfully again and again. We do the same with traditions and holidays. We set and follow meaningful patterns, and add more meaning as we go, and as we learn. Stories and traditions evolve into other stories *sui generis*, with the source stories sometimes becoming masked or lost, and sometimes resurfacing on their own. You can't know how similar two stories are if you're not familiar with both. *Spot a pattern; see a story's source.*

Stories are told and unfold through patterns that we recognize. A story emerges from the *information* coming from the one telling the story, filtered through the *information* available to the one listening. Captured by something, our mind's eye searches for patterns.[4] Finding something familiar, our brains attach and make sense of it. How much sense it makes depends on how much information our algorithmic brains have available to filter through. We'll see an image building before our eyes as the story is told, with the ending unfolding itself before us as well. We hear and experience music the same way. Our brains are pretty well equipped for predicting the future in real time based on what we take as cause and effect. In his book *The Information: A History, a Theory, a Flood*, author James Gleick explained this emergence process:

> In the stream of words past the ear or eye, we sense not just the items one by one but their rhythms and tones, which is to say their music. We, the listener or the reader, do not hear, or read, one word at a time; we get messages in groupings small and large.[5]

What story unfolds from the storyteller is as simple or intricate as the listener cares to make it.

We are influenced by stories that inspire us. The same stories have been told and will be retold with different endings, audiences and agenda, and always will be. They have different characters, with different messages. Beloved characters get recast in new lights and lines along the way. Similar stories are frequently told through the use of motifs and symbolism. The words and message are in the analogies, but only if one recognizes them. Once the connection is made, the stories can be linked.

Take *Romeo and Juliet*, *West Side Story*, *The Outsiders* and *Grease*, to name just a few familiar examples. These are different stories with different people, places and times, and written for completely different audiences. Each is a story about youngsters from different sides of the

Introduction

tracks that fall in love, but society battles it out trying to tell them they can't. These are the same story, aren't they? Well, certainly they share a recognizable motif—one seen as a pattern across the stories.

Pattern recognition is a tool in historical criticism, a critical investigation of the origin of ancient texts to understand "the world behind the text."[6] This is source analysis. More specific areas of critical methodology include textual and source criticism, or trying to ascertain the original wording, meaning, and (if possible), author of a text. Scholars apply the historical-critical method, critically comparing biblical texts against any existing known textual artifacts. They look for and find textual and historical contextual similarities to identify literary genres, and sometimes to confirm authorship. Generally speaking, they look at literary parallels and similarities that resurface as recurring themes, archetypes and features in and among written works. Motifs, patterns, echoes and allusions in literary scripts tell stories within stories, and they are stories behind the stories. Authors use symbols, structure, analogies and themes intentionally because they mean something.

Motifs

Motifs are parallels. In literary works, holy scripture included, "motifs are images, symbols, or themes that are repeated throughout a piece of literature or across more than one piece of literature so as to form a pattern."[7] Biblical scholars refer to textual parallels in terms of "formal and informal quotations, allusions, echoes, and parallels."[8] In his book *Echoes of Scripture in the Letters of Paul*, Richard Hays takes a critical look at Paul's epistles and the parallels to be found in other known literary sources, generalizing them as "quotation, allusion, and echo" used in a "spectrum of intertextual reference, moving from the explicit to the subliminal" to convey the message.[9]

A familiar Bible motif, for example, is that of the barren woman who is miraculously able to conceive. We find our first example in Genesis with Sarah, the wife of Abraham, who is promised to be the father of a great nation with innumerable descendants (Genesis 12:2). The only problem is Sarah is barren and too old (Genesis 11:30). Nevertheless, she becomes pregnant and gives birth to a son, Isaac. After almost being sacrificed by his own father, Isaac survives to marry Rebekah, who is, as you might have guessed, also barren. She nevertheless becomes pregnant and delivers twins, one of whom is Jacob. This is the same Jacob later called Israel, the father of twelve sons who are the heads of the twelve tribes of Israel—that great nation of Abraham's descendants as previously prophesied (Genesis 25:21–24). Miraculous indeed. And it's worth repeating.

The Old Testament motif does in fact continue as Samson's previously barren mother gives him the gift of life (Judges 12:2), and then Ruth, who becomes the no-longer-barren mother of Obed (Ruth 4:17–22). These miraculous conceptions again resulted in some of the heroes of the Hebrew Bible. Samson helped the Israelites defeat the Philistines, and Samuel was the last of the judges, who also had the distinction of anointing King David. This barren woman, miraculous birth and anointed-one motif becomes important both as a literary device for our ancient authors of Hebraic writings, as well as in establishing a claim for divine lineage to be the Messiah ("the anointed"), or the King of the children of Israel. As we learn in the listed genealogies of Jesus in the New Testament, King David was the grandson of Obed, son of the once-barren Ruth (Matt 1:5; Luke 3:32).

We can't help but find this Old Testament motif in the beginnings of the New Testament. Before Jesus was born, Elizabeth is presumed to be barren until being visited by the angel Gabriel and miraculously conceiving, giving birth to John the Baptist. And, of course, we know of the miraculous and immaculate conception of her cousin Mary and birth of her son Jesus, the son of God.

Borrowed Traditions and Cultural Influence

Stories are told in similar frameworks that should be familiar to the reader. Intentionally or subliminally, motifs and echoes have been inserted in oral and literary history since both began. The "barren woman, miraculous birth & resulting hero" motif is not exclusively Jewish or biblical. Miraculous births by the intervention of a deity or the supernatural are found in Hellenistic (Greek) and Greco-Roman mythology. Zeus and Apollo traditions include this same story. Perseus was the son of the god Zeus by the virgin Danae, the daughter of King Argos. Romulus and Remus, founders of Rome, were said to have been born of a Vestal Virgin whose father was Mars, the God of War. It was said that Plato was born of the union of a virgin and Apollo. Even Alexander the Great and the Roman Caesars were claimed to be virgin born. Similar stories infiltrated Palestine societies in the wake of

Introduction

waves of years of imperial predation and exile from the Greeks, Assyrians, Babylonians and Romans. There is little wonder that similar stories span across differing cultures and locations as a result of conquest and assimilation over time.

Case in point, Babylonian tradition in still-existing ancient stone inscriptions hail their kings as gods of divine conception:

> I am Nabu-kuder-usur ... the first-born son of Nebu-pal-sur, King of Babylon. The god Bel himself created me, the god Marduk engendered me, and deposited himself the germ of my life in the womb of my mother.[10]

Not surprisingly, similar traditions of supernatural inception are found in Zoroaster and Egyptian mythology, as well as Hinduism, Buddhism, Islam and various traditions of cultures worldwide.

Patterns, parallels and motifs are found everywhere in ancient Jewish writings, most familiarly the Old Testament. Biblical writing style includes both inserting sub-narrative characters and sub-stories, and actually structuring the text itself in patterns recognizable by the eyes when read, and the ears when heard. The patterns themselves create music—literally—in both sound and rhythm. We've retained our most important stories over time by repeating, reversing and rhyming words and phrases, and adding time and measure. Songs and poetry are written and remembered this way.

Ancient Jewish writers used literary devices known as chiastic structure and parallelism that can be found throughout the Bible. *Chiasmus* (or *chiasm*) is from the Greek word meaning "crossing," or to place crosswise to form the shape of an X. This is a rhetorical device that, very simply speaking, repeats words and phrases in reverse order, or compounds words or phrases with equivalent meanings to add emphasis and draw upon other familiar ideas.

They can be simple or very elaborately structured throughout a text. There are differing versions too, including "synonymous parallelism," when the second line reflects that expressed in the repeating lines, or "parabolic parallelism," the use of simile or metaphor to compare the subjects of corresponding lines. There's also "contrasting parallelism," where opposite ideas, an antithesis, are presented in two (or more) lines. While the field of study was not more widely popularized with available publications until the latter end of the 17th century, Brigham Young University professor John W. Welch writes about chiasm and chiasmus in the ancient Jewish texts, noting that since its discovery among academics, biblical scholars have "identified fascinating chiasms in

Introduction: Patterns and Parallels in Scripture Scholarship

virtually every book of the Bible, whether the poetry of the Psalms or the prose of the Gospels, whether in law, prophecy, or epistolary."[11]

A very simple example of chiasmus is found in Mark 2:27: "The Sabbath was made for man, and not man for the Sabbath." The reversal of words catches your attention and causes you to unscramble it to hear the message. Proverbial wisdom is still taught this way today using the same structural parallelism, often without thinking about it. Common idioms like "no pain; no gain" or "when the going gets tough, the tough get going" are based on this same rhetorical pattern. It has been used by some influential people in very historic moments:

> The only thing we have to fear is fear itself.
> —Franklin D. Roosevelt, March 4, 1933,
> Presidential inaugural address.

> Ask not what your country can do for you but what you can do for your country.
> —John F. Kennedy, January 20, 1961,
> Presidential inaugural address.

> That's one small step for man,[12] one giant leap for mankind.
> —Neil Armstrong, July 20, 1969, Moon landing.

Some of our best-known proverbs, hymns and psalms are structured this way, using parallelism. The most common pattern is composed of just two lines, the second line repeating, comparing, or contrasting that which was expressed in the first line. Directly from a most famous biblical poet and psalmist, King David's Book of Proverbs, we find a few simple examples:

> A false balance is abomination to the Lord;
> But a just weight is his delight
> [Proverbs 11:1].

> As the cold of snow in the time of harvest,
> so is a faithful messenger to them that send him:
> For he refresheth the soul of his masters
> [Proverbs 25:13].

> As the door turneth upon his hinges,
> so doth the slothful upon his bed
> [Proverbs 26:14].

This same chiastic pattern has been spotted in verses of the Book of Mormon. A simple, but more elaborate example (among several

Introduction

others)[13] is found in the Book of Mormon's Alma 34:9. Here, we can both visually spot and hear the chiastic pattern by emphasizing the repeating words or ideas, line by line, where we have a turn, reversal and ending back where we began:

For it is ***expedient*** that an ***atonement should be made***;
    for according to the great plan of the Eternal God ***there must be an atonement made***,
        or else ***all*** mankind must ***unavoidably perish***;
            yea, ***all are hardened***;
        yea, ***all*** are ***fallen and*** are ***lost***, and ***must perish***
    except it be through ***the atonement***
which it is ***expedient should be made***.

The intent is to create a pattern. Presenting the pattern allows the reader to follow in step, gaining the meaning with the message, to express the idea in a way it will be remembered. As Professor John Welch noted, these devices are employed by authors "to enhance appreciation for a composition's logic, impact, and beauty; to link form with substance; to clarify conceptual connections or contrasts; and to aid in studies of comparative literature."[14] These are literary devices mastered by Dr. Seuss. Indeed, our most familiar proverbs, psalms, stories and songs are so memorable because of these ancient literary devices. This is why nursery rhymes rhyme and choruses repeat—so we remember them.

    The authors of our canonical gospels (according to Matthew, Mark, Luke and John) relied heavily on the familiar motifs and language of Old Testament prophecies to structure their own writings, and theology. In addition to rhetorical devices such as chiasmus and antimetabole, biblical stories are replete with repeated themes and stories to draw the reader's attention. Motifs, themes and symbols capture the pattern seeker's attention. The story is then told in the *listener's* mind, embellished by the storyteller's style, use of grammar, vocabulary, sentence structure and word order. It's the embellishments that create the author's signature. The listener will recognize the author's signature in familiar prose between the lines of verse.

    A message draws and builds on the *listener's* ability to hear the motif or message. For example, one might read or hear this verse

> If music be the food of love, play on;
> Give me excess of it, that, surfeiting,
> The appetite may sicken, and so die.

and rightly guess that it is Shakespeare.[15] Or maybe not. But the listener might have heard something more like the commonly misquoted scriptural conflation,

> man hath no better thing under the sun,
> than to eat, and to drink, and to be merry
> [so,] Let us eat and drink;
> for tomorrow we shall die.[16]

Or not. It depends entirely on who thinks so. Did Shakespeare intend any biblical parallel or allusion when he penned these verses in *Twelfth Night*? It's a question worth asking, if we are looking for what literary source materials were available and influential in Shakespeare's written works.

Studying Joseph Smith and Early Mormon Scripture

Joseph Smith was fond of parallels and motifs to supply meaning to his revelations. He borrowed openly and often from the Bible for his own translations, revelations and orations. He often quoted scripture he referred to, or simply noted "as it is written" before reworking a related scriptural verse into his own. Using familiar words and biblical style helped convey a message that was meant to sound as if from a heavenly source. Most of his revealed scripture weaves in biblical motifs, allusions and vocabulary intended to be familiar in sound as well as in the spirit and setting of holy scripture. Joseph was intimately familiar with the Bible and relied on its voice to proclaim his own.

Consider the sound of Joseph's prophetic revelation about his forthcoming church recorded in February 1829, now found in the LDS Church's canonized Doctrine and Covenants, Section 4, and compare it to a few similar biblical verses:

D&C 4:4	Revelation 14:5
For behold the *field is white already to harvest*; and lo, he that *thrusteth in his sickle* with his might, the same layeth up in store that he perisheth not, but bringeth salvation to his soul.	*Thrust in thy sickle*, and reap: for *the time is come* for thee to reap; for *the harvest* of the *earth is ripe*.
	Joel 3:13
	Put ye in the sickle, for the harvest is ripe.

The parallels and allusions are certainly there, but we wouldn't call this copying, would we? At least not slavish copying, like the multi-chapter reproduction of Isaiah in the Book of Mormon. Joseph openly borrowed from scripture, but never intended it to be an identical reproduction. Instead, he adopted a style of imitation and imagery included for the sake of imagery and style. It is meant to sound biblical and prophetic. After all, if revelation comes through inspiration, what is more inspiring than God's word?

The Patternist-Historian Approach

LDS historians and scholars of Mormon studies look for similar patterns, and for different reasons. A contextual approach, including a historical-critical look at Joseph Smith's writings and revelations, was founded in LDS scholarship by the late and revered BYU professor Hugh Nibley. Nibley has been called a "patternist historian."[17] Patternism is a method of comparing teachings and texts of ancient Near East religions, where discovered similarities are presumed to constitute a pattern between them. Similar writings suggest a relation in religions and religious views. Other patternist historians, such as Douglas F. Salmon, have noted that "the number of parallels that Nibley has been unable to uncover from amazingly disparate and arcane sources is truly staggering."[18]

Historian Robert Smith noted of Nibley's approach, "To say anything one way or the other requires a chain of circumstantial evidence—a pattern—and this has been the burden of Hugh Nibley's efforts throughout his career as a patternist historian."[19] Nibley's methods have also been criticized for his selectivity in choosing parallels to compare with Mormon scripture, to the point that his methodology "creates an artificial synthesis that never really existed."[20]

Nibley's work is still recognized as foundational in Mormon studies with respect to Enoch the prophet, 1 Enoch and their influence on Joseph Smith's writings and revelations. Over the course of a thirteen-part series of articles published decades ago in the LDS Church–owned magazine the *Ensign*, Nibley produced parallels and connections between the extracts of Enoch that Joseph Smith added to Genesis 5 in producing the Book of Moses, and other ancient Jewish and Christian writings. His collected essays on Enoch were then republished as *Enoch the Prophet*, a third of a multivolume collection of Nibley's published works.[21] His purpose was to demonstrate that Joseph Smith restored ancient doctrines, practices and scripture that were truly lost. It was certainly faith promoting and erudite in Professor Nibley's time and place.

Introduction: Patterns and Parallels in Scripture Scholarship

Indeed, the danger in searching for patterns is looking for them, or "parallelomania"—when one overdoses on analogies to the point that they are found everywhere, in everything.[22] They become meaningless without some boundaries applied. A patternist's approach, therefore, requires some ground rules for review. That said, extensive similar verbal parallels do tend to speak for themselves.

Along with LDS apologists, Hugh Nibley adamantly denied that Joseph Smith ever had access to 1 Enoch and specifically the English translation published by Professor Richard Laurence in 1821. Some serious LDS scholars and historians still deny Joseph had any access. Preeminent Smith biographer Richard Lyman Bushman finds very few similarities between Joseph's writings and 1 Enoch, concluding, "It is scarcely conceivable that Joseph Smith knew of Laurence's Enoch translation."[23] In their coauthored article "Could Joseph Smith Have Drawn on Ancient Manuscripts When He Translated the Story of Enoch?," Jeffrey M. Bradshaw and Ryan Dahle recognize (but disclaim) that "only a few significant and unique parallels have been identified between the two Enoch chapters of the Book of Moses and the sizable text of *1 Enoch*."[24] LDS historian Jed L. Woodworth finds no important similarities, claiming, "Laurence's 105 translated chapters do not resemble Joseph Smith's Enoch in any obvious way."[25]

All of these disclaimers call for a close comparison between the two texts in the historical context. Their conclusions beg the questions

- Are there any obvious resemblances between Joseph's revelations and Richard Laurence's 1821 Book of Enoch?
- Are there more than just a few significant and unique parallels found between Laurence's text and Mormon scripture?

This book reconsiders these questions.

The intent in looking for literary influences is not to distract from the historical Joseph Smith, the praised man revered by millions as the prophet of the restoration. But he did publish several books of scripture, and there is a bibliography behind every book. This project takes a critical look at a potential literary source (or a unique body of literary sources) that may have influenced Joseph Smith's revelations and teachings about the patriarch Enoch as historically taught as doctrine of the LDS Church, at least in its earliest beginnings. What is readily accessible at our fingertips today is remarkable. Trying to imagine what extrabiblical resources Joseph may have gotten his hands on around 1821 in his own self-searching quest for any information is simply baffling. It's a

Introduction

question worth asking. Joseph's revelations and methodologies remain the subject of serious scholarship, research and writing.

Biblical scholars agree that early Christian authors of the New Testament were influenced by the ancient Jewish apocalyptic writings available to them in their time, which included prophecies of an ancient Jewish author (or group of authors) claiming to write in the name of the even-more-ancient antediluvian patriarch Enoch. The writings of Enoch appear to have been more readily available in ancient Palestine than might have been previously thought. We find Enochic scripture, themes and motifs scattered throughout the New Testament gospels and epistles. However, these direct connections were lost until biblical scholars began comparing ancient texts from different languages.

This book specifically considers whether Joseph Smith had access to Richard Laurence's 1821 Book of Enoch, and how much influence it had (if any) on Joseph Smith's scripture and doctrinal development.[26]

There is an unquestionable influence of apocalyptic writings, including written prophecies of Enoch, among the gospels and epistles of the New Testament. These ancient Jewish visionary traditions and mystical teachings are integral in the origins of Joseph Smith's religion(s). Ancient prophecies of the old prophecies of Enoch that were once believed to have been lost were recovered and incorporated into Joseph's translations. This is, in a sense, a restoration of lost scripture. *Is there a natural explanation for this?* This is perhaps the most intriguing question surrounding early Mormon scripture, and the most historically debated: how did an unlettered farm boy compose the literary works he did? What literature passed through the hands, eyes, or ears of Joseph Smith to make him the author of Mormon scripture that he became?

Intelligence, on at least one level, is a matter of organic data processing. This is why we are sent to school before we can read or write; information input starts somewhere before there's any meaningful output. We have to gather meaningful information if we want to produce any ourselves. Information is gathered bit by bit, word by word, book by book, "line upon line, precept upon precept," etc. Our thoughts and understandings are organized information, run through our personal data settings. We *believe* in what we know, think we know or want to know *is true*. How do we *know* what we know? From all the information we've gathered along the way, whether hard-earned or divinely granted, it's gathered in our quest called life.

On the topic of Joseph's methods or any literary sources he may

Introduction: Patterns and Parallels in Scripture Scholarship

have used in translating scripture, Joseph Smith biographer Richard Bushman explains,

> For the Book of Moses and the inspired revision, Joseph worked from the King James Version of Genesis without promptings from another manuscript. But in the method of their creation *the three translations* were alike. Joseph did not translate in the sense of learning the language and consulting dictionaries. He received the words by "revelation," whether or not a text lay before him.
>
> The three historical translations all grew out of the Bible. They centered on Moses, Enoch, and Abraham, and took place in Bible lands: Jerusalem, Canaan and Egypt. All had the character of expansions, enlarging a few verses in the old scriptures into lengthy accounts unknown to Bible readers.[27]

These "three historical translations" do not include the Book of Mormon. The translation method described here is that "centered on Moses, Enoch, and Abraham," for which purportedly no other text was used. The question remains, were there any other manuscripts, texts, commentaries or any other books lying before him as he conducted these translations?[28] And particularly, did Joseph have access to and read any writings about Enoch when translating his prophecies and visions of Enoch in the Book of Moses? Serious scholarship demonstrates that, at least in later years, Joseph's attempts at composing these historical translations as Mormon scripture were, in fact, made with an attempt at scholarly study, including learning languages and consulting dictionaries and biblical commentaries in his translation projects.[29] This is how we all learn, from available resources. We ask those who have gone before us, and we filter out our own sets of truths and make mental notes for future use. We learn from as much information as we have available and is understandable to us.

Whether 1 Enoch was used as a primary source or not for any of his translations and revelations, Joseph Smith's apocalypticism, Zionism, developing theology, and much of his peculiar cosmology appear to be influenced by the Enochic literature that he availed himself of in his unending quest for intelligence. To reveal the lost writings of the ancient prophet Enoch, you need to know who he was, where he lived and what on earth he would have written about. How would Joseph know? Aside from the Bible, where would Joseph look to learn about Enoch? How would he know what prophecies Enoch ever wrote that needed to be restored? These are honest questions that anyone would ask. In trying to

Introduction

answer these questions, and prompt others, I agree with Richard Bushman that

> hunting for deception can be a distraction. It throws us off the track of Joseph Smith the Prophet. In devising a story of a charlatan, we lose sight of the unprepossessing rural visionary who became a religious leader admired by thousands.[30]

Like the historical Jesus of Nazareth, Joseph Smith was an historical man who lived, ate, grew up asking questions and turning to scripture for answers. They lived in specific times and places, influenced by their own surrounding culture, media, technology and the information available to them in their day. Literary works have literary sources. Jesus quoted the old Hebrew scripture in teaching among both Jews and gentiles, as recorded in our New Testament gospels. The apostle Paul quoted from contemporary poets of his time that inspired him in penning his own epistles. Outside of the KJV Bible, Joseph Smith was likewise influenced by contemporary literature both available to him and meaningful to his developing theology. Which of any of these meaningful literary works found their way into Mormon scripture and doctrine is a question worthy of dialogue.

I propose that Joseph Smith used the Book of Enoch (or contemporary 1 Enoch excerpts) as a literary source, and that it influenced his revelations, translation projects, and early Mormon doctrine and theology. As New Testament scholar Professor Bart. D. Ehrman reminds us, "The burden of proof on such matters, as I've already mentioned, is on the one who claims that an author used another document as a source. The surest indicators of reliance on a source are detailed and extensive verbal parallels."[31] The chapters that follow present a comparative review between Joseph Smith's history of Mormon beginnings, his translated works, cosmology, temple liturgy and some peculiar early Mormon doctrines that we find have a number of verbal and thematic parallels to 1 Enoch available to Smith at the time. Whether these parallels demonstrate the potential for literary borrowing, or are simply perceived, is a question for the reader. The number of similarities is, at least, remarkable.

Having offered a more exhaustive history of the publication of Richard Laurence's 1821 Book of Enoch and its availability to Joseph Smith, it is perhaps best said by the esteemed Brigham Young University professor and Mormon historian D. Michael Quinn,

> Because I accept the unlikely appearance of otherworldly beings to an American farm boy, I cannot deny the earthly possibility that young Joseph

Introduction: Patterns and Parallels in Scripture Scholarship

Smith had knowledge of published works. In my view, the available evidence moves such access beyond probability—to fact.[32]

Discovering how Joseph Smith used available literary sources and what relationship that body of literature had to early Mormon scriptural texts has been called by Mormon studies scholars "the most important historical question at hand"[33] and "one of the most important aspects of Mormon beginnings."[34] The question of Joseph's access to 1 Enoch must consider the extent of parallels between texts. Certainly, when two authors are writing about the same event or idea, there is a likelihood they will use similar language.[35] In this regard, Joseph's familiarity with and reliance on the Bible is unquestioned.

Admittedly, some parallels between Mormon texts and 1 Enoch might also be found in the KJV Bible and the Apocrypha, and some Bible parallels are perhaps a better source for similar scriptural passages and word use in some situations. There are, indeed, many biblical parallels demonstrating borrowing from the prophecies of Enoch, including that of the authors of the gospels of Matthew, Mark and Luke. I offer a few comparative references with similar biblical verses for additional comparison; however, I have not attempted to rule out all other possible literary sources (biblical and extrabiblical) for the sole reason that this project focuses on a single potential source. There is an entire field of current Mormon studies that continues to search for possible sources that Joseph Smith may have been influenced by in his own quest for light, truth and knowledge—his quest for *intelligence.*

CHAPTER ONE

An American Farm Boy

> "What is most interesting about Joseph Smith is that *people believed him*. To understand the emergence of Joseph the Prophet, we must follow the stories told by family and friends who believed they were witnessing a miracle."
> —Richard Lyman Bushman[1]

A favorite story to tell of the "unprepossessing rural visionary who became a religious leader admired by thousands" was that Joseph Smith was practically illiterate and had no formal education to speak of.[2] It is true that he had little formal schooling, if any at all. Of his own schooling, Joseph autobiographically explained that he was "deprived of the benefit of an education," and tutored only in the basics of reading, writing and simple arithmetic.[3] Joseph's simple beginnings have been sentimentalized in Mormon tradition. In a General Conference talk to the members of the LDS Church in October 1977, Apostle Mark E. Peterson reminded us in his talk "It Was a Miracle!" of the ongoing idea in the LDS Church that Joseph hardly handled a book in his life:

> But great as this mighty prophet was, he had but a humble beginning. He was raised as a farm boy, with little formal education.... The work of Joseph Smith was foretold by the prophet Isaiah, who spoke of his humble beginning and his lack of early education. Isaiah actually called him an unlearned man. This is significant in regard to this prophecy, for it becomes an unerring mark of identification.[4]

The "unerring mark of identification" is only unerring as to the lack of any formal educational transcript. Joseph Smith was anything but unintelligent, unread, illiterate or incapable of what he demonstrably accomplished, particularly by relying on resources among the most influential of his closest followers. Literary critic Harold Bloom in his book *The American Religion* famously calls Joseph an "authentic religious genius" with a "religion-making imagination" unsurpassed in American history.⁵

While the unschooled-farm-boy story persists for devotional purposes (and it certainly is faith promoting), the consensus of scholarship in Mormon studies recognizes that Joseph's lack of formal education did little to hinder his intellectual and literary abilities, given available resources. LDS historian Robert F. Smith accepts that Joseph Smith was "an extraordinarily well-read raconteur ... with a well-integrated mind/personality and a lack of formal education who managed to assimilate a tremendous amount of data from the broadest possible range of sources available in his immediate area."⁶ Any attack on his character notwithstanding, Joseph's works reflect undeniable brilliance.

This brilliance was from a thirst to learn. After his baptism with Oliver Cowdery on May 15, 1829, Joseph recorded,

Joseph Smith, Jr., copied from the original daguerreotype ten at the City of Nauvoo, in 1843.

> Our minds being now enlightened, we began to have the Scriptures laid open to our understandings, and the true meaning and intention of their more mysterious passages revealed unto us in a manner which we never could attain to previously, nor ever before had thought of.⁷

The unlettered boy wanted to impress people with his words, and quickly published what he thought were his most important writings. The title page of the 1830 edition of the Book of Mormon touts Joseph Smith, Jr., as the "author and proprietor" of the Book of Mormon. The lauded, but dubious title was removed from subsequent prints. It evidenced, however, that Joseph wanted others to read what he wrote, even declaring his revelations as "solemn proclamations ... to all the kings of the world, to the four corners thereof, to the honorable president-elect, and the high-minded governors of the nation in which you live, and to

Chapter One. An American Farm Boy

all the nations of the earth scattered abroad" (D&C 124:2–3). He wanted everyone to hear what he had to say, and writing was the mass media of the day.

Joseph was a far better and more convincing storyteller than he was a writer. His handwritten memoirs include long rambling sentences without punctuation and no end in sight for the reader looking for a place to breathe. Notwithstanding his intellectual abilities, his lack of formal education is reflected in his attempts to write in his own hand, as opposed to dictating to scribes. Joseph understood his own literary limitations, reflected in a letter he wrote to renowned LDS poet William W. Phelps dated November 27, 1832: "Oh Lord God, deliver us from this prison, almost as it were, of paper, pen and ink, and of a crooked, broken, scattered and imperfect language."[8] He was more comfortable dictating his revelations to a scribe, and his revelations thus recorded are better written. Nick Newman, a journalist writing for the *Desert News* in 2010, shared this forthright insight:

> Joseph Smith was a terrible writer. While that statement might sound foreign to members [of the LDS Church], considering his testimony and revelations have been spread around the world in more than 160 languages, it should come as no surprise when you realize the Prophet had no more than a third-grade education. So how could an uneducated New England farm boy bring to pass a work that would require endless hours of writing and translating? As Joseph transitioned into his role as prophet of God, capable men served as his personal scribes, assistants and secretaries until, at the time of his death, he had amassed an entire office staff. In his collection of 10 journals alone, which consist of 1,500 pages, a mere 35—or 2 percent—are in the prophet's own handwriting.[9]

The individual efforts, contributions and influence of Joseph's scribes have been recognized and are worthy of historical applause entirely of their own. A few of these individuals' contributions are discussed in later chapters. As Joseph developed in his role as prophet and revelator, his best-selling assets remained his persuasive orations, good looks and convincing character. These personality strengths, in light of his limited educational background, underwrote the miraculous in his literary productions.

He certainly was "uneducated" in the modern sense of the term. But available resources in the American frontier days were anything but the modern sense of any education. And for the frontier, the Smiths' modest little home was surrounded with some adequate educational resources of the day. Joseph's father, Joseph Smith, Sr., worked at one time as a schoolteacher and offered some degree of homeschooling, tutoring his son whenever he could, and likely possessed a few books for a family library. His mother, Lucy Mack Smith, was also evidently educated, authoring her own history of her son Joseph. Her writing demonstrates her mastery of reading and writing and evidences the culture of education and literature that she instilled in her home. Joseph's own written history continues this yearning to explore the written word, and relates his reading often from the Bible as a young boy. It was from *reading* the passage in James 1:5 that prompted Joseph to ask questions in seeking truth. He was searching for answers, and he was looking in the books he had available and that he found inspiring. He recorded in his history,

> While I was laboring under the extreme difficulties caused by the contests of these parties of religionists, I was one day reading the Epistle of James, first chapter and fifth verse, which reads: *If any of you lack wisdom, let him ask of God, that giveth to all men liberally, and upbraideth not; and it shall be given him.*[10]

Joseph searched the Bible for truth because he wanted knowledge; he wanted answers to questions. He hungered for *information* in a day and age influenced by 17th-century Enlightenment reasoning. And he read what was available. Regardless of how limited the Smith family library may have been, they had a Bible. It was from reading a Bible that he found answers. "Never did any passage of scripture come with more power to the heart of man than this did at this time to mine." At a time when he was searching for knowledge, truth and light, he found answers by reading.

Lucy Mack Smith wrote that Joseph "had never read the Bible through in his life," but their family must have "presented an aspect as singular as any that ever lived upon the face of the earth" as they all sat in a circle "giving the most profound attention to a boy" telling them wonderous biblical and pseudobiblical stories.[11] Lucy described Joseph as "much less inclined to the perusal of books than any of the rest of our children, *but far more given to meditation and deep study.*"[12] When it came to matters of religion, Joseph told his mother, "I can take my Bible, and go into the woods, and learn more in two hours than you can learn at meeting in two years, if you should go all the time."[13] If these statements reflect anything about his education, they reflect a boy who could read and was raised in a home steeped in a culture of self-learning and religious curiosity.

Chapter One. An American Farm Boy

Joseph's older brother Hyrum's intelligence was recognized at a young age. After the family settled in West Lebanon, New Hampshire, in 1811, Lucy "began to contemplate, with joy and satisfaction, the prosperity which has attended our recent exertions," and felt settled enough to arrange for a formal education for Hyrum.[14] By this time, Joseph was just seven years old, and he and his older siblings (including Hyrum) had only informal home tutoring. "As a child, he showed promise as a student, and at age 11 he entered Moor's Indian Charity School, where he received the most formal education of any of the Smith children."[15] The Moor's Charity School was associated with Dartmouth College in Hanover, New Hampshire, just a few miles north of the Smiths' home.

Hyrum Smith biographer Jeffrey O'Driscoll, in his book *Hyrum Smith: A Life of Integrity*, explains how Hyrum's formal education at the institutional beginnings of Dartmouth College influenced Joseph Smith in his formative years:

> Eleazar Wheelcock founded the Moor's School in Lebanon, Connecticut, in 1754. Its curriculum extended beyond simply educating students; rather, it focused on preparing them to become teachers and preachers. In 1769, the school relocated to Hanover, New Hampshire, and became associated with the newly founded Dartmouth College. With the establishment of a common school in Hanover in 1808, the academy further refined its focus to prepare able students for additional scholarly education. But it maintained its religious influence, and students attended daily chapel services at the White Church on campus. If Hyrum attended in 1811, as Lucy seems to indicate, he joined a class of thirty-one students, which grew to fifty-six by 1814.
>
> School records are incomplete, but the "Hiram Smith" listed in the August 1814 record was one of the "charity scholars" studying arithmetic. Charity scholars were not merely students with limited financial means. The designation also implied remarkable intellectual potential. School president John Wheelcock personally followed the progress of these student scholars, who were supported from his limited funds. Hyrum's designation as a charity scholar in 1814 implies that he performed well academically during his previous years there.
>
> The outbreak of "typhus fever" in late 1812 interrupted Hyrum's education. He came home sick from school, perhaps at the end of the quarter in February 1813. His whole family was eventually infected, but Hyrum, despite his own illness, was determined to do his part to alleviate their suffering. He relieved his mother and sat at Joseph's side for days or weeks until Nathan Smith—an attending surgeon at Dartmouth College, whose daughter Malvina attended class with Hyrum—operated on Joseph's leg to eradicate the infection. Whether Hyrum and Malvina's association was significant or even known to those involved is not recorded.

Joseph Smith and the Book of Enoch

As Joseph's leg improved, his family sent him to his Uncle Jesse's home in Salem, Massachusetts, in hopes that "the sea-breezes would be of service to him."[16]

There are some significantly educated and connected people here in this historical description that might get quickly overlooked. Dr. Nathan Smith, the surgeon who saved Joseph's leg, founded the Dartmouth Medical School, and went on to co-found the University of Vermont Medical School and the medical school at Bowdoin College. He also founded the medical school at Yale. He was profoundly devoted to the spread of education and making higher education more available across the developing American frontier, where most physicians were poorly educated. Over the course of three weeks following the surgery on the young boy's leg, Dr. Smith tenderly visited Joseph almost every day to personally care for him (18 post-op visits over a span of 20 days).[17] Confined to his bed, and recovering with immense pain, the young Joseph was certainly encouraged and influenced by Dr. Nathan Smith's personal attention.

Let's not forget Uncle Jesse, to whose home Joseph was sent to live while his leg, it was hoped, would improve with the aid of the Salem, Massachusetts, sea breezes. Joseph's family had deep roots in Salem, and the family was well established and cultured. Joseph's grandfather, Asael Smith, served as the Salem assessor, selectman and town clerk, and in the Massachusetts state legislature and as a town meeting moderator.[18] His son Jesse Smith (Joseph Jr.'s uncle) followed in the family tradition of civil leadership. Uncle Jesse was the Salem school chancellor. Joseph's recovery in Uncle Jesse's home would have exposed young Joseph to the most educated men in the community, and there were resources available for some formal education during his stay.

Joseph Smith's connections with the Moor's School interestingly go beyond his brother Hyrum. Some other very notable persons with connections to Joseph's past were also students of "early Dartmouth," including Solomon Spaulding (class of 1785), the author of *Manuscript Found* (1812), which was for a time purported to be the literary source (or a source of ideas) for authoring the Book of Mormon.[19] While the Spaulding manuscript theory isn't taken very seriously, the *View of the Hebrews* source theory is.[20] *View of the Hebrews* was published in 1823 by Ethan Smith (no relation to Joseph), who also graduated from Dartmouth in 1790. Ethan Smith was the local minister of Oliver Cowdery's family in Turnbridge, Vermont, before Oliver moved to New York to

Chapter One. An American Farm Boy

help Joseph in the Book of Mormon translation project. Historian Richard K. Behrens recounts,

> Many of Oliver's family were members of Ethan Smith's congregation in Poultney, Vermont, and were aware of *View of the Hebrews* and Ethan's other works. The Cowdery family relationships and the Cowdery family awareness of Ethan Smith were especially good preparation for later events in New York and Pennsylvania.... The later interaction of the Smith and Cowdery families will be integral to the bringing forth of the Book of Mormon.[21]

When Hyrum's education at Moor's Academy was interrupted, he returned home, where he was able to remain at Joseph's side, both comforting and personally tutoring him during his convalescence. In an age of limited media, companionship and discussion filled their time while Hyrum attended to homebound Joseph. As Behrens summarizes,

> Hyrum's education at Moor's school provided a tutor for unschooled Joseph. Hyrum's exposure to Dartmouth's theology, cosmology, ancient language studies, architecture, Ethan Smith's son Lyndon, and Solomon Spaulding's nephew James Spaulding from Sharon, Vermont, who was attending the Medical School, all provided discussion material for tutoring Joseph during his long recovery from leg surgery that kept Joseph at home on crutches until the Smith family reached Palmyra. The future development of Mormon Doctrine so parallels the Dartmouth Lectures that it is hard not to perceive their stimulating possibilities.[22]

After a series of annual crop failures, the Smith family moved to Palmyra, New York, in early 1817. Joseph and Hyrum would have been about the ages of 11 and 17, respectively. This isolated little farming town would soon be connected with a flood of traffic, products, peddlers and information pouring into Palmyra in the prime of Joseph's youth where his family lived. The Erie Canal was completed up to Palmyra in 1822, linking Lake Erie to the Hudson River, and bringing a new flood of modernity.

The publisher of the Cooperstown Bible that Joseph and Oliver purchased to assist in their translation was instrumental in shipping a constant flow of new books, news, pamphlets and products into settlements along the canal, including Palmyra and its bookstores. The Smiths' humble family log home was less than two miles south of the canal, which had to be crossed on the three-mile trip north to the farm of their close friend and Book of Mormon financier Martin Harris. The original 1830 Book of Mormon was published by Egbert B. Grandin at the Grandin Building, located in downtown Palmyra, fittingly just a few hundred meters from the Erie's water's edge.

Commerce and information flowed from East Coast seaports directly west, including new books and literature published in Europe. Kent P. Jackson, professor of ancient scripture at Brigham Young University, notes there was a steady stream of books flowing into Palmyra arriving on traveling "locomotive bookstores" that "had moveable tops and counters, and their shelves were stocked with hundreds of varieties of books."[23] The most "innovative outlet," Professor Jackson says, was a "floating canalboat bookstore" that went back and forth on the canal and "facilitated the fast and convenient transport of passengers and goods that allowed western towns to grow and to share in the unique culture that was developing in the new republic."[24] Books and goods were coming and going faster than local papers could advertise their sale. This flow of information is essential to the question of the literature, books, pamphlets and other media that might have become available and accessible to Joseph Smith during the time he was looking for answers to his own questions and developing his ideas and doctrinal understandings.

The more he pursued his self-education, the more Joseph Smith relished the "uneducated farm boy" epithet because it bolstered his persona and mystique; it supported a supernatural versus a natural explanation for his compositions. He wrote in the *History of the Church*,

> I stood alone, an unlearned youth, to combat the worldly wisdom and multiplied ignorance of eighteen centuries, with a new revelation, which ... would open the eyes of more than eight hundred millions of people, and make "plain the old paths."[25]

Calling someone "educated" implies they had access to whatever published and available literature that may have been within their vicinity at a given time, whereas "uneducated" tends to imply illiteracy and, thus, lack of access to any written information at all, whether immediately at hand or not. It creates a buffer of doubt against any extrabiblical literary influence in Mormon scripture.

As much as the uneducated farm boy story has persisted, LDS Church leaders have come to recognize Joseph's brilliance, intelligence and education. Third president of the LDS Church John Taylor recounted in 1884:

> Joseph Smith was ... uneducated when he was a boy.... The Lord took him into His school, and He taught him things that I have seen puzzle many of the wisest scientists, profoundest thinkers, and the most learned men.[26]

Chapter One. An American Farm Boy

LDS Apostle George Q. Cannon in 1885 said:

> Joseph, a youth, obscure, illiterate in some respects, ... through industry and perseverance, became learned, and if he had lived, he would undoubtedly have become one of the most learned of men through the gifts God gave him.[27]

Joseph Smith was apparently well-read and intellectually gifted. He had a peculiar understanding of the Bible, and particularly the Old Testament and ancient Jewish writings and traditions, especially for a young man of his age and time. His pursuit of knowledge was never-ending, and it became more voracious the more he read and produced written works. In establishing the School of the Prophets, he revealed:

> And as all have not faith, seek ye diligently and teach one another words of wisdom; yea, *seek ye out of the best books* words of wisdom; seek learning, even by study and also by faith.
>
> Organize yourselves; prepare every needful thing; and establish a house, even a house of prayer, a house of fasting, a house of faith, a house of learning, a house of glory, a house of order, a house of God [D&C 88:18–19].

On May 6, 1833, Joseph again recorded his insatiable desire to learn more:

> And, verily I say unto you, that it is my will that you should hasten to translate my scriptures, and to obtain a knowledge of history, and of countries, and of kingdoms, of laws of God and man, and all this for the salvation of Zion [D&C 93:53].

One cannot advise others on which books are good, bad and best without reading just a few to start with. When familiar words and phrases appear in literature that was available to Smith at the time, the question is worth asking: *Could it have been a source?* After all, there are lots of "best books" but not a lot of them have such words of wisdom, word for word, as this:

> The vision which he saw, the second vision of wisdom, which Enoch saw, the son of Jared, the son of Malaleel, the son of Canan, the son of Enos, the son of Seth, the son of Adam. This is the commencement of the *word of wisdom*.... [Enoch XXXV:1].

What do you do when you spot literary parallels like these? It's natural to ask whether or not a particular text lay before Joseph at any time during his translation projects. An attempt to discover what "best books [and] words of wisdom" Joseph Smith ultimately sought, read, heard or

Joseph Smith and the Book of Enoch

was tutored from, and which of those influenced him, is a faithful historical pursuit.

Continuing scholarship on the issue of Joseph Smith's access and use of extrabiblical sources for composing early Mormon literature has opened the pages of a host of available and known publications of excerpts of 1 Enoch in English available even before Laurence's 1821 book was published.[28] In truth, we don't know for sure that Joseph ever handled a copy of Laurence's book, so the question remains. As long as questions remain, critical thinking will continue, and the sources behind Joseph's scriptural texts and translation projects will remain the most mystifying question of Mormon beginnings.

CHAPTER TWO

Who Is Enoch?

"Smith was haunted by the figure of Enoch."
—Harold Bloom[1]

Enoch in the Old Testament

Reading the Bible like a book, from left to right, front to back, one comes across the old patriarch named Enoch in the first few chapters of

"Enoch," by William Blake, 1806–1807 (Purchase, Joseph Pulitzer and Brooke Russell Astor Bequests and 2005 Benefit Fund, 2013, Metropolitan Museum of Art, New York, NY).

Joseph Smith and the Book of Enoch

Genesis. There are actually three Enochs named in the Bible: (1) Enoch the son of Cain, brother of Abel and son of Adam and Eve;[2] (2) a *city* built by Cain and named after his son, Enoch; and (3) Enoch, in the line of Seth, the righteous son of Adam and Eve.[3] The first named Enoch mentioned in Genesis 4 is not the same as the better-known but still enigmatic Enoch of Genesis 5. However, it's easy to see how these homonymous cousins could easily be mistaken for one another.

Taking the Bible at its word, they are two different people, from two different lines descending from Adam, and both having strikingly similar family names. Simply listing the family lines demonstrates the almost mirror image of the genealogies of these two men, keeping in mind that the names are English translations (or transliterations) of the names from the ancient Hebrew, Greek and other texts and sources available to the King James translators in the early 17th century:

Enoch in the line of Cain
- Adam
- Cain (Gen. 4:1)
- **Enoch** (Gen. 4:17)
- Irad (Gen. 4:18)
- Mehujael (Gen. 4:18)
- Methusael (Gen. 4:18)
- Lamech (Gen. 4:18)

Enoch in the line of Seth
- Adam
- Seth (Gen. 4:25; 5:3)
- Enos (Gen. 4:26; Gen. 5:6)
- Cainan (Gen. 5:8)
- Mahalaleel (Gen. 5:12)
- Jared (Gen. 5:18)
- **Enoch** (Gen. 5:19)
- Methuselah (Gen. 5:21)
- Lamech (Gen. 5:25)
- Noah (Gen. 5:28–29)

Even without any particular understanding of Hebrew, Jewish writing or training in Old Testament studies, one can't help but see the similarities between these two genealogies, and how each fits within the context in which it is presented. Genesis 4 ends with verses 25 and 26, establishing "another seed instead of Abel, whom Cain slew. And to Seth, to him also there was born a son; and he called his name Enos: then began men to call upon the name of the LORD." Chapter 4 ends there. Genesis 5 is not just a new chapter; it's the start of a new book.

Genesis 5 begins, again in the beginning, with the creation of Adam and naming his generations:

> 1. This is the book of the generations of Adam. In the day that God created man, in the likeness of God made he him;

Chapter Two. Who Is Enoch?

> 2. Male and female created he them; and blessed them, and called their name Adam, in the day when they were created.
> 3. And Adam lived an hundred and thirty years, and begat a son in his own likeness, after his image; and called his name Seth:

According to Genesis 4:26, it was after Enos was born to Seth that men began calling upon the name of God. The name "Enos" in Hebrew translates to "man," or more specifically "man is his frailty."[4] This parallel to Adam is unmissable. The *Cambridge Bible for Schools and Colleges* commentary on Genesis 4:26 offers, "This word [Enosh], used in Hebrew poetry, means 'man,' and is thus to be compared with Adam."[5] Comparing the two genealogies of Adam, we see they are very similar, particularly if we take out Adam and Seth from the genealogy and start with Enos, another first "man." The two familial lines and names are either directly parallel ("→") or flip-flopped ("X") with one another within the respective orders:

Adam (man fallen) → Enos ("man in his frailty")
Cain → Cainan
Enoch X *Mahalaleel (Mehujael)*
Irad → Jared
Mehujael (Mahalaleel) X *Enoch*
Methusael → Methuselah
Lamech → Lamech

Outside of Genesis 5, we know little to nothing about Enoch. Here's all that the Old Testament has to tell us about Enoch, from Genesis 5:18–24:

> And Jared lived an hundred sixty and two years, and he begat Enoch:
> And Jared lived after he begat Enoch eight hundred years, and begat sons and daughters:
> And all the days of Jared were nine hundred sixty and two years: and he died.
> And Enoch lived sixty and five years, and begat Methuselah:
> And Enoch walked with God after he begat Methuselah three hundred years, and begat sons and daughters:
> And all the days of Enoch were three hundred sixty and five years:
> And Enoch walked with God: and he was not; for God took him.

So far, we know Enoch is a descendent of Adam through the lineage of his righteous son, Seth. He is the son of Jared, and the father of

Methuselah, who was born when Enoch was 65 years old. After that, Enoch "walked with God" for another 300 years; in the meantime he begat more unnamed sons and daughters, and lived until he was 365 years old. What happened to him exactly is unknown, as far as our Hebrew Bible offers. We read that "Enoch walked with God: and he was not; for God took him." There's really nothing more about Enoch in the Old Testament.

Enoch in the New Testament

What does the New Testament say about Enoch? He's mentioned by name three times in the New Testament, once in the gospels (Luke) and twice in the epistles. But strangely, he is referenced as having written scripture, despite the fact that nothing in the Old Testament tells us that Enoch was a writer of any scripture. Enoch's writings are quoted directly by Jude 1:14–15:

> And Enoch also, the seventh from Adam, prophesied of these, saying, Behold, the Lord cometh with ten thousands of his saints,
> To execute judgment upon all, and to convince all that are ungodly among them of all their ungodly deeds which they have ungodly committed, and of all their hard speeches which ungodly sinners have spoken against him.

(*Cf.*, Enoch II; LXI:4.) In authoring his epistle to

"The Translation of Enoch," from the 1728 Figures de la Bible, illustrated by Gerard Hoet (1648–1733) and others, and published by P. de Hondt in The Hague (Wikimedia Commons).

the Hebrews, the Apostle Paul referred to Enoch by name, telling us in Hebrews 11:5,

> By faith Enoch was translated that he should not see death; and was not found, *because God had translated him*: for before his translation he had this testimony, that he pleased God.

From these New Testament verses, we learn that Enoch apparently wrote some inspiring prophecies considered by some as scripture, and that our Christian writers (at least Paul) understood that Enoch was "translated" into the presence of God—whatever that means exactly.

Enoch in the Apocrypha

Among the 15 books in the Apocrypha (noncanonical books included in the Cooperstown Bible that Joseph owned at the time he was revealing the prophecies of Enoch), we find a few references to Enoch, but not many. (*See* Ecclesiasticus 44 & 49, and 2 Esdras 6:49 & 51.) The book of Ecclesiasticus, written about 180–175 BC, endorses the New Testament tradition of Enoch's translation:

> 44:14 But upon the earth was no man created like Enoch; for he was taken from earth.
> 49:16 Enoch pleased the Lord, and was translated, being an example of repentance to all generations.

Reading these verses next to Paul's in Hebrews, we have a good example of Paul borrowing (copying) from other written sources to craft his own epistles, without any reference or citation to his source material. Presumably, Ecclesiasticus was not generally accepted as inspired scripture among the early Christians in Palestine, and therefore Paul does not reference it as authoritative. However, he apparently found it persuasive, influential and consistent with his own understanding regarding the ancient prophet Enoch. The book of Ecclesiasticus was popularized among Greek-speaking Jews after it was taken to Alexandria and translated from Hebrew. Although considered inspired scripture among some, it was later excluded from the 27 books that comprise our canonized New Testament.

Enoch in the Book of Jasher

In June 1840, two years before Joseph published his Book of Abraham, an announcement from the East Coast newspaper the *New York*

Joseph Smith and the Book of Enoch

Star was published in the *Times and Seasons,* the Mormon church's media outlet in Nauvoo, Illinois. The press release announced the publication of an English translation of a lost Book of Jasher:

> We shall shortly have a literary, or rather a Biblical curiosity, to present to the American reader, which we feel confident in predicting, will excite great interest among those who take pleasure in reading and studying the Scriptures. It is the Book of Jasher referred to in the Bible, in Joshua, and in the second book of Samuel, and which has been in the progress of translation from the Hebrew for several years in England, and is now completed, and will be published in a few days in this city, in a very elegant stereotyped edition. There have been several simulated Books of Jasher, a notice of which we find in the Rev. Mr. Horn's Commentaries on the study of the Scriptures; but they bear no analogy to the present work, which is written in the purest Hebrew, and translated with an elegance and fidelity highly creditable to the eminent scholar who has been so long engaged in the work. The preface to the Hebrew edition speaks of it as having been brought from Jerusalem with other sacred rolls and manuscripts, at the destruction of that city, and carried into Spain, where the Jews had their most celebrated colleges up to the eleventh century. On the discovery of printing the manuscript was copied, and carried to Venice, where it was printed by order of the Jewish Consistory of Rabbins, in 1613, and is now for the first time translated into the English language and published. [...] Josephus refers to this Book, and the great Mendelson extracts copiously from it. Recently the Book of Enoch has been discovered, translated from the Ethiopic, and published in England. Professor Stewart has lately reviewed it. The discovery of missing books referred to in Scripture, and the many yet to be discovered, joined to the singular signs of the times in relation to the chosen people, give great interest to this and similar works.—This Book, which makes nearly three hundred pages, clears up some points somewhat obscure in the Bible, and is very full in detailing the events of the reign of Nimrod; the building of the Tower of Babel, and confusion of tongues; the causes preceding the destruction of the doomed cities; the sacrifice of Isaac, and the life of Joseph: and has some curious facts about the deluge.—NEW YORK STAR[6]

This announcement of the 1840 publication confirms that early church leaders were apparently well aware of English productions of scholarly translations of lost books once considered scripture and were still looking for more lost books that might supplement what had been revealed to them. In a world spinning excitedly with the burgeoning era of enlightenment and scholarship, "Egyptomania" in the wake of Napoleonic campaigns, the decipherment of Egyptian hieroglyphs by Jean-Francois Champollion by the light of the trilingual Rosetta Stone, and repeatedly forthcoming English translations of once-thought-lost scriptures, it is easy to imagine how familiar it would sound in that day

Chapter Two. Who Is Enoch?

and age to be told of any ancient scriptures found, translated and published for the English-reading world.

The *Times and Seasons* announcement also suggests that Joseph and his host of scribes relied on extrabiblical, secular and scholarly materials including biblical commentaries in their attempts at scriptural understanding.[7] And it also confirms that, at least by this date in 1840, Joseph and associates in the Mormon-written productions department would have been aware of Richard Laurence's Book of Enoch and the fact that it was given serious scholarly review among academia. Lastly, it shows a specific interest in the Book of Jasher as possible restored scripture, which happens to include a remarkable expansion of the Bible's Enoch story. Jasher's Enoch story is epic, including a 42-verse expansion of the scant 7 verses found in Genesis 5—but with a whole lot more, including Enoch being appointed by all other kings as their King, and teaching everyone his vast knowledge before he must be taken away to ascend into the heavens, after which he rides off on a horse, ascending in a whirlwind and leaving behind a launch pad heaped with ice and snow.

Following the same genealogical lines found in Genesis, Jasher's Enoch is introduced in the last verse of Chapter 2. The expanded Enoch story is the entirety of Jasher, Chapter 3, which is worth reading fully. This fantastic and expanded account gives us insight as to what early 17th-century Jewish authors in western Europe had to say and write about this ancient patriarch:

> 2. And *the soul of Enoch was wrapped up in the instruction of the Lord, in knowledge and in understanding*; and he wisely retired from the sons of men, and secreted himself from them for many days.
> ....
> 5. And Enoch rose up according to the word of the Lord, and went forth from his house, from his place and from the chamber in which he was concealed; *and he went to the sons of men and taught them the ways of the Lord, and at that time assembled the sons of men and acquainted them with the instruction of the Lord.*
> 6. And he ordered it to be proclaimed in all places where the sons of men dwelt, saying, *Where is the man who wishes to know the ways of the Lord and good works? let him come to Enoch.*
> 7. And all the sons of men then assembled to him, for all who desired this thing went to Enoch, *and Enoch reigned over the sons of men according to the word of the Lord, and they came and bowed to him and they heard his word.*

8. And the spirit of God was upon Enoch, and *he taught all his men the wisdom of God and his ways*, and the sons of men served the Lord all the days of Enoch, and *they came to hear his wisdom.*

9. *And all the kings of the sons of men, both first and last, together with their princes and judges, came to Enoch when they heard of his wisdom, and they bowed down to him, and they also required of Enoch to reign over them, to which he consented.*

10. And *they assembled in all,* one hundred and thirty kings and princes, and *they made Enoch king over them and they were all under his power and command.*

11. And *Enoch taught them wisdom, knowledge, and the ways of the Lord; and he made peace amongst them,* and peace was throughout the earth during the life of Enoch.

....

16. And Adam died because he ate of the tree of knowledge; he and his children after him, as the Lord God had spoken.

17. And it was in the year of Adam's death which was the two hundred and forty-third year of *the reign of Enoch,* in that time Enoch resolved to separate himself from the sons of men and to secret himself as at first in order to serve the Lord.

18. And Enoch did so, but did not entirely secret himself from them, but kept away from the sons of men three days and then went to them for one day.

19. And during the three days that he was in his chamber, he prayed to, and praised the Lord his God, and the day on which he went and appeared to his subjects he taught them the ways of the Lord, and all they asked him about the Lord he told them.

20. And he did in this manner for many years, and he afterward concealed himself for six days, and appeared to his people one day in seven; and after that once in a month, and then once in a year, until all the kings, princes and sons of men sought for him, and desired again to see the face of Enoch, and to hear his word; but they could not, *as all the sons of men were greatly afraid of Enoch, and they feared to approach him on account of the Godlike awe that was seated upon his countenance*; therefore no man could look at him, fearing he might be punished and die.

21. And all the kings and princes resolved to assemble the sons of men, and to come to Enoch, thinking that they might all speak to him at the time when he should come forth amongst them, and they did so.

22. And the day came when Enoch went forth and they all assembled and came to him, and Enoch spoke to them the words of the Lord and he taught them wisdom and knowledge, and *they bowed down before him and they said, May the king live! May the king live!*

Chapter Two. Who Is Enoch?

23. And in some time after, when the *kings* and princes and the sons of men were speaking to Enoch, and Enoch was teaching them the ways of God, behold *an angel of the Lord then called unto Enoch from heaven, and wished to bring him up to heaven to make him reign there over the sons of God, as he had reigned over the sons of men upon earth.*

24. When at that time *Enoch heard this he went and assembled all the inhabitants of the earth, and taught them wisdom and knowledge and gave them divine instructions*, and he said to them, *I have been required to ascend into heaven*, I therefore do not know the day of my going.

25. And now therefore *I will teach you wisdom and knowledge and will give you instruction before I leave you*, how to act upon earth whereby you may live; and he did so.

26. And he taught them wisdom and knowledge, and gave them instruction, and he reproved them, and he placed before them statutes and judgments to do upon earth, and he made peace amongst them, and *he taught them everlasting life*, and dwelt with them some time teaching them all these things.

27. And at that time the sons of men were with Enoch, and Enoch was speaking to them, and *they lifted up their eyes and the likeness of a great horse descended from heaven*, and the horse paced in the air;

28. And they told Enoch what they had seen, and Enoch said to them, On my account does this horse descend upon earth; the time is come when I must go from you and I shall no more be seen by you.

29. And the horse descended at that time and stood before Enoch, and all the sons of men that were with Enoch saw him.

30. And Enoch then again ordered a voice to be proclaimed, saying, *Where is the man who delighteth to know the ways of the Lord his God, let him come this day to Enoch before he is taken from us.*

31. *And all the sons of men assembled and came to Enoch that day; and all the kings of the earth with their princes and counsellors remained with him that day; and Enoch then taught the sons of men wisdom and knowledge, and gave them divine instruction*; and he bade them serve the Lord and walk in his ways all the days of their lives, and he continued to make peace amongst them.

32. And it was after this that *he rose up and rode upon the horse; and he went forth and all the sons of men went after him*, about eight hundred thousand men; and they went with him one day's journey.

33. And *the second day he said to them, Return home to your tents, why will you go?* perhaps you may die; and some of them

went from him, and *those that remained went with him six day's journey; and Enoch said to them every day, Return to your tents, lest you may die; but they were not willing to return, and they went with him.*

34. And on the sixth day some of the men remained and clung to him, and they said to him, *We will go with thee to the place where thou goest; as the Lord liveth, death only shall separate us.*

35. And they urged so much to go with him, that he ceased speaking to them; and they went after him and would not return;

36. And when the kings returned they caused a census to be taken, in order to know the number of remaining men that went with Enoch; and it was upon the seventh day that *Enoch ascended into heaven in a whirlwind, with horses and chariots of fire.*

37. And on the eighth day *all the kings that had been with Enoch sent to bring back the number of men that were with Enoch, in that place from which he ascended into heaven.*

38. And all those kings went to the place and *they found the earth there filled with snow, and upon the snow were large stones of snow, and one said to the other, Come, let us break through the snow and see, perhaps the men that remained with Enoch are dead, and are now under the stones of snow, and they searched but could not find him, for he had ascended into heaven.*[8]

Is this the same book of Jasher referenced in the Bible? Joshua 10:13 asks, "Is not this written in the book of Jasher?" Similarly, 2 Samuel 1:18 tells us, "Behold, it is written in the book of Jasher." The Book of Jasher we have today (quoted above) is the 1840 English translation of an older Hebrew work entitled *Sefer Hayasher,* published in Venice, Italy, in 1625.[9] In his 1986 article "The Book of Jasher and the Latter-day Saints," Edward J. Brandt explains the authorship and antiquity of the 1625 production:

> [T]his particular work, called *The Book of Jasher,* is characterized by Jewish scholars as *midrashic agadah* or *haggada*—an exegetical type of legendary or historical narrative—and is generally thought to have been written during the thirteenth century A.D. in Spain. Most of the names of characters in the stories other than the biblical names are of Arabic, Spanish, or Italian origin. Written in a scriptural paraphrase style typical of the Jewish liturgical writing of the late middle ages, the published Hebrew editions (except for the 1923) follow the general pattern of the rabbinical *parashot* (the 54 sections of the Torah read weekly in the synagogue). This suggests that this particular work is the product of later rabbinical writers.[10]

Despite the fact that this work was a later (17th century) production in Spain, the expansion of the Enoch story in the Book of Jasher from the scant verses we find in Genesis is remarkable. And despite the expanded story line devoted to this "King Enoch" and the ascension story, the only similarity to 1 Enoch is (1) Enoch, indeed, possesses great knowledge and offers instruction and writings of his understandings for his son, and (2) the apocalyptic description of the ascension in a whirlwind. But the horse-and-chariots whirlwind sounds more like the apocalyptic descriptions found in the books of Daniel or Ezekiel in the Old Testament, rather than any described in 1 Enoch. Other than these similarities, we won't find quite the same excitement about Enoch's life, and nothing about being "translated," from his own (supposed) ancient writings of 1 Enoch.

Perhaps a more interesting story line to take from the Jasher story is that along with Enoch, it appears that 800,000 men "went after him" after he rode off on his horse, all of whom were determined to follow him to the death if necessary (Jasher 3:32). They devoutly traveled with him for seven days before Enoch, on the eighth day, "ascended into heaven in a whirlwind, with horses and chariots of fire" (Jasher 3:36). When the rest of those that stayed behind in the kingdoms went looking for those that followed Enoch, they found that they were all apparently gone too. They found the spot where Enoch ascended heaped with "stones of snow," and they believed the men were all buried in it and dead, "and they searched but could not find him, for he had ascended into heaven" (Jasher 3:37). Eight hundred thousand people translated with Enoch? *Is this a source for a story about the entire city of Enoch translated into heaven*?

A Bible reader will not find any connection with Enoch and any city translated into heaven. St. John, the Revelator wrote about seeing "the holy city, New Jerusalem, *coming down out of heaven* from God, prepared as a bride adorned for her husband," but nobody wrote of one going up into heaven (Revelation 21:2). We also don't find a direct connection between Enoch and Zion or a New Jerusalem anywhere in the Bible. Curiously, however, we do find these connections, with more specific refence to the ancient writings attributed to Enoch, in even later publications of more apocryphal works.

Enoch in the Book of Jubilees

The Book of Jubilees, published in English after Joseph Smith's lifetime, is another non-canonical lost book that starts with the

Joseph Smith and the Book of Enoch

familiar Jewish creation stories and genealogies of Adam, including the man Enoch. The Book of Jubilees was apparently a popular work of ancient Jewish literature, considered inspired particularly among the Jews who hid their scrolls in the caves at Qumran. Between 1947 and 1956, extensive fragments of 15 scrolls of the Book of Jubilees written in Hebrew were recovered among the Dead Sea Scrolls. Based on references and presumed source materials of its authors, it has been dated as written in the second temple era (about 500 BC to AD 70). And, like other circulated scrolls and prophecies kept and copied in ancient Judea, the Book of Jubilees was considered inspired scripture to some anciently, and is still revered as scripture today for a few Ethiopian religious sects.

The author of the Book of Jubilees apparently had access to (or extensive knowledge of) the ancient writings claimed to be written by Enoch, those same prophecies quoted by our early Christian authors in the Bible. Following a similar description of the Cain vs. Seth genealogies of Adam we find in Genesis, the Book of Jubilees again introduces us to Enoch as the son of Jared, seventh from Adam (Jubilees IV:16). And, again, the authors expand in Chapter IV from the limited verses in Genesis 5, offering many more details about Enoch:

> 17. He was *the first one from among the children of men that are born on the earth to learn writing and knowledge and wisdom.*
> 18. And *he wrote the signs of heaven according to the order of their months in a book,* that the sons of men might know the time of the year according to their separate months.
> 19. He was the first to write a testimony, and *he testified to the children of men concerning the generations of the earth,* and explained the weeks of the jubilees, and made known to them the days of the years, and arranged the months and explained the sabbaths of the years as we made them known to him.
> 20. And what was and what will be *he saw in a vision of the night in a dream, and as it will happen to the children of men in their generations until the day of judgment*; he saw and learned every thing *and wrote it as a testimony and laid the testimony on the earth over all the children of men and for their generations.*
> 21. And in the twelfth jubilee, in the seventh week thereof, he took to himself a wife, and her name was Edna, the daughter of Daniel, the daughter of the sister of his father; and in the sixth year in this week she bore him a son, and he called his name Methusaleh.

Chapter Two. Who Is Enoch?

22. And then *he was with the angels of God* six years of this jubilee, and *they showed him all things on earth and in heaven, the rule of the sun, and he wrote down all things.*

23. And *he testified to the Watchmen, those that sinned with the daughters of men; for they had commenced to mix with the daughters of the earth,* so that they were defiled; and Enoch testified against them all.

24. And he *was removed from the midst of the children of men, and we conducted him into the garden of Eden* for greatness and for honor, and behold here he was engaged in writing down the judgment and the eternal condemnation and all the wickedness of the sons of the children of men.

25. And on his account [God] brought the deluge over the whole land of Eden; for there he was set as a sign and that he should testify over all the sons of the children of men, that he should declare all the deeds of the generations until the day of judgment.

26. And he offered a burnt offering on the west side of the sanctuary which was pleasing before the Lord on the hill of the south; for there are four places to the Lord on earth: the garden of Eden and the hill of the east in it, and this hill on which thou art today, the hill of Sinai, *and the hill of Zion, which will be sanctified in the new creation for a sanctification of the earth*: through it the earth will be sanctified from all its sin and its uncleanness to the generation of eternity.[11]

The author of Jubilees had what we today call 1 Enoch in his library for source material. These descriptions include story lines lifted straight from 1 Enoch, as the author admits to having learned of it "in a book" (a very rare possession in those days) that Enoch wrote. The preceding verse introduces his father, Jared, "for in his days the angels of the Lord descended upon the earth, those that are called Watchmen, that they should teach the children of Men to do judgment and right over the earth." This is the summary version of 1 Enoch, as we'll get into later. What we don't find in 1 Enoch is a direct reference to Zion, a "city of Zion" or a "New Jerusalem." However, the son of God sent to dwell among his chosen saints in their inhabitations, and a "new earth" and "new creation for sanctification of the earth" are both prevalent themes in 1 Enoch. The author of Jubilees' more specific and direct connection of Enoch with Zion is interesting, and noteworthy, considering Joseph Smith's conceptions of Zion in connection with the "city of Enoch," and the lack of a more direct connection that we might expect to find in any other sources, including 1 Enoch itself.

Joseph Smith and the Book of Enoch

Enoch in Mormon Doctrine

LDS doctrine follows the New Testament "translation" tradition, interpreting the Old Testament language "he walked with God" to mean he was translated to some other place, without the taste of death. LDS Apostle Bruce R. McConkie offered the following regarding Enoch as a "translated being" and the translation of his entire city, based exclusively on the LDS standard works of canonized scripture:

> Enoch and his people were translated, probably just a few years after Adam's death (Moses 7:18–21, 31, 63, 69; D. & C. 38:4; 45:11–14; 84:99–100; Gen. 5:22–24; Heb. 11:5). It is apparent from the abbreviated account of the Lord's dealings with Enoch and his people that Zion was a very great and populous city, having perhaps many thousands or even millions of inhabitants (Moses 7). Methuselah, the son of Enoch, was not translated, "that the covenants of the Lord might be fulfilled, which he made to Enoch; for he truly covenanted with Enoch that Noah should be of the fruit of his loins" (Moses 8:2). But during the nearly 700 years from the translation of Enoch to the flood of Noah, it would appear that nearly all of the faithful members of the Church were translated, for "the Holy Ghost fell on many, and they were caught up by the powers of heaven into Zion" (Moses 7:27). That this process of translating the righteous saints and taking them to heaven was still going on after the flood among the people of Melchizedek is apparent from the account in the *Inspired Version* of the Bible. Speaking of the faith and righteousness of those holding the Melchizedek Priesthood in that day, the account says:
>
>> "And men having this faith, coming up unto this order of God, were translated and taken up into heaven. And now, Melchizedek was a priest of this order; therefore he obtained peace in Salem, and was called the Prince of peace. And his people wrought righteousness, and obtained heaven, and sought for the city of Enoch which God had before taken, separating it from the earth, having reserved it unto the latter days, or the end of the world" [*Inspired Version*, Gen. 14:32–34].
>
> As far as we know, instances of translation since the day of Melchizedek and his people have been few and far between. After recording that Enoch was translated, Paul says that Abraham, Isaac, and Jacob, and their seed after them (they obviously knowing what had taken place as pertaining to the people of Melchizedek and others) "looked for a city which hath foundations, whose builder and maker is God" (Heb. 11:5–10), that is, they "sought for the city of Enoch which God had before taken" [*Inspired Version*, Gen. 14:34].[12]

Chapter Three

The Book of Enoch
(1 Enoch)

"Well, someday we will find out the source that Joseph Smith used."

—Professor Matthew Black
Princeton University Old Testament Studies,
editor of the Enoch fragments of the Dead Sea Scrolls[1]

In 1821, Richard Laurence, the Archbishop of Cashel and former Professor of Hebrew at Oxford University, published in England the work verbosely titled *The book of Enoch the prophet: an apocryphal production, supposed to have been lost for ages, but discovered at the close of the last century in Abyssinia: now first translated from an Ethiopic ms. in the Bodleian Library.*[2] As the title suggests, the book translates a handwritten manuscript purporting to be the so-called prophecies of Enoch that was known of anciently, then lost for centuries and rediscovered in northern Africa. It was brought to Europe and rested on the shelves of the Bodleian Library of Oxford University until biblical scholar and professor of Hebrew Richard Laurence took it upon himself to complete the translation and publish this lost book of ancient scripture for the English-reading world.

The title page of the book, and page after page of footnotes and commentary throughout, include samples of the glyphic Ethiopic characters Laurence brilliantly translated.

From cover to cover, the book is about 260 pages, but it's not just the first English translation of the scriptural text. It also included Professor Laurence's preliminary dissertation and commentary on the book's origin, interpretations and a wealth of biblical scholarship for its time. There have been several subsequent English translations of

Joseph Smith and the Book of Enoch

መጽሐፈ: ሄኖክ:

ነቢይ::

THE BOOK OF ENOCH
THE PROPHET:

AN APOCRYPHAL PRODUCTION,

SUPPOSED TO HAVE BEEN LOST FOR AGES;

BUT

DISCOVERED AT THE CLOSE OF THE LAST CENTURY IN ABYSSINIA;

NOW FIRST TRANSLATED FROM

AN ETHIOPIC MS. IN THE BODLEIAN LIBRARY.

BY

RICHARD LAURENCE, LL.D.

REGIUS PROFESSOR OF HEBREW, CANON OF CHRIST CHURCH, ETC.

OXFORD,

AT THE UNIVERSITY PRESS FOR THE AUTHOR:
SOLD BY J. PARKER; AND BY MESSRS. RIVINGTON, LONDON.
1821.

The Book of Enoch, title page, Richard Laurence, 1821.

Chapter Three. The Book of Enoch (1 Enoch)

the same Ethiopic Book of Enoch, all of which are generally referred to as the "First Book of Enoch" or "1 Enoch." Laurence's Book of Enoch is thus also referred to as 1 Enoch, but with the passage of time, with collaboration and refined scholarship, translations often need updating. It makes sense that Enoch scholars generally prefer later translations. For example, R. H. Charles's 1883 translation published in *Apocrypha and Pseudepigrapha of the Old Testament* (Oxford: Clarendon Press, rev. ed., 1913) soon replaced Laurence's as the preferred version and is still often cited in scholarly works. Richard Laurence's was the first in English, and thus primitive in Enoch studies. The book is no longer available in print, but an exact reproduction (facsimile) of the book is scanned and available in the public domain for download online.³

Before Professor Laurence turned his attention to it, the Ethiopic manuscript had sat on the shelves of the Bodleian Library in Oxford since the Scottish traveler James Bruce returned with it from his travels to Abyssinia in 1773. Bruce spent much of his time in northern Africa visiting aging monasteries, looking through libraries for neglected ancient texts. These discovered lost books were scriptural treasure.

The Book of Enoch, based on historical references made by its apparently Jewish authors, is believed to have been originally written in the second temple period (about 516 BC to 70 CE). For example, our synoptic gospels refer to the Roman destruction of the Jerusalem temple in 70 CE, placing their authorship after that time. 1 Enoch predates New Testament writings. It is full of allusions to the coming "Lord" and "Son of man," but it does not reference the destruction of the temple in Jerusalem (AD 70). This places it in the vein of other pre–Christian apocalyptic Jewish writings, like the Book of Daniel and similarly placed writings. Regardless of the

James Bruce (engraving by S. Freeman from a painting by D. Martin, Wikimedia Commons).

exact time of its authorship, we find the prophecies of Enoch accepted as inspired scripture by some of our New Testament authors. Its influence is found in our four gospels, some epistles and John's apocalyptic Book of Revelation (this last one seeming to be a Christianized rewrite of some of Enoch's apocalyptic writings).

The author of the New Testament Epistle of Jude quotes (or paraphrases, borrows, is influenced by, copies from or whatever word works) from the prophecies of Enoch, presumably preserved for him in writing:

Jude 1:14–15.	Enoch II; LXI:4
And Enoch also, the seventh from Adam, prophesied of these, saying, *Behold, the Lord cometh with ten thousands of his saints,* *To execute judgment upon all,* and to convince all that are ungodly among them of all their *ungodly deeds which they have ungodly committed*, and of all *their hard speeches* which *ungodly sinners* have spoken against him.	*Behold, he comes with ten thousands of his saints to execute judgment upon them,* to destroy the wicked, and to reprove all the carnal for every thing *which the sinful and ungodly have done, and committed against him....* *The word of his mouth* shall destroy all the *sinners and all the ungodly*

The close similarity of the language in the Ethiopic Book of Enoch that Bruce found appeared to confirm that it was that lost scripture that New Testament writers and early Church Fathers had used. It was that same book that, except for a few preserved fragments, was considered lost from Europe from the Middle Ages until Bruce returned with three Ethiopic manuscripts from his travels in Africa.

The most exquisite of the three manuscripts Bruce returned with was presented to King Louis XV of France in 1773. The second was donated a year later to the Bodleian Library at Oxford University, and Bruce kept the third copy for his personal collection. After his death in 1794, the third copy joined the second in the Bodleian, where it lay with Bruce's unfinished attempts at translating the text into English until Oxford University Professor of Hebrew Richard Laurence resumed the task, resulting in his 1821 publication that soon became widely available overseas in the United States, and accessible to communities and towns in the stream of commerce and media, like Palmyra, New York.

The first 48 pages of the book include Professor Laurence's "Preliminary Dissertation" with a historical background describing Bruce's journeys looking for lost scripture and finding it in the sands of Africa

Chapter Three. The Book of Enoch (1 Enoch)

and detailing the translation process. Professor Laurence describes how he found it described as catalogued in the Oxford library:

> The subject of the book is a series of visions, respecting the fallen angels, their posterity the giants, the crimes which occasioned the deluge, the mysteries of heaven, the place of the final judgment of men and angels, and various parts of the universe seen by Enoch, and related by him to his son Mathusala.
> The narrative is bold and fabulous, but highly impressive of the sentiments and character of those speculative enthusiasts, who blended the Chaldaic philosophy with the sacred history of the Jews. As a literary relic, it merits attention; and as an Ethiopic book, written in the purest Geez, and venerated by the Abyssinians, as of equal authority with the writings of Moses, it deserves to be laid before the public.[4]

Professor Laurence's 1821 translation is full of scholarly analysis and religious profundity. Laurence expounds on allusions found throughout the Book of Enoch, including heavenly visions with accompanying and inquiring angels to explain the mysteries of the world. He opens his "Preliminary Dissertation" by explaining,

> The apocryphal Book of Enoch, in the last and the preceding century, proved a prolific subject for critical speculation and theological discussion. The circumstance of its having been quoted by an inspired writer of the New Testament augmented the despair of recovering a supposed treasure, which had long been lost. It was known until the eighth century of the Christian era; after which it seems to have sunk into complete oblivion.

Laurence also explains the apocryphal book's apocalyptic visions, where Enoch is shown "all the repositories of the superior and inferior kingdom" of heaven and a vision of a "tree of life."[5] In one paragraph alone, Laurence expounds,

> These allusions of the Zohar to the repositories of the celestial and terrestrial kingdoms, and to the tree of knowledge in the garden of Eden, shewn to Enoch after his ascent into heaven, are distinctly stated to have been taken from a book, entitled the Book of Enoch; and the very same allusions will be found minutely detailed between the sixteenth and thirty-seventh chapters of the present version. The reference to the tree of knowledge in the garden of Eden occurs in the thirty-first chapter. Now the authors of the Cabalistical remains wrote or conveyed down their recondite doctrines in Chaldee. Scarcely therefore, I apprehend, will it be questioned, that the copy of the Book of Enoch which they cited was written either in that language or in Hebrew. For they appear to have regarded it as the genuine work of him whose name it bore, and not as the spurious production of a later age. Presuming therefore that the book before us was the composition of some

Joseph Smith and the Book of Enoch

unknown Jew, under the borrowed name of Enoch, I shall next consider what criteria are afforded us to determine the period at which it may have been written.[6]

For the regular church-going Latter-day Saint of today, this passage is loaded with peculiarly familiar terms that immediately catch the eye. For example, concepts that are so commonly associated with Mormonism that they are almost clichés. Words and phrases like "superior and inferior kingdoms," "repositories of the celestial and terrestrial kingdoms," a vision of a "tree of life," and the whole notion of long-lost ancient scripture, unearthed and translated from an obscure set of symbols into English and published in the ancient prophet's name, which book some consider a "genuine work of him whose name it bore," while others spurn it as "the spurious production of a later age."

There's even more information here that the casual Latter-day Saint reader might not find so peculiar but is nonetheless unique to particular LDS doctrines, temple liturgy and scholarship.[7] In this same paragraph, Laurence mentions special knowledge about our first parents in the garden of Eden that has been "distinctly stated to have been taken from a book, entitled the Book of Enoch," which directly alludes to the special light and knowledge endowed upon members of the LDS Church in the temple. Joseph's Book of Moses and Book of Abraham, found as scripture in the Latter-day Saints' *The Pearl of Great Price*, are restorations of those lost portions of Enoch's prophecies and include specific teachings found in the LDS temple ceremony, discussed in more detail in later chapters.

Laurence's "Preliminary Dissertation" goes on to discuss the doctrine of the "preexistence," a familiar and unique doctrine for Latter-day Saints, quoting the Book of Enoch, (LXI:8–10, 12–13):

> for from the beginning the Son of Man existed in secret, whom the Most High preserved in the presence of his power, and revealed to the elect.... All the kings, the princes, the exalted, and those who rule over the earth, shall fall down on their faces before him, and shall worship him. They shall fix their hopes on this Son of man, and shall pray to him and petition him for mercy.

Laurence expounds on this idea of a "preexistence" found in the Book of Enoch:

> In both these passages the preexistence of the Messiah is asserted in language which admits not the slightest shade of ambiguity. Nor is it such a preexistence as the philosophical Cabbalists attributed to him, who believed the souls of all men, and consequently that of the Messiah, to have

Chapter Three. The Book of Enoch (1 Enoch)

been originally created together, when the world itself was formed; but an existence antecedent to all creation; an existence previous to the formation of the luminaries of heaven; an existence prior to all things visible and invisible, "before every thing concealed." It should likewise be remarked, that the preexistence ascribed to him is a divine preexistence[.]

Laurence's "Preliminary Dissertation" interestingly concludes that the true author of the Book of Enoch was not the real Enoch, the seventh from Adam and pre-flood, great-grandfather of Noah. Instead, this Book of Enoch "was the composition of some unknown Jew, under the borrowed name of Enoch."[8] Later Enoch scholars concur, however ascribing the entirety of 1 Enoch not to a single author but to a handful of authors writing over a span of time. Laurence's "Preliminary Dissertation" confirms that the book of Enoch our early Christian authors were relying on was not only apocryphal, it was pseudepigraphic (forged). He concluded that it was written during the time of the captivity of Babylon, "[f]or the very expressions, as well as the descriptive ideas of Daniel are adopted by it, in the presentation of the Ancient of days coming to judgment with the Son of man."[9] The fact that it was likely known to be pseudepigraphal could be a reason for its exclusion from the canon from the beginning. This, and perhaps because of the Jewish lunar calendar that its author attempts to push on his Hellenistic audience in ancient Palestine, which eventually went with the Gregorian calendar we use today.

Laurence's conclusions about the text's authorship answered the long-lingering question of whether the Book of Enoch, once lost, now found, was truly the inspired written word of God. How could it be inspired scripture if its author is lying about who wrote it and when? Regardless, and like the other books of the Apocrypha and burgeoning contemporary publications on biblical scholarship, Laurence's book was, and remains today, very educational and inspiring to the interested reader.

Chapter Four

Ground Rules for This Historical Question

"Indeed, a copier may be more likely to plagiarize an obscure song from the distant past and a faraway land than a recent well-known hit."

—*Gaste v. Kaiserman*,
U.S. Court of Appeals, 2nd Cir.[1]

In an article acknowledging Joseph Smith's fascination with "lost" or "hidden" books of scripture not found in our Bibles today, Professor Thomas A. Wayment, Brigham Young University professor of ancient scripture, sets down some necessary boundaries when it comes to objective scholarly consideration of what literary sources Joseph Smith availed himself in his own education:

> Before one can answer the most important historical question at hand, *how Joseph Smith used the Apocrypha and what relationship that body of literature had to early Mormon writings*, it seems prudent to first of all establish some controls on the discussion. This is necessary because previous discussions have largely contented themselves with drawing out parallels between apocryphal writings and early Mormon publications without any discussion of whether or not Joseph Smith had access to the texts under discussion. Moreover, a wide variety of modern translations of ancient apocryphal texts are often employed when there is no possible way that someone living in the early nineteenth century could have known them. This is particularly important when citing phrases or words that Joseph Smith might have incorporated into the language of his revelations.[2]

Did Joseph Smith borrow words, draw verbal parallels, themes or story lines from Laurence's 1821 translation of the apocryphal 1 Enoch, or not? Two ground rules for considering this important historical question:

Chapter Four. Ground Rules for This Historical Question

> Rule 1: For purposes of literary source analysis, do not compare Joseph Smith's texts with those to which Joseph Smith had no possible access.

A critical question of whether an author borrowed from another must be limited to determining accessible and available publications or writings. If access was absolutely impossible, there's no point in asking whether the former could have borrowed from the latter. We don't get to probability without a possibility to start. If the text wasn't published and available, copying, borrowing or any measure of influence is not within natural probabilities.

Making a list of parallels between Joseph's revelations and later-published translations of apocryphal works may be faith promoting for devotional purposes, but it's not dispositive for purposes of a historical-critical look at possible literary sources among similar contemporary writings. Some LDS scholars seem to purposely limit their comparisons between Joseph's writings and apocryphal books that were only discovered or published after Joseph's time.[3] They point to latter publications to support their perspective that parallels found with Joseph's revelations are proof of Joseph's prophetic calling as translator, seer and revelator.[4] As it follows, Joseph could not have copied something published after his lifetime and, therefore, any parallels between Joseph's writings and later-published books or translations are irrelevant for considering circumstantial evidence of copying.

Here's an example of how the rule works. We would have no reason to make a list of all the parallels and allusions between Shakespeare's works and the King James Bible to show where Shakespeare may have borrowed from it or was influenced. Why? The King James Bible wasn't published until 1611, long after Shakespeare began penning his plays and sonnets. If there are any biblical allusions in Shakespeare's works (and there are plenty), the source text is the Geneva Bible, not the King James Bible.[5] It's an exercise of confusion and futility for historical-critical purposes—unless you are asking another question, i.e., whether the King James translators borrowed from Shakespeare.

> Rule 2: Avoid using later or more modern translations of ancient apocryphal texts in citing phrases or words that Joseph Smith might have incorporated into his own works.

This obviously restates the first rule, but for a more specific purpose. Using a later translation or revision of prior publication of an apocryphal text to try to prove your point can indicate bias toward trying to prove the point. There are undeniable similarities and parallels

Joseph Smith and the Book of Enoch

between Joseph Smith's writings and Laurence's 1821 Book of Enoch. Yet, some LDS apologists prefer to point out commonalities found in later translations of 1 Enoch published after Joseph's lifetime as additional proof of his prophetic calling.[6]

For example, in a 2014 article, "The LDS Story of Enoch as the Culminating Episode of a Temple Text," LDS scholar Jeffrey M. Bradshaw describes the relationship between 1 Enoch and the LDS temple endowment. Drawing several correlations between the LDS temple and 1 Enoch, he finds "many interesting resemblances." He notes that 1 Enoch is an account of

> Enoch's journeys to the throne of God in the celestial temple, his prophetic commission to pronounce judgment on fallen angels who have corrupted mankind, and revelations regarding the Creation, God's plans for mankind, his vision of the coming of the Son of Man (Chosen One, Righteous One) as an agent of God's judgment, the New Jerusalem, and the final judgment of the world.[7]

Bradshaw's summary of 1 Enoch is spot-on, and his research is excellent and faith promoting. However, due to Bradshaw's reliance on later-published English translations, he seemingly avoids having to address the question of borrowing from Richard Laurence's 1821 English translation of 1 Enoch. Bradshaw's purpose for reliance on later publications is self-stated:

> In addition to *1 Enoch*, other lesser-known ancient Enoch books (*2* and *3 Enoch*, the *Book of the Giants*) add to our understanding of the importance of Enoch among some Jews and Christians and also provide fascinating resonances with LDS scripture.[8]

Relying only on publications produced or found after Joseph Smith's time ignores the fact that many similarities in the latter Enoch writings are because they also stem from earlier Enoch literary sources or traditions—including those found in the 1821 Book of Enoch. The availability of a literary source offers a better explanation based on the number of significant and apparent commonalities found between Joseph's Enoch writings and Laurence's. This also ignores the number of available extracts of the Book of Enoch printed before Professor Laurence's book was published, whether Joseph ever had access to Laurence's book or not.[9]

Modern and better translations of ancient texts are certainly helpful to understand the intended meaning of scripture, but they can skew the results when critically considering any direct verbal parallels between two texts in source analysis. The more direct verbal

Chapter Four. Ground Rules for This Historical Question

connections there are, the more proof there is of influence and possible borrowing. This is not just looking for word-for-word matches. Verbal parallels include similar vocabulary, word order and even punctuation, place-markers and spelling. The more connections between two texts, the more the scale tips toward influence, borrowing and use.

Let's go back to Shakespeare as an example. Some detractors argue Joseph Smith borrowed lines from Shakespeare's *Hamlet* in authoring the Book of Mormon:

"...whose limbs ye must soon lay down in the cold and silent grave, from whence no traveler can return" 2 Nephi 1:14	"But that the dread of something after death, The undiscover'd country from whose bourn No traveller returns" *Hamlet*, 3.1.78–80

It sounds very close, and certainly poetic. Let's compare them. We have matching allusions to death (cold silent grave and the dread of death), followed by a purely metaphorical phrase in almost identical wording "no traveler returns," with different spellings (traveler/traveller). The conclusion that Joseph Smith borrowed from *Hamlet* seems logical, but it falls far short of tipping any scales. It's too myopic and assumes away any other and better available sources that Joseph may have drawn from.

Joseph may have read or heard Shakespeare, who was first published 200 years earlier. But the more probable source of Joseph's revelatory verse and prose was his intimate familiarity with the Bible, both Old and New Testaments. He was familiar with popular stories like Job that were read and reread, told and retold. Familiar Bible stories provided patterns for similar stories. Joseph apparently recognized Hebraic parallelism throughout the biblical poetry and narrative motifs, which was a field of biblical scholarship only in its infancy in Europe in Joseph's lifetime.[10] Professor Thomas Wayment acknowledged,

> For non–LDS scholars, the presence of parallels has been used to draw attention to the possibility that Joseph plagiarized available sources.... The larger reality is that the presence of such parallels may arise out of a much more mundane event: his family, or perhaps even Joseph, was accustomed to reading a Bible in which the Apocrypha were included and that the language of the Apocrypha is echoed in Joseph's early writings.[11]

Lending credence to Professor Wayment's observations, compare the same Book of Mormon language to the Bible passages in the Book of

Joseph Smith and the Book of Enoch

Job in the Old Testament (KJV):

2 Nephi 1:14. "... the cold and silent grave, from whence no traveler can return"	Job 7:9–10. "So he that goeth down to the grave shall come up no more. He shall return no more"
Mosiah 3:25. "... a state of misery and endless torment from whence they can no more return."	Job 10:21. "Before I go whence I shall not return"

Comparing these scriptures, and knowing Joseph was fondly familiar with and borrowed directly from his KJV Bible, it seems a far better case that Joseph was borrowing from the Book of Job rather than Shakespeare. But that still ignores other possible sources.

Others have suggested that Joseph copied from Josiah Priest's *The Wonders of Nature*, published in 1825:

2 Nephi 1:14. "... the cold and silent grave, from whence no traveler can return" Book of Mormon (1830)	"...I had some preparation to make before I went hence to that bourne from whence no traveller returns." *The Wonders of Nature* (1825, 469)

If anyone copied from anyone else, who copied from whom? If we use this chapter's ground rules, it looks at least like Josiah Priest was copying from Shakespeare's *Hamlet*, "from whose **bourn** no **traveller** returns," when we further consider factors including specific word choice and spelling. We'll use these same rules to consider literary parallels between Joseph Smith's compositions and Laurence's Book of Enoch.

CHAPTER FIVE

Joseph Smith's Access to the Book of Enoch

> "Because copiers are rarely caught red-handed, copying has traditionally been proven circumstantially by *proof of access* and *substantial similarity*."
> —United States Court of Appeals Second Circuit[1]

We know that Joseph Smith had access to and read the Apocrypha—or "hidden" books—that aren't found in most printed Bibles today. The Apocrypha is a selection of 15 books originally included in the 1611 publication of the King James Bible but eventually removed from later publications because they were not considered inspired scripture. In Joseph Smith's lifetime, one could expect to find the Apocrypha in nearly half of the Bibles then being published. These 15 obscure books were placed between the Old and New Testaments, and included books of 1 Esdras, 2 Esdras, Tobit, Judith, Additions to Esther, Wisdom of Solomon, Ecclesiasticus, Baruch, Letter of Jeremiah, Prayer of Azariah, Susanna, Bel and the Dragon, Prayer of Manasseh, 1 Maccabees and 2 Maccabees. They were considered inspired scripture at least by some Hellenistic Jews at different times, but rejected as part of the Hebrew Bible by traditional Jews, deemed heretical, pseudepigraphic, uninspired or—worse—political propaganda calling for revolt and insurgency. Sedition was a risky business in Palestine, as we well know.

Whether the Apocrypha are inspired books of scripture or not has always been the question for Bible readers. Martin Luther is said to have described the Apocrypha as "books which are not considered equal to the Holy Scriptures, but are useful and good to read."[2] Joseph Smith similarly recommended their reading, but cautioned of their

Joseph Smith and the Book of Enoch

questionable inspired status. While he was "engaged in the translation of the Old Testament" and "having come to that portion of the ancient writings called the Apocrypha, he inquired of the Lord," and recorded the following revelation in March 1833, now found in D&C Section 91:

> Verily, thus saith the Lord unto you concerning the Apocrypha—There are many things contained therein that are true, and it is mostly translated correctly; There are many things contained therein that are not true, which are interpolations by the hands of men. Verily, I say unto you, that it is not needful that the Apocrypha should be translated. Therefore, whoso readeth it, let him understand, for the Spirit manifesteth truth; And whoso is enlightened by the Spirit shall obtain benefit therefrom; And whoso receiveth not by the Spirit, cannot be benefited. Therefore it is not needful that it should be translated. Amen.

We also know that Joseph Smith personally owned and used a King James translation of the Bible that included the 15 books of the Apocrypha.[3] Oliver Cowdry purchased a Bible to help them in their translation work in October 1829. The new Bible was published the year before by H. and E. Phinney company of Cooperstown, New York. Handwritten notes in the front cover of Joseph and Oliver's Cooperstown Bible record that it was purchased at the Egbert B. Grandin Book Store in Palmyra, New York, where the Book of Mormon was later published. The Cooperstown Bible was encyclopedic, which fueled Joseph's appetite for knowledge. He read the Apocrypha and incorporated bits and pieces of these obscure scriptures into his own revelations and writings.[4]

The consensus among current scholarship is that Joseph Smith had access to Richard Laurence's 1821 Book of Enoch or to published 1 Enoch extracts.[5] Not mincing words, BYU professor Thomas Wayment puts it this way:

> There has been a rather lively debate as to whether or not Joseph Smith used the pseudepigraphical book of 1 Enoch during the time he wrote about Enoch in a work that was later entitled the Book of Moses. Several new stories of Enoch are included in Joseph's Book of Moses, and some have argued that he drew upon a published edition of Enoch while creating the new Enoch material. There was a widely available translation of 1 Enoch that was done in 1821 and was published in England, a book that was potentially available to Joseph.[6]

Laurence's Book of Enoch is not listed in inventories of Joseph Smith's personal library or any of the effects he left behind. But we know that one of Joseph's closest advisors and the first members of Joseph's Quorum of Twelve Apostles, "the Apostle Paul of Mormonism" Parley

Chapter Five. Joseph Smith's Access to the Book of Enoch

P. Pratt, personally owned a copy of the book, as recorded in the LDS Church history.[7]

By June 1830, with the Book of Mormon having been revealed as having been once lost, now found ancient scripture, Smith's flock of followers expected more lost books to surface. And they expected their "prophet, seer and revelator" to reveal and translate more through his revelatory powers. As the LDS *History of the Church* records confirm,

> Much conjecture and conversation frequently occurred among the Saints, concerning the books mentioned, and referred to, in various places in the Old and New Testaments, which were now nowhere to be found. The common remark was, "They are *lost books*"; but it seems that Apostolic Church had some of these writings, as Jude mentions or quotes the Prophecy of Enoch, the seventh from Adam. To the joy of the little flock, which in all ... numbered about seventy members, did the Lord reveal the following doings of olden times, *from the prophecy of Enoch.*[8]

The mention of the "prophecy of Enoch" as a "lost book" is curious, because it is not the only lost book of scripture mentioned in the Bible. In fact, there are a lot of them. They include "the book of the covenant" (Exodus 24:7), "the book of the wars of the Lord" (Numbers 21:14), a book by Samuel (1 Samuel 10:25), "the book of Nathan the prophet" and "the book of Gad the seer" (1 Chronicles 29:29), "the book of Shemaiah the prophet" (2 Chronicles 12:15), "the story of the prophet Iddo" (2 Chronicles 13:22), an additional epistle to the Corinthians (1 Corinthians 5:9), an epistle from Laodicea (Colossians 4:16), and the book of Jasher (Joshua 10:13; 2 Samuel 1:18). In light of the more enigmatic names and stories found in the Book of Mormon, any of these lost books would have been great fodder for revealed scripture from biblical times and places. But it was the prophecies of Enoch—and the named patriarch himself—who was on the mind and lips of Joseph Smith, and disproportionately compared to any other lost books throughout his revelations.

And then, "sometime in December 1830, the bonanza came" and, as Joseph recorded, "to the joy of the little flock ... did the Lord reveal ... the prophecy of Enoch."[9] In his published lecture *The Prophecy of Enoch as Restoration Blueprint,* Professor Terryl Givens writes:

> Smith was excited enough by this prophecy that he rushed it into publication almost as soon as the church had a newspaper to serve as a vehicle. He skipped right over the other six chapters of Genesis he had revised, and published Enoch's prophecy without introduction or explanation. In these passages, we find an impact far out of proportion to its modest textual length.

Joseph Smith and the Book of Enoch

The Enoch text sowed the seeds of Mormonism's most distinctive and vibrant doctrines: It produced the most emphatic version of a passible deity the Christian world then knew (a God of passions and emotions). It catalyzed Latter-day Saint understanding of and enthusiasm for the doctrine of premortal existence. It foreshadowed, and might more vitally inform, the church's distinctive doctrine of *theosis* or divinization. And perhaps most importantly, it provided Joseph with the distinctive contours of his own prophetic vocation as a builder of Zion. If the Book of Mormon lent Joseph his indispensable aura of prophetic authority, the prophecy of Enoch provided a personal role model to inspire him and a blueprint to direct him.[10]

Joseph didn't necessarily hide the fact that he had something he referred to as "the prophecy of Enoch." In a revelation on the priesthood recorded in 1835, Joseph straight out told the saints, "These things were all *written in the book of Enoch*, and are to be testified of in due time" (D&C 107:57). Joseph couldn't have been referring to his earlier revelations of Enoch found in his Book of Moses because they were recorded years earlier, between December 1830 and February 1831.

Joseph knew of the prophecy of Enoch, and of things written in it to be testified of. He even referred to it by its title, the "book of Enoch."

Chapter Six

Substantial (and Important) Similarities

> "Laurence as source material for Joseph Smith does not make much sense if the two texts cannot agree on important issues."
>
> —Jed L. Woodworth
> Latter-day Saint historian[1]

Joseph's First Visions

Joseph Smith recorded that he had a visitation from God and Jesus Christ in the wooded area near his home when he was 14 or 15 years old in the spring of 1820. This is the official date, but the first known recorded account dates from years later, in 1832, in Joseph's own handwriting. It was set aside and forgotten until rediscovered and published in 1965. His first recording says he was from age twelve to fifteen.[2] There are actually several recorded versions of the First Vision, both by Joseph and others. He didn't recount the story often, and it wasn't incorporated into Mormon teachings until there were efforts to make a more detailed history of the LDS Church, particularly after Joseph began to become more nationally renowned. Joseph's own written account in 1832 recounts only a visitation of "the Lord," just one personage, neglecting to mention any visitation from God the father.[3]

The Latter-day Saint official account was published in 1842, just two years before Joseph's martyrdom. Joseph and his scribes worked on versions of the vision between 1838 and 1839 to be serially published in the *Times and Seasons* in Nauvoo, Illinois, beginning on March 15, 1842.

The parallels are significant in both themes and specific language. Here are a few excerpts from the official publication of Joseph's First

Joseph Smith and the Book of Enoch

Vision (1842) side by side with parallels in the visions found in Laurence's 1821 Book of Enoch.[4]

Joseph Smith's *History*: **Beseeching the Lord after Reading**	Laurence's 1 Enoch: **Beseeching the Lord after Reading**
While I was laboring under the extreme difficulties caused by the contests of these parties of religionists, I was one day reading the Epistle of James, First Chapter and fifth verse which reads, "If any of you lack wisdom, let him ask of God, that giveth to all men liberally and upbraideth not, and it shall be given him.["] Never did any passage of scripture come with more power to the heart of man that this did at this time to mine. ... At length I came to the conclusion that I must either remain in darkness and confusion or else I must do as James directs, that is, Ask of God. I at last came to the determination to ask of God, concluding that if he gave wisdom to them that lacked wisdom, and would give liberally and not upbraid, I might venture. So in accordance with this my determination to ask of God, I retired to the woods to make the attempt.	LXXXII. SECT. XVI:1–3 ... I will relate another vision, which I saw before I was married; they resemble each other. The first [vision] was when I was learning a book; and the other before I was married to thy mother. I saw a potent vision; And on account of these things besought the Lord.
Joseph Prayed Vocally It was on the morning of a beautiful clear day early in the spring of Eighteen hundred and twenty. It was the first time in my life that I had<made> such an attempt, for amidst all<my> anxieties I had never as yet made the attempt to pray vocally. After I had retired into the place where I had previously designed to go, having looked around me and	**Enoch Prayed Vocally** XIV:1 & 8 I perceived in my dream, that I was now speaking with a tongue of flesh, and with my breath, which the Mighty One put into the mouth of men, that they might converse with it; ... A vision thus appeared to me.

Chapter Six. Substantial (and Important) Similarities

finding myself alone, I kneeled down and began to offer up the desires of my heart to God,	
Joseph Seized in Terror I had scarcely done so, when immediately I was <seized> upon by some power which entirely overcame me and <had> such astonishing influence over me as to bind my tongue so that I could not speak. Thick darkness gathered around me and it seemed to me for a time as if I were doomed to sudden destruction. But exerting all my powers to call upon God to deliver me out of the power of this enemy which had seized upon me, and at the very moment when I was ready to sink into despair and abandon myself to destruction, not to an imaginary ruin but to the power of some actual being from the unseen world who had such a marvelous power as I had never before felt in any being.	**Enoch Seized in Terror** XV:9 & 12 Behold, in that vision clouds and a mist invited me; agitated stars and flashes of lightning impelled and pressed me forwards, ... terror overwhelmed me, and a fearful shaking seized me. Violently agitated and trembling, I fell upon my face. **LXXXII. SECT. XVI:5–7** And falling to the earth, I saw likewise the earth absorbed by a great abyss; and mountains suspended over mountains. .... and of sinking into the abyss. Being alarmed at these things, my voice faltered. I cried out and said; The earth is destroyed.
Descending in a Pillar of Light Just at this moment of great alarm I saw a pillar [of] light exactly over my head above the brightness of the sun, which descended gradually until it fell upon me. It no sooner appeared than I found myself delivered from the enemy which held me bound.	**Descending in a Cloud of Light** CV:21 There I perceived, as it were, a cloud which could not be seen through; for from the depth of it I was unable to look upwards. I beheld also a flame of fire blazing brightly.... **XV:12, 13, 15, 18, 20–23.** In the vision I looked. ... So greatly did it excel in all points, in glory, in magnificence, and in magnitude, that it is impossible to describe to you either the splendor or the extent of it. The appearance of which was like that of frost; while its circumference resembled the orb of the brilliant sun; To look upon it was impossible.

	One great in glory sat upon it: Whose robe was brighter than the sun, and whiter than snow. ... nor could any mortal behold him. A fire was flaming around him.
Two Personages Appear When the light rested upon me I saw two personages (whose brightness and glory defy all description) standing above me in the air.	**Two Personages Appear** XLVI:1 There I beheld the Ancient of days, whose head was like white wool, and with him another, whose countenance resembled that of man. His countenance was full of grace, like that of one of the holy angels. Then I inquired of one of the angels who went with me, and who shewed me every secret thing, concerning this Son of Man, who he was; whence he was; and why he accompanied the Ancient of days.
Calling upon Him by Name One of [them] spake unto me calling me by name and said (pointing to the other) "This is my beloved Son, Hear him." My object in going to enquire of the Lord was to know which of all the sects was right, that I might know which to join.	**Calling upon Him by Name** XIV:24–25 A fire also of great extent continued to rise up before Him.... Then the Lord with his own mouth called me, saying, Approach hither, Enoch, at my holy word. XV:1–2 Then addressing me, he spoke and said; Hear, neither be afraid, O righteous Enoch, thou scribe of righteousness: approach hither, and hear my voice. He answered and said to me; This is the Son of man, ... who will reveal all the treasures of that which is concealed;
Warn of the Corruption of Man No sooner therefore did I get possession of myself so as to be able to speak, than I asked the personages who stood above me in the light, which of all the sects was right, (for at this time it had never entered into my heart that all were	**Warn of the Corruption of Man** CV:23, 25–26 He said; There, into that place which thou beholdest, shall be thrust the spirits of sinners and blasphemers; of those who shall do evil, and who shall pervert all which God has spoken by the mouth of the

Chapter Six. Substantial (and Important) Similarities

wrong) and which I should join. I was answered that I must join none of them, for they were all wrong, and the Personage who addressed me said that all their Creeds were an abomination in his sight, that those professors were all corrupt, that "they draw near to me ~~to~~ with their lips but their hearts are far from me, They teach for doctrines the commandments of men, having a form of Godliness but they deny the power thereof." He again forbade me to join with any of them and many other thing[s] did he say unto me which I cannot write at this time.	prophets; all which they ought to do..... ... God has said; While they have been trodden down by wicked men, they have heard from them revilings and blasphemies; and have been ignominiously treated, while they were blessing me. And now will I call the spirits of the good from the generation of light, and will change those who have been born in darkness;
"I had seen a vision" It has often caused me serious reflection both then and since, how very strange it was that an obscure boy of a little over fourteen years of age.... But strange or not, so it was, and was often cause of great sorrow to myself. However it was nevertheless a fact, that **I had had a Vision**..... I had actually seen a light and in the midst of that light I saw two personages, and they did in reality speak<un>to me, or one of them did, And though I was hated and persecuted for saying that I had seen a vision, Yet it was true and while they were persecuting me reviling me and speaking all manner of evil against me falsely for so saying, ... **I had seen a vision**,	**"I had seen that vision"** **LXXXIX 48–50** ... This is the vision which I saw, laying down and waking. ... Afterwards I wept abundantly, nor did my tears cease, so that I became incapable of enduring it. While I was looking on, they flowed on account of what I saw; for all was come and gone by; every individual circumstance respecting the conduct of mankind was seen by me. In that night I remembered my former dream; and therefore wept and was troubled, because **I had seen that vision.**

Additional similarities between Joseph's visions and Enoch's are found here and elsewhere in Joseph's history, some of which were foundational for his doctrine, and became recurrent motifs and themes throughout his revelations and teachings.

Joseph Smith's *History*:	Laurence's 1 Enoch:
Joseph Wonders at the Luminaries	**Enoch Wonders at the Luminaries**
... for I looked upon the sun the glorious luminary of the earth and also the moon rolling in their majesty through the heavens and also the stars shining in their courses and the earth also upon which I stood and the beast of the field and the fowls of heaven and the fish of the waters and also man walking forth upon the face of the earth in majesty and in the strength of beauty whose power and intelligence in governing the things which are so exceeding great and marvelous even in the likeness of him who created ~~him~~<them> and when I considered upon these things my heart exclaimed well hath the wise man said ~~the~~<it is a> fool <that> saith in his heart there is no God my heart exclaimed all marvelous these bear testimony and bespeak an omnipotent and omnipreasant power a being who maketh Laws and decreeeth and bindeth all things in their bounds who filleth Eternity who was and is and will be from all Eternity to Eternity.	XCII:20–24 Who [is] capable of contemplating all the workmanship of heaven? Who of comprehending the deeds of heaven? He may behold its animation, but not its spirit. He may be capable of conversing respecting it, but not of ascending to it. He may see all the boundaries of these things, and meditate upon them; but he can make nothing like them. Who of all men is able to understand the breadth and length of the earth? By whom has been seen the dimensions of all these things? Is it every man who is capable of comprehending the extent of heaven; what its elevation is, and by what it is supported? How many are the numbers of the stars; and where all the luminaries remain at rest? XLI:4 I beheld also the receptacles of the moon, whence the moons came, whither they proceeded, their glorious return, and how one became more splendid than another. I marked their rich progress, their unchangeable progress, their disunited and undiminished progress; their observance of a mutual fidelity by a stable oath; their proceeding forth before the sun, and their adherence to the path allotted them, in obedience to the command of the Lord of spirits. Potent is his name for ever and for ever.

Chapter Six. Substantial (and Important) Similarities

Another Vision with Another Angel: The Angel Moroni

Joseph also recorded another vision he had on the night of September 21, 1823, in which he saw an angel named Moroni. The visitation of the Angel Moroni recounted in Joseph Smith's *History* repeats the same descriptions as his First Vision(s), but includes even closer parallels to the descriptions in Enoch's visions of angels and heavenly messengers:

Visitation of Angel Moroni	Angels Described in Enoch's Vision
Joseph Smith *History* 1:30–37	**LXXXIV. SECT. XVII:1**
While I was thus in the act of calling upon God, I discovered a light appearing in my room, which continued to increase until the room was lighter than at noonday, when immediately a personage appeared at my bedside, standing in the air, for his feet did not touch the floor.	And after this I saw another dream, and explained it all to thee, ... I saw a vision on my bed;
	XV:12, 13, 15, 18, 20–23.
	In the vision I looked. ... So greatly did it excel in all points, in glory, in magnificence, and in magnitude, that it is impossible to describe to you either the splendor or the extent of it.
He had on a loose robe of most exquisite whiteness. It was a whiteness beyond anything earthly I had ever seen; nor do I believe that any earthly thing could be made to appear so exceedingly white and brilliant. ... Not only was his robe exceedingly white, but his whole person was glorious beyond description, and his countenance truly like lightning. The room was exceedingly light, but not so very bright as immediately around his person. When I first looked upon him, I was afraid; but the fear soon left me.	The appearance of which was like that of frost; while its circumference resembled the orb of the brilliant sun; To look upon it was impossible. ... Whose robe was brighter than the sun, and whiter than snow. ... nor could any mortal behold him.
	CV:2–4
He called me by name, and said unto me that he was a messenger sent from the presence of God to me, and that his name was Moroni; that God had a work for me to do; and that my name should be had for	... the hair of whose head was white like wool, and long; and whose eyes were beautiful. When he opened them, he illuminated all the house, like the sun; the whole house abounded with light. ... He is not human; but resembling the offspring of the angels of heaven, is of a different nature from ours, being altogether unlike to us. His eyes are bright as the rays of the sun; his

good and evil among all nations, kindreds, and tongues, or that it should be both good and evil spoken of among all people.

... After telling me these things, he commenced quoting the prophecies of the Old Testament. He first quoted part of the third chapter of Malachi; and he quoted also the fourth or last chapter of the same prophecy, though with a little variation from the way it reads in our Bibles. Instead of quoting the first verse as it reads in our books, he quoted it thus:

For behold, the day cometh that shall burn as an oven, and all the proud, yea, and all that do wickedly shall burn as stubble; for they that come shall burn them, saith the Lord of Hosts, that it shall leave them neither root nor branch.

countenance glorious, and he looks not as if he belonged to me, but to the angels.
LXX:12–13
... his head was white as wool, and pure, and his robe was indescribable,
... Then I fell upon my face, ... my spirit became changed.
XLVI:1
... and with him another, whose countenance resembled that of man. His countenance was full of grace, like that of one of the holy angels.
XIV:24–25
A fire also of great extent continued to rise up before Him ... with his own mouth called me, saying, Approach hither, Enoch, at my holy word.
XC. SECT. XVIII:6, 8–11
[O]n earth great punishment shall in the end take place; and that there shall be a consummation of all iniquity, which shall be cut off from its root....
... In those days oppression shall be cutoff from its roots, and iniquity with fraud shall be eradicated, perishing from under heaven. ... with fire shall it be burnt.

Joseph Tells His Father of His Vision

... My father, who was laboring along with me, discovered something to be wrong with me, and told me to go home. I started with the intention of going to the house; but, in attempting to cross the fence out of the field where we were, my strength entirely failed me, and I fell helpless on the ground, and for a time was quite unconscious of anything.

Enoch Tells His Son of His Visions
LXXXII. SECT. XVI
I related to him the whole vision which I had seen. He said to me; Confirmed is that which thou hast seen, my son;
And potent the vision of thy dream respecting every secret sin of the earth. Its substance shall sink into the abyss, and a great destruction take place.
Now, my son, rise up; and beseech the Lord of glory, (for thou art

Chapter Six. Substantial (and Important) Similarities

The first thing that I can recollect was a voice speaking unto me, calling me by name. I looked up, and beheld the same messenger standing over my head, surrounded by light as before. He then again related unto me all that he had related to me the previous night, and commanded me to go to my father and tell him of the vision and commandments which I had received.

I obeyed; I returned to my father in the field, and rehearsed the whole matter to him. He replied to me that it was of God, and told me to go and do as commanded by the messenger.

faithful,) that a remnant may be left upon earth, and that he would not wholly destroy it. My son, all this calamity upon earth comes down from heaven; upon earth shall there be a great destruction.

Then I arose, prayed, and entreated; and wrote down my prayer for the generations of the world, explaining every thing to my son Mathusala.

Metalwork, Stones and Sealed Books
JSH 1:34–35

He said there was a book deposited, written upon gold plates, giving an account of the former inhabitants of this continent, and the source from whence they sprang. He also said that the fulness of the everlasting Gospel was contained in it, as delivered by the Savior to the ancient inhabitants;

Also, that there were two stones in silver bows—and these stones, fastened to a breastplate, constituted what is called the Urim and Thummim—deposited with the plates; and the possession and use of these stones were what constituted "seers" in ancient or former times; and that God had prepared them for the purpose of translating the book.

Metalwork, Stones and Sealed Books
Enoch VIII:1–2

Moreover Azazyel taught men to make swords, knives, shields, breastplates, the fabrication of mirrors, and the workmanship of bracelets and ornaments, ... the use of stones of every valuable and select kind,
Enoch LXXXVII:107–109

In like manner also I saw in the vision him who wrote, how he wrote down one, destroyed by the shepherds, every day. He ascended, remained, and exhibited each of his books to the Lord of the sheep, containing all which they had done, and all which each of them had made away with;

And all which they had delivered up to destruction.

He took the book up in his hands, read it, sealed it, and deposited it.

These are just a few examples of significant similarities in important aspects of the foundation stories for the visionary dreams upon which Joseph Smith built his religion.

Chapter Seven

The Book of Moses

"Moses, my son ... behold, I will raise up another like unto thee."
—Moses 1:40–41

Joseph Smith's Book of Moses, it is said, "is worth close attention because it laid down themes Joseph would return to for the rest of his life."[1] It really does. Familiar themes, patterns and allusions in the Book of Moses remerge throughout Joseph's revelations. Terryl Givens, in his book *The Prophecy of Enoch as Restoration Blueprint*, makes these relevant observations about revelation Joseph Smith received in June 1830, just months after establishing his little Mormon church with a handful of new members:

> [I]n 1830, Smith produces, though he does not at first publish, a version of this encounter, which Latter-day Saints know as Moses 1, which turns out to be most significant for its portent of things to come. In it, Smith understands the Lord to tell Moses that many of his words will be removed from his record, but God promises him a prophet will be raised up, and Moses' words will again be had "among the children of men" [Moses 1:41].[2]

Joseph's December 1830 revelations were in the midst of his Book of Moses project, which is apparently connected with more insight and inspiration from a "prophecy of Enoch," as Givens notes:

> This seems to be all the encouragement Joseph Smith needed to launch himself into a bold new work of scriptural production. Sporadically over the ensuing months, amidst arrests, editorial endeavors, conferencing, and traveling, he made a number of emendations to the text of Genesis. Then, sometime in December 1830, the bonanza came. "To the joy of the little flock ... which numbered about seventy members" (he could not yet have known of the Lamanite mission's success), "did the Lord reveal ... the prophecy of Enoch."[3]

Chapter Seven. The Book of Moses

Joseph received a commandment to begin an inspired translation, or revision, of the King James Version of the Bible. He had shown himself as a translator of ancient lost scripture, and he wanted to reveal more. Starting in June 1830, at 24 years old, he began his career long effort to "translate" the Bible, to restore so "many parts which are plain and most precious; and also many covenants of the Lord [which were] taken away."[4] He surrounded himself with the most gifted and educated among his followers, inviting them into his circle of confidence by calling them as scribes, which allowed him to dictate freely while avoiding the limitations that his own writing imposed.

Between June 1830 and February 1831, Joseph completed translating Genesis 1:1 through 6:13, which is now contained in the LDS Church's *Pearl of Great Price* in the Book of Moses. The Book of Moses was just the beginning. Amongst all the moving, hardship, city-building, land-losing restoration work, Joseph's translation of the Bible from start to finish was his lifelong literary work. Joseph worked on his revisions until the time of his death. His personal effects, including his manuscripts of his never-ending rework through the Bible, remained in the possession of his wife, Emma Smith. Emma kept Joseph's manuscripts when the saints split following Joseph's martyrdom, many of them leaving Nauvoo with Brigham Young to settle in the Salt Lake Valley. But the westward-bound saints didn't have their beloved prophet's revised Bible, the work of his career, as their conduit to God's word.

The leaving saints had with them some copies of some manuscripts with selected portions transcribed from Joseph's translations, but they didn't have his whole inspired Bible rewrite. Brigham Young personally requested that Emma turn the manuscripts over, and Emma politely told him she would think about it. She did, and she kept them in her personal possession for over twenty years following Joseph's death. On May 3, 1866, she turned them over to her son Joseph Smith III, the president and prophet of the Reorganized Church of Jesus Christ of Latter-day Saints (RLDS, renamed the Community of Christ in 2001) for publication as their own scripture.

The LDS Church does not include Joseph's entire translation of his revised Bible as part of the LDS standard works because it was left behind with Emma and eventually became the personal property of the RLDS. They had the manuscripts, and thus the copyrights. The RLDS published Joseph's New Translation of the Bible in 1867, and reverently refer to it simply as the *Inspired Version*. Joseph's insertions are not distinguishable from the original Bible text in the published version, and identifying which words and verses were revised, deleted or otherwise changed requires a side-by-side, word-for-word comparison.[5]

Latter-day Saints' scriptures only include portions of Joseph Smith's translation of Matthew from the New Testament, and the Book of Moses (Chapters 1–8), Moses 2 through 5 corresponding mostly with the first six chapters of the Genesis in the Old Testament. Chapters 1, 6, 7 and 8 expound on Genesis and incorporate the theophany of Moses (mirroring that of Enoch's), introducing the prophet Enoch into Joseph's additional lost-and-found scriptures.

Moses 1: The Prologue to Genesis

"In the beginning," there was Genesis 1:1 and that's how it once all started. Or maybe it all just *came to pass*, as it begins in Joseph's *Inspired Version*.[6] Because now we have Moses 1, which is the pre-beginning to the beginning in Genesis. So, let's begin.

Joseph's Moses 1 is a prequel. It's been called a "prologue to Genesis," just as the apocryphal Book of Jubilees has been called a "Lesser Genesis."[7] E. Douglas Clark, an attorney and LDS scholar, draws impressive parallels between Moses 1 and the Book of Jubilees in his 2006 article "A Prologue to Genesis: Moses 1 in Light of Jewish Traditions."[8] Finding parallels between Joseph's revealed scripture and later-published apocryphal works is of particular interest for proving the inspired origin of Joseph's revelations, even if those later published works relied on are considered heretical and pseudepigrapha themselves. Any significant parallels between Joseph's works and any extra-biblical ancient Jewish writings would be remarkable.

Like the Book of Enoch, the Book of Jubilees was originally written by Jewish authors in the second temple era (about 500 BC to AD 70) and considered inspired and accepted among some Jews at the time. Like Enoch, Jubilees was excluded from the canonized Bible. Unlike the Book of Enoch, the Book of Jubilees was only published in English after Joseph Smith's lifetime, so Joseph couldn't have had any access to it as a source. Notwithstanding, Clark found five "striking similarities" between Jubilees 1 and Moses 1, including these impressive parallel points:

1. Both constitute "an entire prefatory chapter providing the setting for the subsequent divine revelation to Moses about the creation and early history of the world" (Moses 1; Jubilees 1);

Chapter Seven. The Book of Moses

2. In both, Moses is atop a mountain when the Lord speaks to Moses and manifests his glory to him (Moses 1:1–2, 7–8; Jubilees 1:1–3);

3. Both prologues say that Moses sees all things, including things come and gone and those yet to come (Moses 1:7–8; Jubilees 1:4);

4. In both versions, Moses is instructed to write what he sees in a book for the benefit of those who live in a future time (Moses 1:40–42; Jubilees 1:5–6); and

5. Both mention a future age of divine revelation to for their followers (Moses 1:41–42; Jubilees 1:22–25).

These are, indeed, several and important parallels between the two works, and Clark goes on, in the true style of the rhetorician that his profession has honed within him, to make a very compelling closing argument for his case:

> As I see it, the emergence of numerous parallels to Moses 1 in a host of previously unknown ancient sources yields evidence for the authenticity and antiquity of Moses 1. The evidence is compelling enough that a burden of proof would now rest on those who would argue against the prophetic calling of both Moses and Joseph Smith.[9]

Both for Clark's and our own purposes, we are comparing for any evident parallels, themes and verbal similarities. In that sense, a side-by-side look at Moses 1 and Jubilees 1[10] helps to show how tightly or loosely any claimed parallels really correspond. Here are similarities that Clark finds compelling:

1. Similar Openings and Settings

Moses 1:1–2	Jubilees 1 (Prefatory Comments)
The words of God, which he spake unto Moses at a time when Moses was caught up into an exceedingly high mountain, And he saw God face to face, and he talked with him, and the glory of God was upon Moses; therefore Moses could endure his presence.	These are the words of the division of days, according to the law and testimony, according to the events of the years, according to their sevens, according to their Jubilees, to all the years of the world, according to the word of the Lord on Mount Sinai to Moses, when he ascended to receive the stone tablets of the law and the commandments by the voice of the Lord when he said to him: "Ascend to the top of the mountain!"

2. Moses Atop a Mountain, Speaks with God and Sees His Glory

Moses 1:1–2, 7–8.	**Jubilees 1:1–3**
The words of God, which he spake unto Moses at a time when Moses was caught up into an exceedingly high mountain, And he saw God face to face, and he talked with him, and the glory of God was upon Moses; therefore Moses could endure his presence.	And it happened in the first year of the exodus of the children of Israel out of Egypt, in the 3rd month, on the 16th of this month, and the Lord spoke to Moses saying: "Ascend to me here on the mountain, and I will give to thee the two stone tablets of the law and the commandments; as I have written them, thou shalt make them known. And Moses ascended the mountain of the Lord, and the glory of the Lord dwelt on the mountain of Sinai, and a cloud overshadowed it six days. And the Lord called to Moses on the seventh day in the midst of the cloud; and he saw the glory of the Lord like a flaming fire on the top of the mountain.

3. Moses Is Shown All Things of the Past and Things Yet to Come

Moses 1:7–8	**Jubilees 1:4**
And now, behold, this one thing I show unto thee, Moses, my son, for thou art in the world, and now I show it unto thee. And it came to pass that Moses looked, and beheld the world upon which he was created; and Moses beheld the world and the ends thereof, and all the children of men which are, and which were created; of the same he greatly marveled and wondered.	And Moses was there on the mountain forty days and forty nights, and the Lord instructed him in regard to what was past and what would be, the words of the division of days, both in the law and the testimony.

4. Moses Is Commanded to Write

Moses 1:40–41	Jubilees 1:5–6
And now, Moses, my son, I will speak unto thee concerning this earth upon which thou standest; and thou shalt write the things which I shall speak. And in a day when the children of men shall esteem my words as naught and take many of them from the book which thou shalt write, behold, I will raise up another like unto thee; and they shall be had again among the children of men—among as many as shall believe.	And he said to him: "Incline thy heart to every word which I shall speak to thee, and write them into a book, in order that their generations may see how I have left them on account of all the evil which they do, in rebelling and in deserting the covenant which I established between me and thee this day on Mount Sinai for their generations. And it will be and these words shall declare it thus when all the punishments shall come over them, and they will know that I am more righteous than they in all their judgments and their desires, and they will know that I was with them.

5. Revelations for His Followers

Moses 1:41–42	Jubilees 1:22–23
And in a day when the children of men shall esteem my words as naught and take many of them from the book which thou shalt write, behold, I will raise up another like unto thee; and they shall be had again among the children of men—among as many as shall believe. (These words were spoken unto Moses in the mount, the name of which shall not be known among the children of men. And now they are spoken unto you. Show them not unto any except them that believe. Even so. Amen.)	And thou, write down for thyself all these words which I have this day make known to thee on this mountain, the first and the last and what is future, according to all the division of days in the law and in the testimony, and according to the weeks' of the jubilees to eternity, until I descend and dwell with them in all eternity. And he said to the angel of the face; Write for Moses from the beginning of creation until my sanctuary shall have been established in their midst for all eternity, and the Lord will have appeared to the eyes of all, and all will know that I am the God of Israel and the Father of all of the children of Jacob and King on Mount Zion from eternity to eternity. And Zion and Jerusalem will be holy.

Joseph Smith and the Book of Enoch

These really are striking similarities, and admittedly faith promoting considering the parallels with a book that Joseph could not have possibly known of, let alone borrow from, as a source for Moses 1. In his comparative analysis, Clark professes that these five correlations are "compelling enough [evidence] that a burden of proof would now rest on those who would argue against the prophetic calling of both Moses and Joseph Smith."[11] Moses's calling doesn't need to get mixed up with Joseph's for purposes of the text comparison, but I agree that the parallels are compelling evidence that might carry the day in a legal argument.

And anyone arguing against his case could simply point out that the same five corresponding parallels found between Joseph's Moses and Jubilees can also be found in the Book of Enoch—and with even tighter correspondences and verbal parallels. The similarities between these two unrelated texts—Moses and Jubilees—naturally results from the fact that they both draw from the same source material, the Book of Enoch.

Whoever wrote Jubilees admittedly had the Book of Enoch and incorporated into the later work similar and popular apocalyptic themes. If Joseph was influenced by the Book of Enoch in writing Moses 1, then parallels between Jubilees and Moses are not surprising, since Jubilees expressly references the Book of Enoch and its importance:

> **Jubilees IV:16–20**
> And in the eleventh jubilee Jared took to himself a wife, and her name was Baraka, a daughter of Rasujel, a daughter of the sister of his father, in the fourth week of this jubilee; and she bore for him a son in the fifth week, in the fourth year, of this jubilee, and he called his name Enoch.
>
> He was the first one from among the children of men that are born on the earth to learn writing and knowledge and wisdom.
>
> And he wrote the signs of heaven according to the order of their months in a book, that the sons of men might know the time of the year according to their separate months.
>
> He was the first to write a testimony, and he testified to the children of men concerning the generations of the earth, and explained the weeks of the jubilees, and made known to them the days of the years, and arranged the months and explained the sabbaths of the years as we made them known to him.
>
> And what was and what will be he saw in a vision of the night in a dream, and as it will happen to the children of men in their generations until the day of judgment; he saw and learned every thing and wrote it as a testimony and laid the testimony on the earth over all the children of men and for their generations.

Chapter Seven. The Book of Moses

A reader familiar with Laurence's 1 Enoch should find this a remarkable summary of what we find in the Book of Enoch, leaving no question that the author of Jubilees read it, considered it inspired and was familiar with it enough to offer a brief summation. More compelling, and in contrast to Jubilees, the book of 1 Enoch describes the theophany of Enoch (instead of Moses) with substantial verbal similarities found in Joseph's Moses that jump off the page from Laurence's 1 Enoch when one looks at the texts side by side:

1. Similar Openings and Settings

Moses 1:1–2	Enoch 1:1, 3 & 4.
The words of God, which he spake **unto Moses** at a time when Moses was **caught up into an exceedingly high mountain,** **And he saw God face to face, and he talked with him**, and the glory of God was upon Moses; therefore Moses could endure his presence.	**The word of** the blessing **of Enoch**, how he blessed the elect and the righteous, who were to exist in the time of trouble; rejecting all the wicked and ungodly. **Enoch**, a righteous man, **who was with God, answered and spoke**, while his **eyes were open**, and while **he saw a holy vision in the heavens.** This the angels shewed me. ... Upon their account **I spoke and conversed with him,** who will go forth from his habitation, the Holy and Mighty One, the God of the world: Who will hereafter tread **upon Mount Sinai; appear with his hosts**; and be **manifested in the strength of his power from heaven.**

2. Taken Atop a Mountain to Speak with God and Sees His Glory

Moses 1:1–2	Enoch XVII. SECT. IV:2 & 1
The words of God, which he spake unto Moses at a time when Moses was **caught up into an exceedingly high mountain,** And he **saw God face to face, and**	They **carried me to a lofty spot, to a mountain**, the top of which reached to heaven. They raised me up into a certain **place, where there was the**

he talked with him, and the glory of God was upon Moses; therefore Moses could endure his presence.	appearance of a burning fire; and when they pleased they **assumed the likeness of men.**

3. Moses and Enoch Are Shown All Things Past and Things Yet to Come

Moses 1:7–8	Enoch 1:1–2
And now, behold, this one thing I show unto thee, Moses, my son, for thou art in the world, and now I show it unto thee. And it came to pass that **Moses looked, and beheld the world upon which he was created**; and Moses beheld **the world and the ends thereof**, and **all the children of men** which are, and which were created; of the same he greatly marveled and wondered.	... **Enoch,** a righteous man, who was with God, answered and spoke, while **his eyes were open, and while he saw a holy vision in the heavens.** This the angels shewed me. From them **I heard all things**, and understood what I saw; **that which will not take place in this generation, but in a generation which is to succeed at a distant period**, on account of the elect. Enoch XL:1 After this I beheld thousands of thousands, and myriads of myriads, and an infinite number of people, standing before the Lord of spirits.

4. Moses and Enoch Are Both Commanded to Write Books

Moses 1:40–41	Enoch LXXX:1 & 9
And now, Moses, my son, I will speak unto thee concerning this earth upon which thou standest; and **thou shalt write the things which I shall speak** And in a day when the children of men shall esteem my words as naught and take many of them from the book which thou shalt write, behold, I will raise up another. like unto thee; **and they shall be had again among the children**	He said; **O Enoch,** look on the book which heaven has gradually dropped down; and, reading that which is written in it, understand every part of it. ... **that thou mayest instruct they family, write these things, and explain them to all thy children.** Enoch LXXXI:1–3 Now, **my son Mathusala**, all these things I speak unto thee,

Chapter Seven. The Book of Moses

of men—among as many as shall believe.

(*Cf.* Abraham 1:31: But **the records of the fathers**, even the patriarchs, concerning the right of Priesthood, **the Lord my God preserved in mine own hands**; therefore a knowledge of the beginning of the creation, and also of the planets, and of the stars, **as they were made known unto the fathers**, have I kept even unto this day, and **I shall endeavor to write some of these things upon this record, for the benefit of my posterity that shall come after me**.)

and write for thee. To thee I have revealed all, and have given thee books of every thing.

Preserve, my son Mathusala, the books written by thy father that thou mayest transmit them to future generations.

Wisdom have I given to thee, to thy children, and thy posterity, that they may transmit to their children, for generations for ever, this wisdom in their thoughts;

5. Both Are to Write Books for Their Followers "Who Believe"

Moses 1:41–42	Enoch CIV:10–11
And in a day when the children of men shall esteem my words as naught and take many of them from the book which thou shalt write, **behold, I will raise up another like unto thee; and they shall be had again among the children of men—among as many as shall believe.** (These words were spoken unto Moses in the mount, the name of which shall not be known among the children of men. **And now they are spoken unto you. Show them not unto any except them that believe**. Even so. Amen.)	... And all **the righteous shall be rewarded**, who from these shall acquire the knowledge of every upright path. Another mystery also I point out. **To the righteous** and the wise **shall be given books** of joy, of integrity, and of great wisdom. **To them shall books be given, in which they shall believe;**

Whether or not the five examples of similarities between Moses 1 and Jubilees 1 are compelling evidence of anything, it would seem these even tighter correspondences between Moses 1 and 1 Enoch start to tip the scales. If Joseph had no access to Laurence's 1 Enoch, these parallels should be heralded as more faith promoting than the similarities found in other apocryphal books like Jubilees—because there are many, and many more.

Devotionally flavored scholarship avoids talking about the evidence of similarities between Joseph's Book of Moses and Laurence's Book of Enoch because the higher incidence of correspondences tends to prove a case of borrowing, if Joseph had access. The problem one runs into is that *when there is opportunity for access*, the more evidence you offer of important and extensive similarities, the more compelling a case of borrowing you begin to build. That's why the rules for critical review are necessary in the context of objective consideration on the issue of influence versus inspiration. The more verbal parallels between two writings, the more likely there was an influence or borrowing, rather than an ephemeral touchdown and emergence of the same information in two texts without any earthly source. It can happen. But it's hard to prove your point when the more evidence you consider tends to prove the other side's case.

We've just scratched the surface of the comparative similarities between Joseph's Book of Moses and Laurence's 1 Enoch, and we haven't yet left Chapter 1:

6. Transfiguration to Speak with God Face to Face

Moses 1:2 & 11.	Enoch I:1 & 3
And he saw **God face to face, and he talked with him**, and the glory of God was upon Moses; therefore Moses could endure his presence. But **now mine own eyes have beheld God**; but **not my natural, but my spiritual eyes**, for my natural eyes could not have beheld; for I should have withered and died in his presence; but his glory was upon me; **and I beheld his face**, for I was transfigured before him.	Enoch, a righteous man, who was with **God, answered and spoke, while his eyes were open**, ... Upon their account **I spoke and conversed with him**, Enoch XIV:1 I perceived in my dream, that I was now speaking with a tongue of flesh, and with my breath, which **the Mighty One put into the mouth of men, that they might converse with it**;

7. Falling to the Ground

Moses 1:9	Enoch XIV:12–13
And the presence of God withdrew from Moses, that his glory was	... terror overwhelmed me, **and a fearful shaking seized me**.

not upon Moses; **and Moses was left unto himself. And as he was left unto himself, he fell unto the earth.**	Violently agitated and trembling, I fell upon my face. In the vision I looked.

8. Satan Is Rebuked, He Fears and Departs

This is an interesting addition to Joseph's Book of Moses not found anywhere in our Bible. At least not a struggle directly between Moses and Satan, but it's an obvious take on the temptation of Jesus in Matthew 4 of the Old Testament. Joseph's revelatory style was to incorporate familiar biblical stories, even word-for-word transcriptions, or use similitudes and allegories in his own works. Moses's temptation and struggle with the devil compares neatly with Matthew as its source:

Moses 1:12–22	**Matthew 4:1, 7–11**
And it came to pass that when Moses had said these words, behold, Satan came tempting him, saying: Moses, son of man, worship me.	Then was Jesus led up of the Spirit into the wilderness to be tempted of the devil.
And it came to pass that Moses looked upon Satan and said: Who art thou? For behold, I am a son of God, in the similitude of his Only Begotten; and where is thy glory, that I should worship thee?	Jesus said unto him, It is written again, Thou shalt not tempt the Lord thy God.
	Again, the devil taketh him up into an exceeding high mountain, and sheweth him all the kingdoms of the world, and the glory of them;
For behold, I could not look upon God, except his glory should come upon me, and I were transfigured before him. But I can look upon thee in the natural man. Is it not so, surely?	And saith unto him, All these things will I give thee, if thou wilt fall down and worship me.
Blessed be the name of my God, for his Spirit hath not altogether withdrawn from me, or else where is thy glory, for it is darkness unto me?	Then saith Jesus unto him, Get thee hence, Satan: for it is written, Thou shalt worship the Lord thy God, and him only shalt thou serve.
And I can judge between thee and God; for God said unto me: Worship God, for him only shalt thou serve.	Then the devil leaveth him, and, behold, angels came and ministered unto him.
Get thee hence, Satan; deceive me not; for God said unto me: Thou art after the similitude of mine Only Begotten.	

Joseph Smith and the Book of Enoch

> And he also gave me commandments when he called unto me out of the burning bush, saying: Call upon God in the name of mine Only Begotten, and worship me.
>
> And again Moses said: I will not cease to call upon God, I have other things to inquire of him: for his glory has been upon me, wherefore I can judge between him and thee. Depart hence, Satan.
>
> And now, when Moses had said these words, Satan cried with a loud voice, and ranted upon the earth, and commanded, saying: I am the Only Begotten, worship me.
>
> And it came to pass that Moses began to fear exceedingly; and as he began to fear, he saw the bitterness of hell. Nevertheless, calling upon God, he received strength, and he commanded, saying: Depart from me, Satan, for this one God only will I worship, which is the God of glory.
>
> And now Satan began to tremble, and the earth shook; and Moses received strength, and called upon God, saying: In the name of the Only Begotten, depart hence, Satan.
>
> And it came to pass that Satan cried with a loud voice, with weeping, and wailing, and gnashing of teeth; and he departed hence, even from the presence of Moses, that he beheld him not.

Interestingly, there is a quarrel with Satan "about the body of Moses" when he is also rebuked found in the Jude:

> Yet Michael the archangel, when contending with the devil he disputed about the body of Moses, durst not bring against him a railing accusation, but said, The Lord rebuke thee [Jude 1:9].

Jude, remember, is also our only New Testament writer who directly quoted the ancient Jewish book of Enoch. So now we have a

Chapter Seven. The Book of Moses

direct connection with an Enoch story and the devil causing carnal concerns with the sons of men.

There is a devil stirring sin and getting rebuked in 1 Enoch. In Enoch's story, angels fell from heaven among the children of men and became enamored with women, so they "took wives, each choosing for himself; whom they began to approach, and with whom they cohabited; teaching them sorcery, incantations, and the dividing of roots and trees" (Enoch VII. SECT. II:10). One among the fallen angels in 1 Enoch is named Azazyel.

Azazyel is known in Jewish tradition and the Old Testament as the male goat cast out in the desert, the same "scapegoat" and fallen angel recognized as or sympathized with our Christian devil, Satan or Lucifer. Here's what the ancient Jewish (pre–Christian) writer of the Book of Enoch has to say about Azazyel, with Laurence's translation:

> **Enoch VIII:1–2**
> Moreover Azazyel taught men to make swords, knives, shields, breastplates, the fabrication of mirrors, and the workmanship of bracelets and ornaments, the use of paint, the beautifying of the eyebrows, the use of stones of every valuable and select kind, and of all sorts of dyes, so that the world became altered. Impiety increased; fornication multiplied; and they transgressed and corrupted all their ways.
>
> **Enoch IX:5 & 9**
> Thou hast seen what Azazyel has done, how he has taught every species of iniquity upon earth, and has disclosed to the world all the secret things which are done in the heavens. Thus has the whole earth been filled with blood and with iniquity.
>
> **Enoch X:12**
> All the earth has been corrupted by the effects of the doctrine of Azazyel. To him therefore ascribe the whole crime.

And, like Joseph's Moses, Enoch rebukes Azazyel for being the devil he is, Azazyel also fears and departs hence:

> **Enoch XIII:1–4 & 6**
> Then Enoch passing on said to Azazyel; Thou shalt not obtain peace. A great sentence has gone forth against thee. He shall bind thee; Neither shall relief, mercy, and supplication be thine, on account of the oppression which thou hast taught; And on account of every act of blasphemy, tyranny, and sin, which thou hast discovered to the children of men. Then departing from him I spoke to them all together; ... And they all became terrified, and trembled;

Joseph Smith and the Book of Enoch

9. Beholding the Numberless on the Earth, from the Beginning and Without End

Moses 1:27–29	Enoch 1:1–2
And it came to pass, as the voice was still speaking, Moses cast his eyes and beheld the earth, yea, even all of it; and there was not a particle of it which he did not behold, discerning it by the Spirit of God. And he beheld also the inhabitants thereof, and there was not a soul which he beheld not; and he discerned them by the Spirit of God; and their numbers were great, even numberless as the sand upon the sea shore. And he beheld many lands; and each land was called earth, and there were inhabitants on the face thereof.	... Enoch, a righteous man, who was with God, answered and spoke, while his eyes were open, and while he saw a holy vision in the heavens. This the angels shewed me. From them I heard all things, and understood what I saw; that which will not take place in this generation, but in a generation which is to succeed at a distant period, on account of the elect. **Enoch XXXIX:4–6 & 10** There I saw another vision; I saw the habitation and dormitory of the saints. There my eyes beheld their habitation with the angels, and their dormitory with the holy ones..... At that time my eyes beheld the dwelling of the elect, of truth, faith, and righteousness. Countless shall be the number of the holy and the elect in the presence of God for ever and for ever. ... That place long did my eyes contemplate. I blessed and said; Blessed be He, blessed from the beginning for ever. In the beginning, before the world was created, and without end is his knowledge.

10. Moses and Enoch Both Ask What Is This World? And Why Creation?

Moses 1:30–32, 36–38	Enoch XXXIX:10–11
And it came to pass that Moses called upon God, saying: Tell me, I pray thee, why these things are so, and by what thou madest them?	That place long did my eyes contemplate. I blessed and said; Blessed be He, blessed from the beginning for ever. In the beginning, before

And behold, the glory of the Lord was upon Moses, so that Moses stood in the presence of God, and talked with him face to face. And the Lord God said unto Moses: For mine own purpose have I made these things. Here is wisdom and it remaineth in me. And by the word of my power, have I created them, which is mine Only Begotten Son, who is full of grace and truth. And it came to pass that Moses spake unto the Lord, saying: Be merciful unto thy servant, O God, and tell me concerning this earth, and the inhabitants thereof, and also the heavens, and then thy servant will be content. And the Lord God spake unto Moses, saying: The heavens, they are many, and they cannot be numbered unto man; but they are numbered unto me, for they are mine. And as one earth shall pass away, and the heavens thereof even so shall another come; and there is no end to my works, neither to my words.	the world was created, and without end is his knowledge. What is this world? **Enoch XCII:20–24** ... Who capable of contemplating all the workmanship of heaven? Who of comprehending the deeds of heaven? He may behold its animation, but not its spirit. He may be capable of conversing respecting it, but not of ascending to it. He may see all the boundaries of these things, and meditate upon them; but he can make nothing like them. Who of all men is able to understand the breadth and length of the earth? By whom has been seen the dimensions of all these things? Is it every man who is capable of comprehending the extent of heaven; what its elevation is, and by what it is supported? How many are the numbers of the stars; and where all the luminaries remain at rest?

11. The Purpose: Eternal Life and Everlasting Glory of Mankind

Moses 1:39 For behold, this is my work and my glory—to bring to pass the immortality and eternal life of man.	**Enoch XV:6** But you from the beginning were made spiritual, possessing a life which is eternal, and not subject to death for ever. **Enoch XCL. SECT. XIX:3** Let the righteous man arise from slumber; let him arise, and proceed in the path.... In goodness and in righteousness shall he exist, and shall walk in ever lasting light.

	Enoch XXXV:3
	... I blessed the Lord of glory, who had made those great and splendid signs, that they might display the magnificence of his works to angels and to the souls of men; and that these might glorify all his works and operations; might see the effect of his power; might glorify the great labour of his hands; and bless him for ever.

12. A Warning That the Children of Men Will Turn Against God's Books

Moses 1:40–42	Enoch LXXXI:2
And now, Moses, my son, I will speak unto thee concerning this earth upon which thou standest; and thou shalt write the things which I shall speak. And in a day when the children of men shall esteem my words as naught and take many of them from the book which thou shalt write, behold, I will raise up another like unto thee; and they shall be had again among the children of men—among as many as shall believe. (These words were spoken unto Moses in the mount, the name of which shall not be known among the children of men. And now they are spoken unto you. Show them not unto any except them that believe. Even so. Amen.)	Preserve, my son Mathusala, the books written by thy father that thou mayest transmit them to future generations. **Enoch CIV:7, 10–11** ... Many sinners shall turn and transgress against the word of uprightness. ... To the righteous and the wise shall be given books of joy, of integrity, and of great wisdom. To them shall books be given, in which they shall believe; And in which they shall rejoice.

That's all just from Moses Chapter 1.

Moses 2–5 (Genesis 1–4)

Following the Prologue to Genesis, Moses Chapters 2–5 are mostly word-for-word transcriptions directly from Genesis 1–4, with very few

Chapter Seven. The Book of Moses

insertions or changes. Moses 5 takes a turn, as Adam and Eve's family members are introduced (paralleling Genesis), expanding on their stories.

Joseph's "translation" methodology becomes clearer when you follow along with reading the Bible side by side with Joseph's *Inspired Version*. Since Moses 1 is our prologue, Moses 2 corresponds and begins with Genesis 1, with few changes from Bible verses for the next few chapters. Following along between Moses and Genesis (or Genesis and the *Inspired Version*), word for word, you see where the King James authors' words are interrupted and Joseph's interpolations begin. Dragging our fingers down the column, reading horizontally, we can distinguish what Joseph added and, more importantly, catch a glimpse of his thought process.

Patterns of Joseph's method for character building and story lines emerge. We can watch as specific names and topics catch Joseph's eye as he drew his finger down the page, reading word for word from the KJV Bible before stopping to interpolate God's lost words on the subject. An example of this is his development of the bad-guy story line of Cain. Joseph's Moses (and *Inspired Version* of the Bible) inserts 12 verses of scripture about Cain in Genesis 4. Genesis 4:24–25 in our KJV Bible reads:

> 24. If Cain shall be avenged sevenfold, truly Lamech seventy and sevenfold.
> 25. And Adam knew his wife again; and she bare a son, and called his name Seth: For God, said she, hath appointed me another seed instead of Abel, whom Cain slew.

Joseph's Moses enlightens us, reinserting what was God's word lost and removed by scribes over thousands of years of preserving the scripts. Between verses 24 and 25, it is revealed to us apparently just how bad and cursed Joseph's revealed Cain really was, sprinkled with some Masonic seasoning:

> 48. If Cain shall be avenged sevenfold, truly Lamech shall be seventy and seven fold; [end Genesis 4:24, insert Moses 5:49–6:1]
> 49. For Lamech having entered into a covenant with Satan, after the manner of Cain, wherein he became Master Mahan, master of that great secret which was administered unto Cain by Satan; and Irad, the son of Enoch, having known their secret, began to reveal it unto the sons of Adam;
> 50. Wherefore Lamech, being angry, slew him, not like unto Cain, his brother Abel, for the sake of getting gain, but he slew him for the oath's sake.

51. For, from the days of Cain, there was a secret combination, and their works were in the dark, and they knew every man his brother.

52. Wherefore the Lord cursed Lamech, and his house, and all them that had covenanted with Satan; for they kept not the commandments of God, and it displeased God, and he ministered not unto them, and their works were abominations, and began to spread among all the sons of men. And it was among the sons of men.

53. And among the daughters of men these things were not spoken, because that Lamech had spoken the secret unto his wives, and they rebelled against him, and declared these things abroad, and had not compassion;

54. Wherefore Lamech was despised, and cast out, and came not among the sons of men, lest he should die.

55. And thus the works of darkness began to prevail among all the sons of men.

56. And God cursed the earth with a sore curse, and was angry with the wicked, with all the sons of men whom he had made;

57. For they would not hearken unto his voice, nor believe on his Only Begotten Son, even him whom he declared should come in the meridian of time, who was prepared from before the foundation of the world.

58. And thus the Gospel began to be preached, from the beginning, being declared by holy angels sent forth from the presence of God, and by his own voice, and by the gift of the Holy Ghost.

59. And thus all things were confirmed unto Adam, by an holy ordinance, and the Gospel preached, and a decree sent forth, that it should be in the world, until the end thereof; and thus it was. Amen.

Ch. 6:1 And Adam hearkened unto the voice of God, and called upon his sons to repent.

. 2. [*End Moses 6:1, resume Genesis 4:25*] And Adam knew his wife again, and she bare a son, and he called his name Seth. And Adam glorified the name of God; for he said: God hath appointed me another seed, instead of Abel, whom Cain slew.[12]

Aside from the obvious Masonic connections that have been made with this and other revelations,[13] surprisingly similar themes are found in Laurence's Book of Enoch. Even ardent LDS apologists recognize the direct parallels here of "the oaths of the conspirators," and "the rise of secret combinations" found inserted here into the Genesis texts as Joseph's Moses 5.[14] Rather than applaud these striking similarities for faith-promoting purposes, apologists avoid these literary parallels because they draw similar questions and raise similar issues about source material for the same peculiar story lines, themes and word choice found in the Book of Mormon.

Chapter Seven. The Book of Moses

The parallels between secret combinations in Joseph's Moses and Laurence's 1 Enoch are noteworthy:

Moses 5:49–50	Enoch LIV:9–10:
For Lamech having entered into a covenant with Satan, after the manner of Cain, wherein he became Master Mahan, master of that great secret which was administered unto Cain by Satan; and Irad, the son of Enoch, having known their secret, began to reveal it unto the sons of Adam; Wherefore Lamech, being angry, slew him, not like unto Cain, his brother Abel, for the sake of getting gain, but he slew him for the oath's sake. *For, from the days of Cain, there was a secret combination*, and their works were in the dark, *and they knew every man his brother.*	*Then shall princes combine together, and conspire.* ... They shall rise up to destroy each other; their right hand shall be strengthened; *nor shall a man acknowledge his friend or his brother.*

Joseph's Master Mahan (Cain), became "master of that great secret that was administered by Satan," and then Joseph's Irad (through Cain's lineage, *see* Genesis 4:18) began telling the secret to everyone, so he was killed "for the oath's sake" (Moses 5:50). Apparently, secrets, secret names, death-penalty oaths and evil combinations were all risky business by 1830 in upstate New York, and spurred anti–Masonic sentiments.

The disappearance and murder of anti–Mason William Morgan of Batavia, New York, for revealing Masonic secrets and oaths eventually made national news, but it was all the buzz in the surroundings of the Smith family's hometown. Morgan had infiltrated his local Masonic lodge and was threatening to publish an exposé titled *Illustrations of Masonry*. He never personally got to see his work, which was later published "[i]n the absence of the author, or rather compiler of the following work, who was kidnapped and carried away from the village of Batavia, on the 11th day of September, 1826, by a number of Freemasons[.]"[15] He was never seen again.

But the secret names, secret combinations, secret oaths motif is not just a Masonic thing, it's also found in Laurence's Book of Enoch with a number of direct verbal parallels to Joseph's Book of Moses.

Secret Combinations and Death Penalty Oaths

Enoch LXVIII:19–23
[T]he principal part of the oath which the Most High, dwelling in glory, revealed to the holy ones.

... He spoke to holy Michael to discover to them the secret name, that they might understand that secret name, and thus remember the oath; and that those who pointed out every secret thing to the children of men might tremble at that name and oath.

This is the power of that oath; for powerful it is, and strong.

And he established this oath of Akae by the instrumentality of the holy Michael.

These are the secrets of this oath, and by it were they confirmed.
Enoch LIV:9–10:
Then shall princes combine together, and conspire.....

They shall go up, and tread upon the land of their elect. The land of their elect shall be before them. The threshing floor, the path, and the city of my righteous people shall impede the progress their horses. They shall rise up to destroy each other; their right hand shall be strengthened; nor shall a man acknowledge his friend or his brother.

Continuing the story of Adam and his children in Moses 6 (Genesis 4:25), we find additional interpolations into the Genesis story by Joseph that include Enochic themes, more corresponding illusions and verbal parallels—and we haven't been introduced to Joseph's version of Enoch yet.

Chapter Eight

Joseph Smith's Enoch
(Moses 6–8)

> "...there is a strange thing in the land,
> a *wild man* hath come among us."
> —Moses 6:38

Joseph's translation of Moses 1 was written in the hand of Oliver Cowdery, acting as Joseph's scribe. Oliver, Joseph's distant cousin about his same age but better educated, had already proved he could write well in his work with Joseph's Book of Mormon translation project. Together, they worked on transcribing Moses 1 through Moses 5:43 between the months of June and September 1830. The work stopped there—at that verse.

For some reason, Oliver and Joseph had been quibbling about whether or not Oliver had what it takes to "translate" like Joseph. Joseph offered him the opportunity, but Oliver failed. Section 9 of the Doctrine & Covenants records the scorning Oliver received:

> 2. And then, behold, *other records have I*, that I will give unto you power that you may assist to translate.
> 3. Be patient, my son, for it is wisdom in me, and it is not expedient that you should translate at this present time.
> 4. Behold, the work which you are called to do is to write for my servant Joseph.
> 5. And, behold, it is because that you did not continue as you commenced, when you began to translate, that I have taken away this privilege from you.
> 6. Do not murmur, my son, for it is wisdom in me that I have dealt with you after this manner.

Where were they again in their translation of the Bible? They stopped at Moses 5:43, which corresponds with Genesis 4:18. *What is that verse?* What prompted the interruption?

Joseph Smith and the Book of Enoch

The first mention of anyone named "Enoch" in the Bible is in Genesis 4:17, and it's Enoch the city builder. But there's some confusion about who the Enoch in this verse is, given the similar and different names in their family lines (third from Adam through Cain, versus the better-known seventh from Adam, son of Seth and that patriarch who "walked with God"). But that's where it stopped, at the first mention of someone named Enoch.

A side-by-side review of Genesis 4:17–18, and Moses 5:42–43, again demonstrates Joseph's meticulous review of each verse, word by word. Following the revisions of these final verses also indicates the last of Joseph's revelations recorded by Oliver as his faithful scribe, and what their topic of discussion was prompting this interruption (with Joseph's interpolations italicized):

Genesis 4:17–18	Moses 5:42–43
And Cain knew his wife; and she conceived, and bare Enoch: and he builded a city, and called the name of the city, after the name of his son, Enoch. And unto Enoch was born Irad: and Irad begat Mehujael: and Mehujael begat Methusael: and Methusael begat Lamech.	And Cain knew his wife, and she conceived and bare Enoch, *and he also begat many sons and daughters.* And he builded a city, and he called the name of the city after the name of his son, Enoch. And unto Enoch was born Irad, *and other sons and daughters.* And Irad begat Mahujael, *and other sons and daughters.* And Mahujael begat Methusael, *and other sons and daughters.* And Methusael begat Lamech.

With emphasis on the specific words Joseph is restoring here from those "many parts that are plain and most precious" that were taken away and lost, a pattern appears of Joseph's creation of plotlines and characters, inserting the potential for additional scripture narratives. These interpolations accommodate additional revelation, expanding story lines and characters, and connecting people and places in biblical literature. Richard Bushman characterized Joseph's translations of Moses, Enoch and Abraham, as all having "the character of expansions, enlarging a few verses in the old scriptures into lengthy accounts unknown to Bible readers."[1]

In Genesis 4:17 (Moses 5:42), we have introduced Enoch, the son of Cain, who "builded a city" and called it "after the name of his son, Enoch." Then, interpolated after Enoch's name, we have numberless unnamed sons and daughters from this otherwise unknown and short-lived cast of characters. And among this family line, we find the obscurely referenced Mehujael, found only in Genesis 4:18. Or is it Mahujael (with an "a") that we find in Moses 5:43? Is it Mahujah-*el*?

Mahujah, Mahijah and Mehujael

A less-than-casual reader might not catch this change of spelling (or misspelling) from "M̲ehujael" in Genesis to "M̲ahujael" in the Book of Moses—at least in what became officially published in the LDS Church's canonical scriptures. *How and why the spelling change?*

The original handwritten "Old Testament Revision 1" ("OT1") and "Old Testament Revision 2" ("OT2") manuscripts, including historical notations and scribal changes, are scanned and available online through the Joseph Smith Papers Project.[2] The original OT1 manuscript still remains in the possession and ownership of the reorganized LDS Church (Community of Christ) and has been generously made available for public perusal. These original and earliest manuscripts are the best source for any serious source criticism and historical-critical analysis, and making original historical records fully accessible must be commended and continued for objective historical research.

A close review of the original handwritten manuscripts of OT1[3] indicates that Oliver Cowdery spelled "Mehujael" correctly in transcribing Joseph's dictation as they came across the name first in Genesis 4:18. That is where Cowdery's work as scribe ended. John Whitmer was then called as Joseph's scribe, and picked back up in the middle of verse 18, with the first words from his quill: "& Mahujael begat...." John Whitmer misspelled the name. And it carried over into all other manuscripts. The Joseph Smith Papers Project offers this historical background in relation to these manuscripts:

> Before his move to Ohio in early January 1831, John Whitmer made a copy of the first 19 pages and first five lines of page 20 of the manuscript, possibly indicating that JS and Rigdon had finished through Genesis chapter 5 when they moved to Ohio. It is unknown why Whitmer made this copy. When both the Old Testament Revision manuscript and Whitmer were in Ohio, Whitmer made a second copy of the completed manuscript (known as Old Testament Revision 2). He documented his work by inserting a final date at the end of this copy: "April 5th 1831 transcribed thus far." This original manuscript (Old Testament Revision 1) was then retired and JS and Rigdon continued the ambitious Bible revision using Whitmer's second copy.[4]

In the OT1 manuscript, John Whitmer had picked up as scribe right after Oliver Cowdery left off after Genesis 4:18. Oliver's transcription ending with "... & unto Enoch was born Irad & other sons & daughters & Irad begat *Mehujael* & other sons & daughters."[5] The very next entry on the page is in a different handwriting and darker ink, beginning with John Whitmer writing the date October 21, 1830, and picking up where Cowdery left off mid-verse, writing, "& *Mahujael* begat Mathusael & other sons & daughters...."[6]

Thus started the misspelling in OT1, which was carried over entirely throughout the OT2 and Book of Moses manuscripts. The misspelling from "Mehujael" in Genesis 4:18 to "Mahujael" in both the OT2 and the Book of Moses became part of the LDS Church's official publications and canonized scripture as a result of John Whitmer's transcription error.[7] Joseph Smith completed his Bible revision using Whitmer's second copy, the OT2 manuscript. Because the OT1 was "retired" (set aside not to be used for publishing Joseph's revised Bible or the Book of Moses), it was the copied Book of Moses manuscript with Whitmer's misspelling that made its way west with Brigham Young's contingency of saints that left Nauvoo, Illinois, after Joseph's martyrdom in 1844. The OT1 manuscript with the original correct spelling stayed behind with Emma Smith and the saints who stayed and reorganized there.

A misspelling in the transcription—big deal, right? Who cares? It makes all the difference when looking at derivative names later used in Josephs' Enoch revelations. The change in spelling to "Mahujael" carries over to the derivative names "Mahujah" and "Mahijah" found nowhere else but the Book of Moses. While briefly acting as scribe for Joseph between John Whitmer's transcriptions, Emma Smith transcribed in what is now Moses 6:40: "...there came a man unto him, whose name was Mahijah."[8] Shortly after, in December 1830, Sidney Rigdon was then called to transcribe for Joseph, picking up in Moses 7. In verse 2, Enoch journeyed to a place called "Mahujah" where he heard the voice of the Lord, another derivative name from Mehujael, with the change of spelling carrying through.

This Mahijah person at a place called Mahujah was a point of passion for the venerable Brigham Young University professor Hugh Nibley. Like-minded apologists cling to the idea that Joseph could not have possibly conjured up such an enigmatic character/place names of "Mahujah" and "Mahijah," never before having read it, and thus these are proof positive of a revelation of restored ancient Jewish texts. The patternist scholar that he was, Nibley published a series of installments titled "A Strange Thing in the Land," in the *Ensign*, the LDS monthly magazine, drawing connections (parallels) between the Book of Moses and

Chapter Eight. Joseph Smith's Enoch

the ancient Enoch texts and traditions.[9] Nibley argued that the name "Mahawai" (or "Mahaway") found in the texts among Dead Sea Scrolls in 1947 was so close in the original Hebrew to the "Mahuja" or "Mahijah" found in Joseph's Book of Moses that it had to be proof of a restored ancient text, confirmed by ancient texts found after Joseph's lifetime.

This argument ignores the accidental misspellings first under the hand of John Whitmer and then by later scribes who, while transcribing, had the manuscript in hand to refer to for prior language and spellings.[10] If "Mehujael" had not been misspelled by Whitmer in continuing where Oliver Cowdery left off in OT1, and in creating the OT2 and Book of Moses manuscripts with the name misspelled throughout, one wonders whether Professor Nibley would have pursued it as passionately as he did.

Biblical (and Jewish) scholar Colby Townsend most succinctly concludes: "The name Mahujah in Moses 7:2 likely comes from Gen. 4:18, 'And unto Enoch was born Irad: and Irad begat Mehujael: and Mehujael begat Methusael: and Methusael begat Lamech.'"[11] This is the simplest explanation for the origin of the name. Townsend expounds:

> Mahijah/Mahujah, which are the same name, come from the root החמ, "destroyed" or "smitten" one, and Mahawai from the *Book of Giants* comes from the root היה, "to be," "to happen," "to occur," or "to come to pass." These are two completely separate names that are easily confused when transliterated into English from the Hebrew. Nibley relied too heavily on his English transcription of both names—MHWY—and failed to recognize that the H represents two distinct letters.

We have to remember that Professor Nibley's argument is founded on the Hebrew spelling of the name MHWY and not the Anglicized spelling as written in Joseph's revelations. Nibley argued that MHWY found among the Dead Sea Scrolls, and derivative references (i.e., "Mahaway" or "Mahawai") found specifically in the Qumran Book of Giants (*4Q203*), was so similar to "Mahijah" and "Mahujah" in Moses 6:40 and 7:2 that they must derive from the same source, and therefore be ancient and not conceivable to Joseph Smith absent revelation. Professor Nibley ultimately concedes, however, that the Anglicized "Mahaway" from its Hebrew script is very similar and related to the names "Mahuja" and "Mahija"—if they are related at all.[12] And, if they are related, there should be little surprise to find similarly named persons in stories included among Enochic literature that might surface sometime and somewhere else.

In his article "Returning to the Sources: Integrating Textual Criticism in the Study of Early Mormon Texts and History," Townsend offers an alternative literary source widely available to Joseph Smith at the time, which includes the same variant spellings:

> [T]he idea that if Smith intended the two separate names Mahijah and Mahujah that he would need to be dependent on an ancient manuscript or source is also unlikely. In his commentary on the Bible Adam Clarke, whose commentary was known to Smith while he worked on his revision of the Bible, created a table he called "Same Names Differing in the Hebrew," and the first examples he shared were from Gen. 4:18: "Mehujael" and "Mehijael."[13]

Joseph's Enoch Found in Translation

Getting back to the lineage of Adam and the patriarch named Enoch in Joseph's translation, recall that Oliver Cowdery's transcription stopped at Genesis 4:18 (Moses 5:43), the first verse in their Old Testament revision work where anyone named Enoch is mentioned. This Enoch, however, is not our patriarch Enoch, the seventh from Adam and great-grandfather of Noah. This first-mentioned Enoch is the son of Cain, the murderous son of Adam.

For whatever reason, Joseph receives revelation in September 1830—just three months into translating the Book of Moses—that Oliver must go away "unto the Lamanites and preach my gospel unto them" (D&C 28:8). What was going on between them prompting the interruption is not entirely known and left purely for speculation. But these two had a history together, as deep as it goes with respect to Mormon origins and scriptures. And it's interesting that the interruption comes right in the middle of a verse—at the first mention of a man named Enoch.

This was a pivotal point and time in their Bible revision project. The general "cut-and-paste" straight from Genesis 1–4, mingled with modifications here and there, was about to end and a new story line was to be introduced. Smith and Cowdery were about to turn back to the free flow of revelation/transcription method they had used in translating the Book of Mormon. And they were about to pick that back up with the introduction of another forgotten prophet of old who allegedly scripted revelations that have since been lost; Enoch, the heretofore little-known biblical figure who happened to be having quite the literary comeback at the time.

Richard Bushman notes in his biography of Smith:

> In redoing the early chapters of Genesis, the stories of Creation, of Adam and Eve, and the Fall were modified, but with less extensive interpolations than in the revelation to Moses. Joseph wove Christian doctrine into the

Chapter Eight. Joseph Smith's Enoch

text without altering the basic story. But with the appearance of Enoch in the seventh generation from Adam, the text expanded far beyond the biblical version. *In Genesis, Enoch is summed up in 5 verses; in Joseph Smith's revision, Enoch's story extends to 110 verses.*

... In 1821, Richard Laurence, the Archbishop of Cashel and Professor of Hebrew at Oxford, published an English translation of an early Ethiopic text discovered in Abyssinia by James Bruce and deposited in Oxford's Bodleian Library. Called the Book of Enoch, or later, *1 Enoch*, the text purported to be the teachings and visions of the ancient patriarch, though its true authorship was unknown. [...] It is scarcely conceivable that Joseph Smith knew of Laurence's Enoch translation, but the coincidence of their appearance within a few years of each other is a curiosity.

Within the previous year, Cowdery was Joseph's scribe and closest confidant in translating and publishing the Book of Mormon. He witnessed Joseph's gift in revealing lost ancient scripture, and he wanted to try. *Who wouldn't want to experience such a miracle, after witnessing one after another?* After all, Oliver *was* the writer between them. And it wasn't strange for Oliver to believe he too could translate by a divine spiritual gift. The Smith and Cowdery families lived in a culture steeped in biblical ideas, language and practices, including the use of a divining rod as an instrument for revelation. It was magical times in those parts in them days.[14] It is no secret that Oliver was "among those who believed in and used a divining rod."[15] Just as Joseph manifested gifts of seeing and translating, Oliver was recognized for his gift of the divining rod. In April 1829, Joseph received revelation directly for Oliver Cowdery in the course of translating the Book of Mormon, after Oliver asked to try his hand at translating. The revelation is recorded today in D&C Section 8, which describes Joseph's encouraging Cowdery to exercise his gift, and promising him the chance to translate "from *all* those ancient records, which have been hid up":

> 6. Now this is not all thy gift; for you have another gift, which is *the gift of Aaron*; behold, it has told you many things;
> 7. Behold, there is no other power, save the power of God, that can cause this gift of Aaron to be with you.
> [...]
> 11. Ask that you may know the mysteries of God, and that you may translate and receive knowledge from all those ancient records which have been hid up, that are sacred; and according to your faith shall it be done unto you.

The revelation originally referred to Oliver's "gift of working with the sprout," not the "gift of Aaron."[16] Sidney Rigdon changed "sprout" to "rod" in preparation for the revelation's publication in the Book of Commandments in 1833. The reference to the gift of working with the diving "rod" was replaced in 1835, replacing the magical sounding language with more spiritual, calling it instead "the gift of Aaron." While this meant something to him, Cowdery continued asking to translate and reveal scripture. His request was granted in April 1829, as recorded now in D&C Section 6:

> 10. Behold thou hast a gift, and blessed art thou because of thy gift. Remember it is sacred and cometh from above—
> 11. And if thou wilt inquire, thou shalt know mysteries which are great and marvelous; therefore thou shalt exercise thy gift, that thou mayest find out mysteries, that thou mayest bring many to the knowledge of the truth, yea, convince them of the error of their ways.
> 12. Make not thy gift known unto any save it be those who are of thy faith. Trifle not with sacred things.
> [...]
> 25. And, behold, *I grant unto you a gift, if you desire of me, to translate, even as my servant Joseph.*

For whatever reason, Oliver's attempt at translation did not go well. In the LDS Church's publication titled *Revelations in Context,* we learn the following:

> Though we know very few details about Oliver Cowdery's attempt to translate, it apparently did not go well. His efforts quickly came to naught. In the wake of Oliver's failure, Joseph Smith received another revelation, counseling Oliver, "Be patient my son, for it is wisdom in me, and it is not expedient that you should translate *at this present time.*"[17]

This history between Joseph and Cowdery and the quibble over translating, and with Oliver still being promised a chance to translate other "ancient records which have been hid up," raises the question *what caused their abrupt interruption in the Old Testament revision?* Oliver's duties as scribe for Joseph end in the middle of transcribing Genesis 4:18, where we first read about any man named Enoch, and at a time when a Book of Enoch, believed to be lost, had been recovered and published to the English-reading world. *Did Oliver want another attempt at revealing lost scripture relating to Enoch?*

We don't know, but the timing of the abrupt commandment for Oliver to leave town seems suspect. It wasn't unusual for Joseph to send some of his closest confidants and apostles away on missions or assignments out of town to chastise them. For example, in June 1833, Joseph

Chapter Eight. Joseph Smith's Enoch

sent several of his apostles away to "chasten" them, as recorded in D&C 95:10:

> Nevertheless, my servants sinned a very grievous sin; and contentions arose in the school of the prophets; which was very grievous unto me, saith your Lord; therefore I sent them forth to be chastened.

With Oliver out of the picture, Joseph picked up the work of translating, trudging through clumsily at times and lacking the fluidity of prose that Oliver offered as his scribe.

Joseph called on John Whitmer in Oliver's absence. Whitmer started transcribing on October 21, 1830. They translated and transcribed through the end of the next month, recording Moses 5:43 through Moses 6:18, which includes a "book of the generations of Adam" corresponding with and expounding on Genesis 5:1–2. Whitmer's work as a scribe here ends on November 30, 1830, just three verses shy of introducing Joseph's Enoch—this same Enoch who Joseph had been contemplating since the interrupting confusion with Oliver broke out while translating Genesis 4:18, where our first Enoch appeared.

After Whitmer's transcription ends at Moses 6:18, Joseph's wife, Emma, comes on board once again to act as scribe for her husband. In these next few verses, Joseph and Emma were introduced to Enoch, the seventh from Adam, the patriarch "who walked with God." We keep hearing that, as if that's all we really know about Enoch. It turns out, yes—that's pretty much it in the Bible.

Joseph received later revelation that perhaps offers the best description of who the patriarch Enoch was to him, reflecting similar roles in their respective dispensations. In D&C 76:100 it reads:

> These are they who say they are some of one and some of another—some of Christ and some of John, and some of Moses, and some of Elias, and some of Esaias, and some of Isaiah, and some of Enoch.

Joseph's Enoch as Another Elias

Emma picked back up as Joseph's scribe in December 1830, transcribing Joseph's dictations found in Moses 6:19–52. These are only a few, but significant, verses as they introduce for us Joseph's Enoch. During the same month, John Whitmer returns to his work as scribe, relieving Emma and continuing from Moses 6:53 through Moses 7:1.

Joseph Smith and the Book of Enoch

Their collective work offers the first verses where Joseph's Book of Moses becomes a book of the visions of Enoch.

As Joseph is introduced to Enoch, we can follow his method for developing the Enoch story. As we follow his revisions to Genesis and his lost/restored scripture in Moses, we can watch how Joseph familiarized himself with the man Enoch and found a story line for his introduction in Moses. We can also see the presence of parallels, influence and borrowing from the Bible, and particularly from the Apocrypha found in Joseph's 1828 Cooperstown Bible. Following along with Joseph's insertions in Genesis, we begin to see a perfect example of how Joseph weaves in familiar Bible and Apocrypha narratives and verbiage into these early writings.[18] We can see Joseph reflecting upon himself, and inflecting himself into the allusions, characters and verses as he dictates.

We also find some parallels, allusions and influence from Laurence's Book of Enoch scattered through these verses here where Enoch is first introduced through Joseph at the hands of Emma and John Whitmer—but not nearly as many parallels to Laurence as we find later when Sidney Rigdon is called as Joseph's scribe in December 1830. This introductory version of Enoch we learn of is through Joseph's aggrandized version of the Genesis story. Compare the two, side by side, with Joseph's reinsertions emphasized:

Genesis 5:19–20	**Moses 6:21–24**
18. And Jared lived an hundred sixty and two years, and he begat Enoch:	21. And Jared lived one hundred and sixty-two years, and begat Enoch; and Jared lived, after he begat Enoch, eight hundred years, and begat sons and daughters. *And Jared taught Enoch in all the ways of God.*
19. And Jared lived after he begat Enoch eight hundred years, and begat sons and daughters:	
20. And all the days of Jared were nine hundred sixty and two years: and he died.	22. *And this is the genealogy of the sons of Adam, who was the son of God, with whom God, himself, conversed.*
	23. *And they were preachers of righteousness, and spake and prophesied, and called upon all men, everywhere, to repent; and faith was taught unto the children of men.*
	24. *And it came to pass that* all the days of Jared were nine hundred and sixty-two years, and he died.

Chapter Eight. Joseph Smith's Enoch

Enoch's Patriarchal Lineage

Joseph would discover his Enoch by understanding where he fit in the line of patriarchs, the prophets of dispensations from Adam to Jesus Christ, and for any dispensations to come. Where can we find a genealogy from Adam to Jesus? Look for Jesus's genealogy. Where is that found? Only the gospels of Matthew and Luke in the New Testament include the genealogies of Jesus.

Matthew's gospel opens our New Testament with a "book of the generation of Jesus Christ, the son of David, the son of Abraham" (Matt. 1:1). Jesus's divine lineage is explained through a particular number of generations, eventually back through King Solomon, King David, and Jacob, Isaac to Abraham. But it stops short there. Matthew doesn't connect Jesus's generations with Adam. Luke's gospel fixes that. And Luke's opening seems more aligned with Joseph's style of introducing characters and story lines.

The gospel of Luke does not immediately start with Jesus or an explanation of his genealogy. It opens with a forerunner—a familiar biblical character with a particular purpose, also known as "firstfruits," who goes before another who is to yet to come, preparing the way. This motif is found in Adam as the forerunner of mankind itself, Noah our first savior of mankind, and Abraham and Moses as our Hebrew fathers, both literally and figuratively. Other biblical characters have been specifically identified as forerunners, including Elijah, Elias, John the Baptist and Jesus Christ. This biblical forerunner motif found its way more formally into LDS doctrine, referred to as the "spirit of Elias," symbolizing the forerunner who prepares the way for greater things to come and the restoration of things lost. To turn the present towards the past, in preparation for the future.

In Luke 1, Zacharias and Elisabeth are visited by the archangel Gabriel (aka Noah in LDS doctrine), promising her that she will bear a son whom she will name John, whom we know as John the Baptist (Luke 1:11–19). They are told to rejoice at his birth,

> For he shall be great in the sight of the Lord, and shall drink neither wine nor strong drink; and he shall be filled with the Holy Ghost, even from his mother's womb.
> And many of the children of Israel shall he turn to the Lord their God.
> And he shall go before him in the spirit and power of Elias, to turn the hearts of the fathers to the children, and the

disobedient to the wisdom of the just; to make ready a people prepared for the Lord [Luke 1:15–17].

The story of Luke begins with the John the Baptist, going before the birth and ministry of the Lord in the spirit and power of Elias. Joseph understood what this meant.

Joseph, too, was an Elias, restoring lost scripture for his little flock. He was a Moses of his dispensation. An Enoch. He and his revelatory characters are all forerunners in their own stories, for the cause of something greater to come. He knew that he had specifically been called and raised up "as another like unto Moses," another Elias figure (Moses 1:41). This was a doctrine Joseph was intimately familiar with, as he noted of his own calling:

> ...but that my ordination was a preparatory work, or a going before, which was the spirit of Elias; for the spirit of Elias was a going before to prepare the way for the greater, which was the case with John the Baptist. He came crying through the wilderness, "Prepare ye the way of the Lord, make his paths straight. ... Messiah is above the spirit and power of Elijah, for He made the world, and was that spiritual rock unto Moses in the wilderness." Elijah was to come and prepare the way and build up the kingdom before the coming of the great day of the Lord, although the spirit of Elias might begin it.[19]

Luke's genealogy of Jesus follows in Chapter 3, and indeed takes us from Jesus back through another particular number of generations all the way back to "Adam, which was the son of God" (Luke 3:23–38). And here, for the first time, we find Enoch specifically named in this divine genealogy of 76 purported generations from God creating Adam to Jesus (or 75 is you don't include God in the tally). Appropriately found in the beginnings of Luke's gospel, where Enoch's divine lineage is made sure, Joseph's Enoch in Moses 6 also emerges as an Elias in similar fashion, language, allusions and allegory starting with John's story in Luke 3, with a weave of other apocryphal stories apparently familiar to Joseph.

The Wild Man Out of the Wilderness

Joseph's Elias (Enoch) follows in the footsteps of Luke's Elias (John the Baptist). Compare with the parallels of John in Luke 3 with Enoch in Moses 6:

Chapter Eight. Joseph Smith's Enoch

Luke 3:2–5; 21–22	Moses 6:25–27
... the word of God came unto John the son of Zacharias in the wilderness. And he came into all the country about Jordan, preaching the baptism of repentance for the remission of sins; As it is written in the book of the words of Esaias the prophet, saying, The voice of one crying in the wilderness, Prepare ye the way of the Lord, make his paths straight. Every valley shall be filled, and every mountain and hill shall be brought low; and the crooked shall be made straight, and the rough ways shall be made smooth; .... Now when all the people were baptized, it came to pass, that Jesus also being baptized, and praying, the heaven was opened, And the Holy Ghost descended in a bodily shape like a dove upon him, and a voice came from heaven, which said, Thou art my beloved Son; in thee I am well pleased.	And it came to pass that Enoch journeyed in the land, among the people; and as he journeyed, the Spirit of God descended out of heaven, and abode upon him. And he heard a voice from heaven, saying: Enoch, my son, prophesy unto this people, and say unto them—Repent, for thus saith the Lord: I am angry with this people, and my fierce anger is kindled against them; for their hearts have waxed hard, and their ears are dull of hearing, and their eyes cannot see afar off;

In addition to the direct Elias parallels with Luke, these same verses show Joseph's incorporation (and influence) of other familiar biblical phrases, vocabulary and texture. Compare Moses 6:27 (above) with Matthew 13:15:

Matthew 13:15	Moses 6:27
For this people's heart is waxed gross, and their ears are dull of hearing, and their eyes they have closed; lest at any time they should see with their eyes, and hear with their ears, and should understand with their heart, and should be converted, and I should heal them.	... for thus saith the Lord: I am angry with this people, and my fierce anger is kindled against them; for their hearts have waxed hard, and their ears are dull of hearing, and their eyes cannot see afar off;

Joseph Smith and the Book of Enoch

As Moses 6 continues, more biblical allusions continue to emerge, starting with the familiar biblical story of Moses doubting his ability to speak and lead, echoed by Enoch in Joseph's Moses, then continuing with his story, drawing on both biblical and apocryphal influences:

Moses 6:31	Exodus 4:10
And when Enoch had heard these words, he bowed himself to the earth, before the Lord, and spake before the Lord, saying: Why is it that I have found favor in thy sight, and am but a lad, and all the people hate me; for I am slow of speech; wherefore am I thy servant?	And Moses said unto the Lord, O my Lord, I not eloquent, neither heretofore, nor since thou hast spoken unto thy servant: but I slow of speech, and of a slow tongue.
Moses 6:32 And the Lord said unto Enoch: Go forth and do as I have commanded thee, and no man shall pierce thee. Open thy mouth, and it shall be filled, and I will give thee utterance, for all flesh is in my hands, and I will do as seemeth me good.	**Tobit 5:1** Tobias then answered and said, Father, I will do all things which thou has commanded me: **Psalms 81:10; Psalms 71:8** I am the LORD thy God, which brought thee out of the land of Egypt: open thy mouth wide, and I will fill it. Let my mouth be filled with thy praise and with thy honour all the day.
Moses 6:33 Say unto this people: Choose ye this day, to serve the Lord God who made you.	**Joshua 24:15** ... choose you this day whom ye will serve; ... but as for me and my house, we will serve the Lord.

Following a familiar theme, Joseph's Enoch is introduced as an Elias, another John the Baptist, preaching out of the wilderness, coming to clear the ways and paths for something greater. Riding this familiar character is the related motif he carries, being "the voice of one crying in the wilderness" (Mark 1:3). Isaiah also foretold and warned of "the voice of him that crieth in the wilderness, Prepare ye the way of the Lord, make straight in the desert a highway of our God" (Isaiah 40:3). And in true fashion, John the Baptist is described in our New Testament as wearing clothes of camel's hair and living on locusts and wild honey.

Chapter Eight. Joseph Smith's Enoch

Moses 6:34 takes us back to the Elias story in Luke 3, where John was sent to prepare the way and "make his paths straight," reminiscent of Isaiah:

Moses 6:34	Luke 3:5
Behold my Spirit is upon you, wherefore all thy words will I justify; and the mountains shall flee before you, and the rivers shall turn from their course; and thou shalt abide in me, and I in you; therefore walk with me.	Every valley shall be filled, and every mountain and hill shall be brought low; and the crooked shall be made straight, and the rough ways shall be made smooth

A particularly interesting phrase Joseph uses here is "the rivers shall turn from their course." Luke speaks of mountains and hills, and the crooked shall be made straight, but not specifically about waters and their courses. But Joseph returns to the same metaphor in Moses 7:13, again in connection with the wilderness when Enoch "spake the word of the Lord, and the earth trembled, and the mountains fled, ... and the rivers of water were turned out of their course; and the roar of the lions was heard out of the wilderness."

More biblical and apocryphal allusions and stories begin to more fully weave their way into Joseph's Enoch story in Moses 6, coming forward in the spirit of Elias, the man coming out of the wilderness:

Moses 6:35–36	John 9:6
And the Lord spake unto Enoch, and said unto him: Anoint thine eyes with clay, and wash them, and thou shalt see. And he did so. And he beheld the spirits that God had created; and he beheld also things which were not visible to the natural eye; and from thenceforth came the saying abroad in the land: A seer hath the Lord raised up unto his people.	When he had thus spoken, he spat on the ground, and made clay of the spittle, and he anointed the eyes of the blind man with the clay,
Moses 6:37–38 & 40	Tobit 5:6–16
And it came to pass that Enoch went forth in the land, among the people, standing upon the hills and the high places, and cried with a	To whom the angel said, I will go with thee, and I know the way well: for I have lodged with our brother Gabael.

> loud voice, testifying against their works; and all men were offended because of him.
>
> And they came forth to hear him, upon the high places, saying unto the tent-keepers: Tarry ye here and keep the tents, while we go yonder to behold the seer, for he prophesieth, and there is a strange thing in the land; a wild man hath come among us.
>
> ... And there came a man unto him, whose name was Mahijah, and said unto him: Tell us plainly who thou art, and from whence thou comest?
>
> And he said unto them: I came out from the land of Cainan, the land of my fathers, a land of righteousness unto this day. And my father taught me in all the ways of God.
>
> And it came to pass, as I journeyed from the land of Cainan, by the sea east, I beheld a vision; and lo, the heavens I saw, and the Lord spake with me, and gave me commandment; wherefore, for this cause, to keep the commandment, I speak forth these words.

> Then Tobias said unto him, Tarry for me, till I tell my father.
>
> Then he said unto him, Go and tarry not. So he went in and said to his father, Behold, I have found one which will go with me. Then he said, Call him unto me, that I may know of what tribe he is, and whether he be a trusty man to go with thee.
>
> So he called him, and he came in, and they saluted one another.
>
> Then Tobit said unto him, Brother, shew me of what tribe and family thou art. To whom he said, Dost thou seek for a tribe or family, or an hired man to go with thy son? Then Tobit said unto him, I would know, brother, thy kindred and name.
>
> Then Tobit said, Thou art welcome, brother; be not now angry with me, because I have enquired to know thy tribe and thy family; for thou art my brother, of an honest and good stock:
>
> So they were well pleased. Then said he to Tobias, Prepare thyself for the journey, and God send you a good journey. And when his son had prepared all things for the journey, his father said, Go thou with this man, and God, which dwelleth in heaven, prosper your journey, and the angel of God keep you company.

This Elias character preaching out of the wilderness is not a new Enoch story. Enoch is mentioned in Hebrews 11, which is accompanied with the familiar spirit of Elias motifs, including a "strange" and "wild man" who tarries in the desert preaching out of the wilderness:

> 5. By faith Enoch was translated that he should not see death; and was not found, because God had translated him: for before his translation he had this testimony, that he pleased God.
>
> 9. By faith he [Abraham] sojourned in the land of promise, as in a strange country, dwelling in tabernacles [tents] with Isaac and Jacob, the heirs with him of the same promise:

Chapter Eight. Joseph Smith's Enoch

10. For he looked for a city which hath foundations, whose builder and maker is God.

37. ... they wandered about in sheepskins and goatskins; being destitute, afflicted, tormented;
38. ... they wandered in deserts, and in mountains, and in dens and caves of the earth.
39. And these all, having obtained a good report through faith, received not the promise.

Literary Parallels Between Moses and Enoch

In addition to insertions from the Apocrypha, we also find a few similar allusions from Laurence's 1821 Book of Enoch here and Joseph's Enoch story. Backing up to verse 31 in Moses 6, for example, we find these examples of corresponding themes:

Bowing or Falling to the Earth

Moses 6:31	Enoch XIV:12 & 13; XV:9 & 12; LXXXII. SECT. XVI:5–7
And when Enoch had heard these words, he bowed himself to the earth, before the Lord, and spake before the Lord,	... I fell upon my face. In the vision I looked. ... Behold, in that vision clouds and.... I fell upon my face. ... And falling to the earth, I saw likewise

Waters in Their Course and Turning Their Ways

Moses 6:34	Enoch LXXVI
Behold my Spirit is upon you, wherefore all thy words will I justify; and the mountains shall flee before you, and the rivers shall turn from their course; and thou shalt abide in me, and I in you; therefore walk with me. **Moses 7:13** And so great was the faith of Enoch that he led the people of God,	Seven rivers I beheld upon earth, greater than all rivers, one of which takes its course from the west; into a great sea its water flows. **Enoch LXVII:13–15** In those days shall the waters of that valley be changed; for when the angels shall be judged, then shall the heat of those springs of water experience an alteration.

and their enemies came to battle against them; and he spake the word of the Lord, and the earth trembled, and the mountains fled, even according to his command; and the rivers of water were turned out of their course;	And when the angels shall ascend, the water of the springs shall again undergo a change,.... For these waters of judgment shall be for their healing, and for the death of their bodies. But they shall not perceive and believe that the waters will be changed, and become a fire, which shall blaze for ever.

A "Spirit Prison"

Moses 6:38 & 57 But behold, these which thine eyes are upon shall perish in the floods; and behold, I will shut them up; a prison have I prepared for them.... And as many of the spirits as were in prison came forth, and stood on the right hand of God; and the remainder were reserved in chains of darkness until the judgment of the great day.	**Enoch XVIII:15; XIX:2**[20] Then the angel said; This place, until the consummation of heaven and earth, will be the prison of the stars, and of the host of heaven. And being numerous in appearance made men profane, and caused them to err; so that they sacrificed to devils as to gods. For in the great day there shall be a judgment, with which they shall be judged, until they are consumed; and their wives also shall be judged, who led astray the angels of heaven without resistance

God's "Earth Is His Footstool"

Moses 6:43–44 And Enoch continued his speech, saying: The Lord which spake with me, the same is the God of heaven, and he is my God, and your God, and ye are my brethren, and why counsel ye yourselves, and deny the God of heaven? *The heavens he made; the earth is his footstool*; and the foundation thereof is his. Behold, he laid it, an host of men hath he brought in upon the face thereof.	**Enoch LXXXIII.** ... I spoke with the breath of my mouth, and with a tongue of flesh, which God has formed for all the sons of mortal men, that with it they may speak; giving them breath, a mouth, and a tongue to converse with. Blessed art thou, O Lord, the King, great and powerful in thy greatness. Lord of all the creatures of heaven. King of kings, God of the whole world,

Chapter Eight. Joseph Smith's Enoch

	whose reign, whose kingdom, and whose majesty endure for ever and ever. From generation to generation shall thy dominion exist. *All the heavens are thy throne for ever, and all the earth thy footstool* for ever and for ever.

Men Are Carnal and Devilish

Moses 6:49–51	Enoch XV:1–3
Behold Satan hath come among the children of men, and tempteth them to worship him; and men have become carnal, sensual, and devilish, and are shut out from the presence of God. But God hath made known unto our fathers that all men must repent. And he called upon our father Adam by his own voice, saying: I am God; I made the world, and men before they were in the flesh.	Wherefore have you forsaken the lofty and holy heaven, which endures for ever, and have lain with women; have defiled yourselves with the daughters of men; have taken to yourselves wives; have acted like the sons of the earth, and have be gotten an impious offspring? You being spiritual, holy, and possessing a life which is eternal, have polluted yourselves with women; have begotten in carnal blood; have lusted in the blood of men; and have done as those who are flesh and blood do.

Moses 6 continues after the passages cited here, ending with verse 68. Moses 7:1 is where John Whitmer's transcription services as scribe for Joseph ended and a new scribe was called in December 1830. Joseph's Enoch in the final two chapters of Moses come at the hand of Sidney Rigdon, an Elias himself, and scribe just like Enoch of old. And it seems to be almost a new Enoch, with a clearer start and with some more tightly knit correspondences to Laurence's Enoch.

A Scribe of Righteousness

In December 1830, the bonanza arrived with Sidney Rigdon at the Whitmer's home in Fayette, New York, where Joseph was then living and working on his translation of the Bible. After sending his schoolteacher

Joseph Smith and the Book of Enoch

scribe, Oliver Cowdery, off to the edges of Indian territory, as noted, Joseph juggled the transcription work between Emma and John Whitmer and struggled to bring forth an Enoch with his own stories. Things changed on December 7, 1830, when Rigdon arrived seeking out the young prophet Joseph Smith. Rigdon is probably the most "unsung hero" in the history of the development of Mormon doctrine—what it was in its infancy and where it could have gone from there, in contrast to what it would eventually become—as he contributed heavily to crafting the Mormon apocalyptic doctrines and Zionism. Where Joe Smith was the presumed unlettered farm boy, Rigdon was not. A farm boy, yes. But he was well-read and had an encyclopedic understanding of biblical verse.

Rigdon biographer Richard S. Van Wagoner notes of Joseph's fortuitous introduction to his new scribe:

> That Rigdon could have been merely "Sidney the Scribe," a penman whose sole function was to take down dictation, is implausible. A biblical scholar with a reputation for erudition, he was more learned, better read, and more steeped in biblical interpretation than any other early Mormon, despite his common school education. Any number of Smith's followers could have served as clerk, but only Rigdon could have functioned as a scribe in the historical Jewish sense of the word: "a man of learning; one who read and explained the law to the people."[21]

Scholars and Mormon historians have long recognized that "Rigdon held sway over Smith intellectually," providing Joseph with a formidable resource for doctrine, biblical history and (most importantly) literary sources that Joseph utilized at different times in his "translation" of the Bible and his composition of pseudobiblical[22] literature, such as the Book of Moses and Book of Abraham.[23] Rigdon was 12 years Joseph's senior, and not only could claim a far better education but was also more experienced in running a congregation. Joseph hardly went to organized church at all, and he had only a few month's experience leading the handful of his few followers. Rigdon, on the other hand, had been preaching for more than eleven years as a licensed Baptist minister.

In 1822, Rigdon had accepted the pastorate of the First Baptist Church in Pittsburgh under the recommendation of Alexander Campbell, well-known leader of the reformative Restoration Movement. The Restoration Movement began in the early 19th century in the United States. Restorationists wanted to reform the Christian church into a more unified church patterned after that in the New Testament. Campbell's 1826 publication *The Living Oracles*, his translation of the New Testament, was also widely distributed and discussed. Sidney Rigdon

Chapter Eight. Joseph Smith's Enoch

was a Campbellite and a Restorationist, the latter having a profound effect on Joseph's concepts of communal living and his Zionism. Having heard of the young farm boy restoring lost scriptures and plain and simple truths, Rigdon went to find him.

Rigdon was introduced to Mormonism by a former member of his own congregation, Parley P. Pratt—the same Parley P. Pratt who we know owned a copy of Laurence's 1821 1 Enoch in his personal library at least by 1840, probably procured during his missionary efforts to England. In the fall of 1830, Pratt was baptized into the Mormon church and began a mission himself to proclaim its new gospel. He visited Rigdon at his home in Ohio and gave him a copy of the Book of Mormon. Rigdon read the book in two weeks and was baptized on November 14, 1830, in Mentor, Ohio, without ever meeting the young prophet Joseph Smith. After he was converted, he converted hundreds of members of his own congregation to this new Mormon religion. Within a month of his conversion to the newfound religion, he left Ohio to travel to New York to meet Joseph Smith.

Upon arriving, Sidney Rigdon soon learned that Joseph Smith was not the presumed and so-called "uneducated farm boy" he had been so portrayed as.[24] Whatever it was they discussed, Joseph was impressed and immediately received a revelation calling Sidney Rigdon to act as his scribe. Section 35 of D&C was revelation received by Joseph and Sidney on December 7, 1830; and "thus spake the Lord":

> And I have given unto him [Joseph] the keys of the mystery of those things which have been sealed, even things which were from the foundation of the world, and the things which shall come from this time until the time of my coming, if he abide in me, and if not, another will I plant in his stead.
> Wherefore, watch over him that his faith fail not, and it shall be given by the Comforter, the Holy Ghost, that knoweth all things.
> And a commandment I give unto thee [Sidney]—that thou shalt write for him; and the scriptures shall be given, even as they are in mine own bosom, to the salvation of mine own elect.[25]

Rigdon's arrival proved to be a turning point for Joseph's prophecies. Transitioning from the deflections of anti–Masonic themes and his clumsy revelations at the hand of several shuffled scribes over the few months prior, Joseph's revelations again found fluidity and purpose. The revelations flowing from the hand of Joseph's newest trusted friend, Sidney the scribe, resumed with a quicker pace and—even more apparent—an elegance that Joseph's prior writings wanted.

Consider the revelation received at the hand of Sidney soon after he began writing for Joseph, received in preparation for a conference of all the church members. Recorded in D&C Section 38:1–4, we hear the familiar recycling of where to begin again, anew with reference to creation, the cosmic expanse and the coming of heavenly angels preparing the way to build a kingdom of God upon the earth:

> Thus saith the Lord your God, even Jesus Christ, the Great I Am, Alpha and Omega, the beginning and the end, the same which looked upon the wide expanse of eternity, and all the seraphic hosts of heaven, before the world was made;
> The same which knoweth all things, for all things are present before mine eyes; I am the same which spake, and the world was made, and all things came by me.
> I am the same which have taken the Zion of Enoch into mine own bosom.

This calling of Sidney the scribe is resounding of Laurence's Enoch, who is also referred to as "Enoch the scribe" and "Enoch, scribe of righteousness" in Enoch XIII:4–5. It is also fitting that his calling as a scribe is recorded as being for the "salvation of mine own elect," a prevalent theme throughout the Book of Enoch (Enoch 1:1). ("The word of the blessing of Enoch, how he blessed the elect and the righteous, … Upon their account I spoke and conversed with him.")

They had work to do. Joseph was busy to get back to fluid translation, and particularly back to Enoch and building Zion.

Joseph and Sidney Rigdon's Enoch Emerges

Sidney picked up his pen for Joseph, and immediate verbal parallels with Laurence's Enoch begin to emerge with a greater fluidity and rate. Patterning the same "begin at the beginning" refresher, we are introduced to a clearer version of Joseph's Enoch.

Again, Speaking with God and Seeing All Generations of the World

Moses 7:1–4 & 21	Enoch. XXXIX:1
1. And it came to pass that Enoch continued his speech, saying: Behold, our father Adam taught these things, and many have believed and become the sons of	In those days shall the elect and holy race descend from the upper heavens, and their seed shall then be with the sons of men. Enoch received books of indignation and

Chapter Eight. Joseph Smith's Enoch

God, and many have believed not, and have perished in their sins, and are looking forth with fear, in torment, for the fiery indignation of the wrath of God to be poured out upon them. 2. And from that time forth Enoch began to prophesy, saying unto the people, that: As I was journeying, and stood upon the place Mahujah, and cried unto the Lord, there came a voice out of heaven, saying—Turn ye, and get ye upon the mount Simeon. 3. And it came to pass that I turned and went up on the mount; and as I stood upon the mount, I beheld the heavens open, and I was clothed upon with glory; 4. And I saw the Lord; and he stood before my face, and he talked with me, even as a man talketh one with another, face to face; and he said unto me: Look, and I will show unto thee the world for the space of many generations. 21. And it came to pass that the Lord showed unto Enoch all the inhabitants of the earth; and he beheld, and lo, Zion, in process of time, was taken up into heaven. And the Lord said unto Enoch: Behold mine abode forever.	wrath, and books of hurry and agitation. **Enoch IV:12** They shall not be condemned the whole period of their lives, nor die in torment and indignation; but the sum of their days shall be completed, and they shall grow old in peace; while the years of their happiness shall be multiplied with joy, and with peace, for ever, the whole duration of their existence. **Enoch 1:1, 3–4** Enoch, a righteous man, who was with God, answered and spoke, while his eyes were open,.... ... Upon their account I spoke and conversed with him, ... Who will hereafter tread upon Mount Sinai; appear with his hosts.... **Enoch XIV:1** I perceived in my dream, that I was now speaking with a tongue of flesh, and with my breath, which the Mighty One put into the mouth of men, that they might converse with it; **Enoch LXXX:1–3** He said; O Enoch, look.... Then I looked on all which was written, and understood all, ... And of all the children of flesh upon earth, during the generations of the world.

Angels Declaring Wo! Wo! to the Inhabitants of the Earth

Moses 7:25 And he saw angels descending out of heaven; and he heard a loud voice saying: Wo, wo be unto the inhabitants of the earth.	Enoch XCIII:6–7 Wo to those who build up iniquity and oppression, and who lay the foundation of fraud; for suddenly shall they be subverted, and never obtain peace. Wo to those who build up their houses with crime; for from their

	very foundations shall their houses be demolished, and by the sword shall they themselves fall. Those, too, who acquire gold and silver, shall justly and suddenly perish. Wo to you who are rich, for in your riches have you trusted; but from your riches you shall be removed because you have not remembered the Most High in the days of your prosperity: **Enoch XCVI:6 & 19** Wo unto you, sinners, who in the midst of the sea, and on dry land, are those against whom an evil record exists. But are destined to the day of the great judgment, to the day of distress, and the extreme ignominy of your souls.

Heavenly Weeping on Account of the Earth

Moses 7:28–29	Enoch XCIII:9–10; XCIV:1–3
And it came to pass that the **God of heaven looked upon** the residue of **the people, and he wept**; and Enoch bore record of it, saying: How is it that **the heavens weep, and shed forth their tears as the rain** upon the mountains? And Enoch said unto the Lord: **How is it that thou canst weep,** seeing thou art holy, and from all eternity to all eternity?	This I declare and point out to you, that **he who created you** will destroy you. When you fall, he will not shew you mercy; but **your Creator** will rejoice in your destruction. **O that my eyes were clouds of water, that I might weep over you, and pour forth my tears like rain[b], and rest from the sorrow of my heart!** Who has permitted you to hate and to transgress? Judgment shall overtake you, ye sinners. The righteous shall not fear the wicked; because God will again bring them into your power, that you may avenge yourselves of them according to your pleasure. (fn. b: *"a cloud of water."*)

Chapter Eight. Joseph Smith's Enoch

Enoch's Son Methuselah Prophesies in Moses and the Book of Enoch

Moses 8: –3	Enoch LXXX:8–9
And it came to pass that Methuselah, the son of Enoch, was not taken, that the covenants of the Lord might be fulfilled, which he made to Enoch; for he truly covenanted with Enoch that Noah should be of the fruit of his loins. And it came to pass that Methuselah prophesied that from his loins should spring all the kingdoms of the earth (through Noah), and he took glory unto himself.	And they said unto me; Explain every thing to Mathusala thy son; and inform all thy children, that no flesh shall be justified before the Lord; for he is their Creator. During one year we will leave thee with thy children, until thou shalt again recover thy strength, that thou mayest instruct thy family, write these things, and explain them to all thy children. **Enoch LXXXI:2–3** Preserve, my son Mathusala, the books written by thy father that thou mayest transmit them to future generations. Wisdom have I given to thee, to thy children, and thy posterity, that they may transmit to their children, for generations for ever, this wisdom in their thoughts;

Enoch Foretells of Noah Building an Ark, and His Family Saved from the Flood

Moses 7:42–45	Enoch LXXXVIII:1, 4–8 & 11
And Enoch also saw Noah, and his family; that the posterity of all the sons of Noah should be saved with a temporal salvation; Wherefore Enoch saw that Noah built an ark; and that the lord smiled upon it, and held it in his own hand; but upon the residue of the wicked the floods came and swallowed them up. ... And it came to pass that Enoch looked; and from Noah, he beheld all the families of the earth; and he	While the cow was trembling, it was born, and became a man [a "Noah"], and fabricated for himself a large ship. In this he dwelt, and three cows ["Shem, Ham and Japhet"] dwelt with him in that ship, which covered them. The water began to boil up, and rose over the earth; so that the village was not seen, while its whole soil was covered with water. Much water was over it, darkness, and clouds. Then I surveyed the

cried unto the Lord, saying: When shall the day of the Lord come? When shall the blood of the Righteous be shed, that all they that mourn may be sanctified and have eternal life?
Moses 8:25–26
And thus Noah found grace in the eyes of the Lord; for Noah was a just man, and perfect in his generation; and he walked with God, as did also his three sons, Shem, Ham, and Japheth.
And the Lord said: I will destroy man whom I have created, from the face of the earth, both man and beast, and the creeping things, and the fowls of the air; for it repenteth Noah that I have created them, and that I have made them; and he hath called upon me; for they have sought his life.

height of this water; and it was elevated above the village.
It flowed over the village, and stood higher than the earth.
Then all the cows which were collected there, while I looked on them, were drowned, swallowed up, and destroyed in the water.
But the ship floated above it. All the cows, the elephants, the camels, and the asses, were drowned on the earth, and all cattle. Nor could I perceive them. Neither were they able to get out, but perished, and sunk into the deep.
The ship remained on the earth; the darkness receded and it became light.

Corruption of "Sons of Men," "Giants" and Choosing Wives Among Daughters of Men

Moses 8:13–15; 17–18.
And Noah and his sons hearkened unto the Lord, and gave heed, and they were called the **sons of God.**
And when these men began to multiply on the face of the earth, **and daughters were born unto them,** the **sons of men saw that those daughters were fair, and they took them wives, even as they chose.**
And the Lord said unto Noah: **The daughters of thy sons have sold themselves;** for behold mine anger is kindled against the **sons of men,** for they will not hearken to my voice.

Enoch VII. SECT. II:1–2; 10–11
It happened after the **sons of men** had multiplied in those days, that **daughters were born to them elegant and beautiful.**
And when the angels, **the sons of heaven,** beheld them, they became enamoured of them, saying to each other; Come, **let us select for ourselves wives** from the progeny of men, and let us beget children.
Then they took wives, each choosing for himself....
And the women conceiving brought forth giants;
Enoch CV:13–16
Then I, Enoch, answered and

Chapter Eight. Joseph Smith's Enoch

And the Lord said unto Noah: My Spirit shall not always strive with man, for he shall know that all flesh shall die; yet his days shall be an hundred and twenty years; and if men do not repent, I will send in the floods upon them. **And in those days there were giants on the earth**, and they sought Noah to take away his life, but the Lord was with Noah, and the power of the Lord was upon him. Moses 8: 28–30 The earth was corrupt before God, and it was filled with violence. **And God looked upon the earth, and, behold, it was corrupt, for all flesh had corrupted its way upon the earth.** And God said unto Noah: The end of all flesh is come before me, for the earth is filled with violence, and behold I will destroy all flesh from off the earth.	said; The Lord will effect a new thing upon the earth. This have I explained, and seen in a vision. I have shewn thee that in the generations of Jared my father, those who were from heaven disregarded the word of the Lord. Behold they committed crimes; laid aside their class, and intermingled with women. With them also they transgressed; married with them, and begot children. A great destruction therefore shall come upon all the earth; a deluge, a great destruction, shall take place in one year. This child which is born to you shall survive on the earth, and his three sons shall be saved with him. When all mankind who are on earth shall die, he shall be safe. **And his posterity shall beget on the earth giants**, not spiritual, but carnal. **Upon the earth shall a great punishment be inflicted, and it shall be washed from all corruption.** Now therefore inform thy son Lamech, that he who is born is his child in truth; and he shall call his name Noah, for he shall be to you a survivor. He and his children shall be saved from the corruption which shall take place in the world; from all the sin and from all the iniquity which shall be consummated on earth in his days.

Enoch Foresees the Coming of the Son of Man

The "Son of man" motif is something that can be said to be specifically related to Enochic literature. Or at least to pre–Christian apocalyptic Jewish literature. The specific phrase "Son of man" found its ways into our New Testament gospels as naturally as so many other ideas and phrases taken from Old Testament writings by New Testament writers to shore up their narrative. Mark 14:21 tells us, "The Son of man indeed goeth, as it is written of him." Matthew identically writes, "The Son of man goes as it is written of him" (Matthew 26:24), whereas Luke tells us that "truly the Son of man goeth, as it was determined" (Luke 22:22). The synoptic authors, and at least Mark, had access to written scriptures or writings about the "Son of man" who would be coming. John's gospel asks, "The Son of man must be lifted up?" (John 12:34).

Who is this Son of man? The phrase is synonymous with and sounds like "Son of God," and used so closely in that context, we hardly hear the difference. But what does "Son of *man*" mean? Jesus was *not* the son of a man.

The term is used as a title in Ezekiel and Daniel of the Old Testament. Daniel is of particular interest because of its significant similarities with the Book of Enoch. Both are pre–Christian apocalyptic prophecies about the "Ancient of Days" in snow white garments, seated on his throne, with a stream of thousands and ten thousands of his angels coming to establish the heavenly kingdom here upon the earth. Both stories include troubling visions that leave the authors terrified and trembling. And both stories follow the same accompanying and interpreting angel motif. Compare Daniel's description of the Ancient of Days to Enoch's:

> **Daniel 7:9–16**
> I beheld till the thrones were cast down, and the Ancient of days did sit, whose garment was white as snow, and the hair of his head like the pure wool: his throne was like the firey flame, and his wheels as burning fire.
> A fiery stream issued and came forth from before him: thousand thousands ministered unto him, and ten thousand times ten thousand stood before him: the judgment was set, and the books were opened.
> I beheld then because of the voice of the great words which the horn spake: I beheld even till the beast was slain, and his body destroyed, and given to the burning flame.
> As concerning the rest of the beasts, they had their dominion taken away: yet their lives were prolonged for a season and time.
> I saw in the night visions, and, behold, one like the Son of man came with the clouds of heaven, and came to the Ancient of days, and they brought him near before him.
> And there was given him dominion, and glory, and a kingdom, that all people, nations, and languages, should serve him: his dominion is an everlasting dominion, which shall not pass away, and his kingdom that which shall not be destroyed.

Chapter Eight. Joseph Smith's Enoch

> I Daniel was grieved in my spirit in the midst of my body, and the visions of my head troubled me.
>
> I came near unto one of them that stood by, and asked him the truth of all this. So he told me, and made me know the interpretation of the things.

Compare the preceding to Enoch LIX, SECT. X:1–2

> ... in that parable, I saw that the heaven of heavens shook; that it shook violently; and that the powers of the Most High, and the angels, thousands of thousands, and myriads of myriads, were agitated with great agitation.
>
> And when I looked, the Ancient of days was sitting on the throne of his glory, while the angels and saints were standing around him. A great trembling came upon me, and terror seized me. My loins were bowed down and loosened; my reins were dissolved; and I fell upon my face. The holy Michael, another holy angel, one of the holy ones, was sent, who raised me up.
>
> And when he raised me, my spirit returned; for I was incapable of enduring this vision of violence, its agitation, and the concussion of heaven.

"Ancient of Days" and "Son of man" are expressions associated specifically with Jewish apocalyptic literature in which the author is swept away in a vision and sees the end of times or end of ages revealed by an angel or heavenly messenger. Apocalyptic prophecies are found throughout the New Testament, in Matthew 24, Mark 13, 2 Thessalonians 2, 1 Timothy 4, 2 Peter 3, Jude 14–15 and the Book of Revelation. The Book of Enoch is apocalyptic Jewish literature, telling of the coming of a Son of man who is going to set in action cosmic reversals, where the first will be the last and the last first.

Joseph's Moses 7 and 8 include a much more pronounced apocalyptic flavor than the earlier chapters, specifically incorporating the Son of man motif:

> **Moses 7:24–56**
>
> And there came generation upon generation; and Enoch was high and lifted up, even in the bosom of the Father, and of the Son of Man; and behold, the power of Satan was upon all the face of the earth.
>
> And he saw angels descending out of heaven; and he heard a loud voice saying: Wo, wo be unto the inhabitants of the earth.
>
> And he beheld Satan; and he had a great chain in his hand, and it veiled the whole face of the earth with darkness; and he looked up and laughed, and his angels rejoiced.

And Enoch beheld angels descending out of heaven, bearing testimony of the Father and Son; and the Holy Ghost fell on many, and they were caught up by the powers of heaven into Zion.

And behold, Enoch saw the day of the coming of the Son of Man, even in the flesh; and his soul rejoiced, saying: The Righteous is lifted up, and the Lamb is slain from the foundation of the world; and through faith I am in the bosom of the Father, and behold, Zion is with me.

And the Lord said: Blessed is he through whose seed Messiah shall come; for he saith—I am Messiah, the King of Zion, the Rock of Heaven, which is broad as eternity; whoso cometh in at the gate and climbeth up by me shall never fall; wherefore, blessed are they of whom I have spoken, for they shall come forth with songs of everlasting joy.

And it came to pass that Enoch cried unto the Lord, saying: When the Son of Man cometh in the flesh, shall the earth rest? I pray thee, show me these things. And the Lord said unto Enoch: Look, and he looked and beheld the Son of Man lifted up on the cross, after the manner of men;

And he heard a loud voice; and the heavens were veiled; and all the creations of God mourned; and the earth groaned; and the rocks were rent; and the saints arose, and were crowned at the right hand of the Son of Man, with crowns of glory;

Enoch, also, prophesies of the cosmic coming of the Son of man:

Enoch XLVIII:2–5, 7 & 11

In that hour was this Son of man invoked before the Lord of spirits, and his name in the presence of the Ancient of days.

Before the sun and the signs were created, before the stars of heaven were formed, his name was invoked in the presence of the Lord of spirits.

He shall be the hope of those whose hearts are troubled. All, who dwell on earth, shall fall down and worship before him; shall bless and glorify him, and sing praises to the name of the Lord of spirits.

Therefore the Elect and the Concealed one existed in his presence before the world was created, and for ever.

... For in his name shall they be preserved; and his will shall be their life.

... In his presence shall they fall, and not be raised up again; nor shall there be any one to take them out of his hands, and to lift them up; for they have denied the Lord of spirits, and his Messiah. The name of the Lord of spirits shall be blessed.

Enoch XCL. SECT. XIX:3

Let the righteous man arise from slumber; let him arise, and proceed in the path.... In goodness and in righteousness shall he exist, and shall walk in ever lasting light.

Enoch LXVIII:40

According to their ranks of corruption shall they be imprisoned, and all their works shall disappear from the face of the earth; nor thenceforward shall there be any to corrupt; for the Son of Man has been seen, sitting on the throne of his glory.

Chapter Nine

Zion—A New Jerusalem

> *"Bible readers had always been curious about Enoch and the city transported into heaven."*
> —Richard Lyman Bushman[1]

God's biblical children—Israel—are a chosen people with a promised land. This is a repeat story found in the Old Testament, and the same motif is found woven into the Book of Mormon stories. In the Old Testament, Abraham is promised to be the father of innumerable descendants, and promised a land for his progenies as a lasting heritage (Genesis 12: 1–3, 7). This promised land geographically extended from Egypt's Nile to the Euphrates (Exodus 15:18) and was inhabited by Canaanites, Amorites, Hittites, Perizzites, Hivites, and Jebusites (Judges 3:5). Today, this land includes modern-day Israel, Gaza, the West Bank, Jordan, and some of Egypt, Syria, Saudi Arabia and Iraq. God's promise was that his chosen children—if they remain righteous—would establish a nation of their own and even an earthly Kingdom of God in their promised land.

God's promised-land covenant with Abraham was confirmed with his son, Isaac (Genesis 26: 2–3). And the same promise was confirmed to Isaac's son, Jacob, with similarly sounding genetic potency promised to Abraham:

> And, behold, the LORD stood above it, and said, I *am* the LORD god of Abraham thy father, and the God of Isaac: the land whereupon thou liest, to thee will I give it, and to thy seed;
> And thy seed shall be as the dust of the earth, and thou shalt spread abroad to the west, and to the east, and to the north, and to the south: and in thee and thy seed shall all the families of the earth be blessed [Genesis 28: 13–14].

Recall, this is the same Jacob also named Israel, the father of the 12 tribes of Israel. This land was promised to the seed of Jacob if they

Chapter Nine. Zion—A New Jerusalem

trusted their God, who in return demanded their faithful worship (Deut. 7: 12–15).

The Israelites became enslaved in Egypt when Jacob took his famished family there in search of food. But, true to his word, God raised another leader, Moses, who led the Israelites out of Egypt and into the desert, on their way again to the promised land. They wandered for 40 years before Moses died, and another hero rose. Joshua, in military command and conquest, leads God's children toward their promised land. But they were never far from warring neighbors, like the Philistines. David "triumphed over the Philistine with a sling and a stone" (1 Samuel 17:50). King David had his flaws, but he was a great king and poet. It was David who captured the Canaanite hill fortress called "Zion,"[2] thereafter establishing the permanent city for God's chosen and their leader.

Jerusalem became a political and religious capital. It symbolically stood as the dwelling place of God, God's tabernacle. "Zion" eventually became synonymous with the Jewish temple itself, the hill upon which the temple stood, all of Jerusalem, or the entire land belonging to Israel. Zion was God's kingdom on earth, in every sense. And it was through David's lineage that the Israelites were promised an anointed one, a Messiah, even a King to reign and rule in God's earthly kingdom.

Establishing themselves as the "tribes of Israel," all named after the sons or grandsons of Jacob, the Israelites divided into two independent kingdoms, the Kingdom of Israel in the northern half (consisting of ten tribes and territories) and the Kingdom of Judah (the remaining two tribes) in the southern half. The northern Kingdom of Israel was conquered by the Babylonians and Assyrians, and the Israelites were taken into captivity. The Babylonians destroyed the Jerusalem temple. Over time, the peoples known as those ten tribes were thought to have become "lost" to the word as a result of gradual assimilation by conquest and mixed cultures.

Jerusalem was the promised land for the Israelites—the Jews. Under different Israelite kings and kingdoms, their devotion to the Hebrew god was lost to the worship of idols and false gods. Jewish prophets arose to remind people to repent, concluding with John the Baptist. And, again as promised in the Jewish hero story, we have the Son of man. And Christianity was born.

Joseph Smith was a restorationist of what he believed to be primitive Christianity. He also believed in a literal gathering of Israel as a people, in a place, to re-establish God's divine city, where there would be a tabernacle and dwelling place for God among his people. He knit the promised land, lost tribe and God's city story into his translation projects, particularly the Book of Mormon and revealed prophecies of Enoch in his Book of Moses.

Book of Mormon readers are familiar with a "promised land" motif. Book of Mormon prophet Lehi is told, "Ye shall be led to a land of promise" (1 Nephi 2:20; 1 Nephi 5:5). Lehi is told that if his descendants keep God's commandments, they will prosper in the land of promise (2 Nephi 1: 5–9). As the Book of Mormon is understood, Lehi's promised land is the American continent. As the Book of Mormon storyline plays out, just as Jerusalem was the promised land for the descendants of Abraham, the Americas were a land of promise for those Israelites that left Jerusalem by way of boat with Lehi and his family—the "seed of Jacob" (Mormon 7:10) ("And ye will also know that ye are a remnant of the seed of Jacob; therefore ye are numbered among the people of the first covenant"). These "other sheep" left the fold in Jerusalem and were scattered across the sea to their own land of inheritance, the other "promised land" and new Zion.

Gathering God's elect and scattered sheep is a common biblical theme for both Jews and Christians. The Hebrew bible repeatedly reminds us of God's promise to his chosen people:

> [T]he Lord thy God will turn thy captivity, and have compassion upon thee, and will return and gather thee from all the nations whither the Lord thy God hath scattered thee. If any of thine be driven out unto the outmost parts of heaven, from thence will the Lord thy God gather thee, and from thence will He fetch thee [Deut. 30: 1–4].

In Isaiah 11:12 we read "he shall set up an ensign for the nations, and shall assemble the outcasts of Israel, and gather together the dispersed of Judah from the four corners of the earth." New Testament writers echo this gathering, as Matthew 24:31 tells us, "And he shall send his angels with a great sound of a trumpet, and they shall gather together his elect from the four winds, from one end of heaven to the other." Mark 13:27 similarly says, "And then shall he send his angels, and shall gather together his elect from the four winds, from the uttermost part of the earth to the uttermost part of heaven." John's Revelation also speaks of "four angels standing on the four corners of the earth, holding the four winds of the earth" (Revelation 7:1).

The Book of Enoch also refers to angels on the "fourth quarter [of] the winds to the west," and describes "the four quarters of heaven" (Enoch LXXVL: 10 & 12). Notice Enoch's use of the word "quarters," and not "corners" as Isaiah and John the Revelator use. The Book of Enoch

Chapter Nine. Zion—A New Jerusalem

also describes the gathering of the "elect," his saints, and the Son of man coming to live among them, scattered over the earth:

> There I saw another vision; I saw the habitation and dormitory of the saints. There my eyes beheld their habitation with the angels, and their dormitory with the holy ones. They were entreating, supplicating, and praying for the sons of men, while righteousness like water flowed before them, and mercy like dew was scattered over the earth. And thus shall it he with them for ever and for ever. At that time my eyes beheld the dwelling of the elect, of truth, faith, and righteousness. Countless shall be the number of the holy and the elect in the presence of God for ever and for ever [Enoch XXXIX: 4–5].

Joseph's prophecies of Enoch in the Book of Moses similarly reference the "elect," those saints that are scattered on the earth. Joseph's Enoch declares:

> And the day shall come that the earth shall rest, but before that day the heavens shall be darkened, and a veil of darkness shall cover the earth; and the heavens shall shake, and also the earth; and great tribulations shall be among the children of men, but my people will I preserve;
>
> And righteousness will I send down out of heaven; and truth will I send forth out of the earth, to bear testimony of mine Only Begotten; his resurrection from the dead; yea, and also the resurrection of all men; and righteousness and truth will I cause to sweep the earth as with a flood, to gather out mine elect from the four quarters of the earth, unto a place which I shall prepare, an Holy City, that my people may gird up their loins, and be looking forth for the time of my coming; for there shall be my tabernacle, and it shall be called Zion, a New Jerusalem [Moses 7: 61–62].

Interpreting the supposed meaning of his own revealed translation, Joseph Smith explained Enoch's prophecy:

> Now I understand by this quotation, that God clearly manifested to Enoch the redemption which He prepared, by offering the Messiah as a Lamb slain from before the foundation of the world; and by virtue of the same, the glorious resurrection of the Savior, and the resurrection of all the human family, even a resurrection of their corporeal bodies, is brought to pass; and also righteousness and truth are to sweep the earth as with a flood. And now, I ask, how righteousness and truth are going to sweep the earth as with a flood? I will answer. Men and angels are to be co-workers in bringing to pass this great work, and Zion is to be prepared, even a new Jerusalem, for the elect that are to be gathered from the four quarters of the earth, and to be established an holy city, for the tabernacle of the Lord shall be with them.
>
> Now Enoch was in good company in his views upon this subject: "And I heard a great voice out of heaven, saying, Behold, the tabernacle of God is

with men, and He will dwell with them, and they shall be His people and God Himself shall be with them, and be their God" [quoting Book of Revelation 21:3].

I discover by this quotation, that John [the Revelator] upon the isle of Patmos, saw the same things concerning the last days, which Enoch saw. But before the tabernacle can be with men, the elect must be gathered from the four quarters of the earth.[3]

This is strange, because there is nothing in the Bible connecting Enoch with the City of Zion. This is uniquely Joseph Smith's—and a purely Mormon doctrine. In his biography of Joseph Smith, Richard Bushman interestingly reflects on the LDS understanding of Enoch in connection with any city of Enoch:

> Bible readers had always been curious about Enoch and the city transported into heaven. Joseph's expansion appeared when a vast apocryphal literature on Enoch was first being rediscovered.... Up until that time, modern biblical commentators on Enoch had been restricted to the five verses in Genesis and the three in the New Testament that speak of Enoch's genealogy, prophecy of judgment, and ascent into heaven without dying.[4]

Notice *who* would be "curious about Enoch and the city transported into heaven." *Bible readers.* Bible readers should be curious about a city of Enoch transported into heaven, because there is no city of Enoch, and none transported into heaven in the Bible. As Bushman implies, if we are Bible-*only* readers, then these stories are curious from perspectives of religious historicity or scriptural connection. But readers of Mormon scripture, including the Bible, the Book of Mormon, Book of Moses and Joseph's *Inspired Version* of the Bible, are not so surprised by the "City of Enoch" (or "Zion of Enoch") (D&C 38:4) teachings and stories, and his entire city and its inhabitants transported into and/or coming down from heaven.

In fact, the Mormon promise of a City of Zion—a New Jerusalem—finds a repeat appearance in the early Mormon scriptures offering the alternative origin story for indigenous Americans. In 3 Nephi 20: 22, Christ, while preaching to the Nephites, tells us, "And behold, this people will I establish in this land, unto the fulfilling of the covenant which I made with your father Jacob; and it shall be a New Jerusalem. And the powers of heaven shall be in the midst of this people; yea, even I will be in the midst of you." Book of Mormon prophet, Ether, also wrote about "the New Jerusalem upon this land" (Ether 13: 4). Ether wrote:

> And that it was the place of the New Jerusalem, *which should come down out of heaven*, and the holy sanctuary of the Lord. ...

Chapter Nine. Zion—A New Jerusalem

> And he spake also concerning the house of Israel, and the Jerusalem from whence Lehi should come—after it should be destroyed it should be built up again, a holy city unto the Lord; wherefore, it could not be a new Jerusalem for it had been in a time of old; but it should be built up again, and become a holy city of the Lord; and it should be built unto the house of Israel.
>
> And that a New Jerusalem should be built upon this land, unto the remnant of the seed of Joseph, for which things there has been a type.
>
> For as Joseph brought his father down into the land of Egypt, even so he died there; wherefore, the Lord brought a remnant of the seed of Joseph out of the land of Jerusalem, that he might be merciful unto the seed of Joseph that they should perish not, even as he was merciful unto the father of Joseph that he should perish not.
>
> Wherefore, the remnant of the house of Joseph shall be built upon this land; and it shall be a land of their inheritance; *and they shall build up a holy city unto the Lord, like unto the Jerusalem of old*; and they shall no more be confounded, until the end come when the earth shall pass away.
>
> *And there shall be a new heaven and a new earth*; and they shall be like unto the old save the old have passed away, and all things have become new.
>
> And then cometh the New Jerusalem; and blessed are they who dwell therein, for it is they whose garments are white through the blood of the Lamb; and they are they who are numbered among the remnant of the seed of Joseph, who were of the house of Israel [Ether 13: 3, 5–10, emphasis added].

This "new heaven" and "new earth" parallel in Joseph's revelations echoes scripture in the Book of Enoch, where "[t]he former heaven shall depart and pass away, a new heaven shall appear" (Enoch XCII: 17). It should, because Joseph admittedly borrowed it from the Book of Revelation, whose author apparently borrowed it from the scrolls of Enoch.[5] Again, explaining from his own translations and revelations, Joseph Smith taught:

> ... Now we learn from the Book of Mormon the very identical continent and spot of land upon which the New Jerusalem is to stand, and it must be caught up according to the vision of John upon the isle of Patmos.
>
> Now many will feel disposed to say, that this New Jerusalem spoken of, is the Jerusalem that was built by the Jews on the eastern continent. But you will see, from Revelation 21:2, *there was a New Jerusalem coming down from God out of heaven*, adorned as a bride for her husband; that after this, the Revelator was caught away in the Spirit, to a great and high mountain, *and saw the great and holy city descending out of heaven from God*. Now there are two cites spoken of here. As everything cannot be had in so narrow a compass as a letter, I shall say with brevity, that there is a New Jerusalem to be established on this continent, and also Jerusalem shall be rebuilt on the eastern continent (*see* Book of Mormon, Ether 13:1-12). "Behold, Ether saw

the days of Christ, and he spake also concerning the house of Israel, and the Jerusalem from whence Lehi should come; after it should be destroyed, it should be built up again, a holy city unto the Lord, wherefore it could not be a New Jerusalem, for it had been in a time of old." This may suffice, upon the subject of gathering, until my next.[6]

In a bit more modern times of our latter days, LDS apostle and author of the encyclopedic compendium *Mormon Doctrine*, Bruce R. McConkie, offered the following comments on "Zion," connecting it with Enoch and his holy city:

> *Zion* is the name given by the Lord to his saints; it is the name by which the Lord's people are always identified. Of the saints in Enoch's day the record says: "And the Lord called his people ZION, because they were of one heart and one mind, and dwelt in righteousness; and there was no poor among them" (Moses 7:18). After the Lord had called his people Zion, Enoch "built a city that was called the City of Holiness, even Zion." This "Zion, in process of time," after 365 years, "was taken up into heaven, ... for God received it up into his own bosom; and from thence went forth the saying, ZION IS FLED." Between that time and the flood "many" persons "were caught up by the powers of heaven into Zion." It is this City of Zion which is to return in the last days, probably shortly after the ushering in of the millennial era (Moses 7: 18; D&C 38:4).[7]

The *Guide to the Scriptures* published by the LDS church offers its current doctrinal position on Enoch and the City of Zion, explaining,

> Enoch was a great person and had a more significant ministry than the Bible's brief account of him indicates. ... Latter-day revelation explains much more of Enoch, specifically of his preaching, his city called Zion, his visions, and his prophecies (D&C 107:48–57; Moses 6–7). Zion was taken to heaven because of the righteousness of those who lived in it (Moses 7:69).

This understanding about the Holy city of Zion is revealed in Joseph Smith's Book of Moses in the chapters where the prophet Enoch is introduced:

> And righteousness will I send down out of heaven; and truth will I send forth out of the earth, to bear testimony of mine Only Begotten; his resurrection from the dead; yea, and also the resurrection of all men; and righteousness and truth will I cause to sweep the earth as with a flood, *to gather out mine elect from the four quarters of the earth, unto a place which I shall prepare, an Holy City*, that my people may gird up their loins, and be looking forth for the time of my coming; for there shall be my tabernacle, *and it shall be called Zion, a New Jerusalem.*
>
> *And the Lord said unto Enoch: Then shalt thou and all thy city meet them there*, and we will receive them into our bosom, and they shall see us; and

Chapter Nine. Zion—A New Jerusalem

we will fall upon their necks, and they shall fall upon our necks, and we will kiss each other; ... And there shall be mine abode, and it shall be Zion, which shall come forth out of all the creations which I have made; and for the space of a thousand years the earth shall rest.[8]

Elder McConkie also offered the following explanation of Joseph's City of Enoch in *Mormon Doctrine:*

> All the inhabitants of Zion—being devoted members of the Lord's Church, with Enoch at their head—were translated and taken to heaven (Moses 7:69). Their callings and elections were made sure, and they were all assured of membership in the Church of the Firstborn and of an inheritance of exaltation in the eternal worlds. Those so favored were, of course, with Christ in his resurrection (D. & C. 133:54-56). They are spoken of as "the general assembly and *church of Enoch*" (D. & C. 76:67), and all those who gain exaltation will be joined with them.

The motif of Enoch, a prophet of a dispensation and builder of the city of Zion for the gathering of the righteous and elect, would endure in the hearts of the early saints and become a lasting legacy of Joseph Smith. His early followers assembled, lived communally and built cities of Zion, the Kingdom of God and gathering place and divine abode on Earth. As Joseph grew in his role as leader of the small band of followers, so did his vision for building God's Kingdom. They even anointed him King in their Kingdom of Nauvoo.

His revelations continued with both Enoch and Zion emerging connected in the patterns of Joseph's restoration, and his preparation for a second coming of Jesus. Joseph's revelations, including the corresponding themes, verbal parallels and similarities with the Book of Enoch and apocalyptic traditions, demonstrate Joseph's affinity for Enoch the prophet, and certainly a longing for the restoration of *any* of his long-lost teachings.

Chapter Ten

The Mormon Temple Endowment

> "...the house of glory and of dominion shall be erected for ever.
> The tree of knowledge also was there, of which if any one eats, he becomes endowed with great wisdom."
> —Book of Enoch XCII:9; XXXI:3

In a biographical description of his studies and publications, LDS historian David John Buerger is described as having "linked an understanding of doctrinal questions with personal self-discovery, and saw doctrinal speculation as an essential component of his own spiritual quest."[1] In his 1987 article titled "The Development of the Mormon Temple Endowment Ceremony," Buerger offered this introductory explanation concerning his research and writing about the LDS temple endowment ceremony:

> Some people may feel that any discussion whatsoever of the temple may be inappropriate. My understanding of the temple ceremony is that certain names, signs, tokens, and penalties are guarded by vows of secrecy. I respect these limitations both as a Latter-day Saint and as a historian. However, it is not my understanding that these prohibitions extend to other areas of the temple ceremony, even though such reticence has become the custom among Latter-day Saints in general. I do not wish to offend any who may have a more restricted view than I about what is appropriate to discuss in relationship to the temple and its ceremonies and have worked toward an effective balance of scholarly objectivity, reverence for this sacred institution, regard for the scruples of others, and adequate documentation and development of the points to be discussed.[2]

I echo David Buerger's sentiment in this regard on this subject.[3] We find enlightenment, knowledge and truth in continued study concerning historical and doctrinal questions, and finding answers is essential in

Chapter Ten. The Mormon Temple Endowment

Nauvoo Temple, Nauvoo, Illinois (*Harper's Magazine*, 1853).

our quest. After all, it was a simple question and a quest for an answer that led an unprepossessing farm boy to his knees, resulting in a miraculous vision and the establishment of a worldwide religion.

A Temple-Building People with a Promised Endowment

In January 1841, the saints in Nauvoo, Illinois, were commanded "to build a house unto me ... [f]or therein are the keys of the holy priesthood ordained, that you may receive honor and glory."[4] In D&C 124:40–42, Joseph revealed in a solemn proclamation to the world,

> And verily I say unto you, let this house be built unto my name, that I may reveal mine ordinances therein unto my people;
> For I design to reveal unto my church things which have been

> kept hid from before the foundation of the world, things that pertain to the dispensation of the fulness of times.
> And I will show unto my servant Joseph all things pertaining to this house, and the priesthood thereof, and the place whereon it shall be built.

Joseph was promising his saints the same special gift he had received: an endowment of knowledge from God. Their own "theophany." An assurance beyond faith. A visionary confirmation that God lives. Each member could have a personal witness, if they believed. And they did. They believed they would receive something to be experienced, not just spoken about. These experiences were promised through ordinances that would be restored and revealed through temples, "which my people are always commanded to build unto my holy name" (D&C 124:39).[5] And Mormon saints did build them always, at least they toiled to, wherever they found themselves gathered, and from whatever they had to offer. The LDS temples are said to be "the crowning jewel" of Joseph Smith's restored gospel, and they are still being built prophetically throughout the world.[6]

Mormon apostle Bruce R. McConkie described the individual's temple endowment ordinance as "certain special, spiritual blessings given worthy and faithful saints in the temples … because in and through them the recipients are *endowed* with power from on high."[7] The word "endowed" first appears in Joseph Smith's revelations on January 2, 1831, from the pen of his newly called scribe Sidney Rigdon, recorded in D&C 38:32:

> Wherefore, for this cause I gave unto you the commandment that ye should go to the Ohio; and there I will give unto you my law; and there you shall be *endowed* with power from on high.

Joseph then relocated the headquarters of his church from Fayette, New York, to Kirtland, Ohio, in February 1831; here, the saints laid the first foundation to build a temple. The complete endowment ordinance was not revealed to Joseph Smith during the saints' time in Kirtland. Only part of the temple endowment, including a ceremonial washing and anointing, was ever performed in the Kirtland temple. What has become known as the temple "endowment" today was not revealed before the saints were driven from Kirtland, forced to abandon their temple. LDS historians refer to ordinances performed in the Kirtland temple as a "pre-endowment ritual" consisting of "a simple, staged ceremony clearly patterned after similar washings and anointings described

Chapter Ten. The Mormon Temple Endowment

in the Old and especially the New Testament."[8] In October 1835, Joseph reminded his apostles that he was still awaiting an "endowment" that would grant them that promised "power from on high."[9]

After relocating his Zion to Nauvoo, Illinois, Joseph revealed that if they built a temple there, God would "reveal mine ordinances therein unto my people" (D&C 124). They followed and gave to build their "City of Zion" both physically and spiritually wherever they went, looking forward to receiving their promised blessing, a gift of a personal revelation and heavenly visions of the mysteries of the universe.

This gathering of saints and temple-building pattern is also found in the Book of Enoch. The first mention of Enoch in the Doctrine & Covenants is found in Section 38, recorded January 2, 1831. Verse 4 calls Enoch's communal followers "the Zion of Enoch," the "same which [was] taken ... into mine own bosom, and verily, I say, even as many as have believed in my name." Joseph's Zionism has an apparent connection with that of Enoch, a gathering of his "elect" and city building as God's kingdom on earth. Joseph's Zion was a gathering place for the saints in the latter days, a New Jerusalem.

The Book of Enoch also tells of the "latter days" when "saints" would be gathered as an "elect and holy race" in the kingdom of God established on earth—a city of the saints—where God would dwell among them:

> There I saw another vision; I saw the habitation and dormitory of the saints. There my eyes beheld their habitation with the angels, and their dormitory with the holy ones.....
> At that time my eyes beheld the dwelling of the elect, of truth, faith, and righteousness.
> Countless shall be the number of the holy and the elect in the presence of God for ever and for ever.
> Their residence I beheld under the wings of the Lord of spirits.
> ....
> The tree of knowledge also was there, of which if any one eats, he becomes endowed with great wisdom.[10]

In the Book of Enoch, the prophet is taken up into a vision and given a guided tour of God's holy temple. Enoch then writes that "the order of generation after generation shall take place" and "the house of glory and of dominion shall be erected for ever" (XCII:9). Joseph's saints likewise built temples where God would dwell among them, a heavenly sanctuary on earth where Enoch's celestial and terrestrial cities of Zion coexist. As discussed further below, these are not the only parallels between Joseph's temple theology and many themes and examples of specific language found in the Book of Enoch.

Before the Nauvoo temple was completed, Joseph was anxious to get the work underway. The first "endowment" was administered by Joseph to a select group of just nine men on May 3, 1842, in the upper room of the newly finished, distinctive Red Brick Store owned by Joseph Smith. Until their more grandiose temple was completed, the modest brick building still offered a very stately edifice, warranting the reverence Joseph had for the makeshift temple setting. Joseph personally decorated and arranged the upper room to look like "the interior of a temple as much as the circumstances would permit."[11] He performed the ceremony for each of the men participating, all of whom were bound by secrecy regarding what they experienced. What this first endowment ceremony was exactly, or what specific words or blessings were pronounced, was not recorded. However, we know it involved allegorical religious instruction and symbolic rites with mutual promises among those members participating. It was initially committed to memory and solemnly secreted among those who received the ordinance. The endowment ceremony developed over time, and several changes have been made, but the substance of the original has been retained.

For members of the LDS Church, the "endowment" is a ceremony performed only within LDS temples. It is performed for each individual as a saving ordinance, necessary for each recipient's personal salvation. The more fully revealed ceremony in Nauvoo expanded on the washing and anointing ceremony that Joseph introduced in the Kirtland Temple earlier in 1836.[12] The ordinance includes personal directions to each of the participants in a format including symbolic instruction and solemn promises. Brigham Young University professor John W. Welch explains LDS temple theology as an understanding of "signs, symbols, and patterns (semiotics)" and "ritual instruction ... for purposes of protection, healing, blessing, and ultimate exaltation."[13] And, Professor Welch suggests, it gives us context and meaning to what it means to *be*—to exist, "to project the fullness of the past ... to give bearings in answering the so-called terrible questions of where we came from, why we are here, and where we are going: things as they were, as they are, and as they will be."

The LDS Church today offers this description of the temple endowment and how it is presented:

> In contrast to written scripture, the endowment taught participants by inviting them to symbolically reenact key aspects of the plan of salvation, including "the most prominent events of the creative period, the condition

of our first parents in the Garden of Eden, their disobedience and consequent expulsion from that blissful abode, their condition in the lone and dreary world when doomed to live by labor and sweat, the plan of redemption by which the great transgression may be atoned." During the course of this reenactment, they covenant to obey God's commandments, commit to devote themselves fully to His work, and acquire knowledge needed to "walk back to the presence of the Father."[14]

We don't know exactly how the endowment ceremony materialized in writing because Joseph never described or recorded any revelation outlining its content—or if it was written, it has never been made public.[15] It was revealed just after Joseph Smith was initiated into the Freemasonry fraternity in Nauvoo in March 1842, and there are unmistakable similarities in the rituals exchanged.[16] Scholars have also connected the ancient patriarch Enoch with Freemasonry history and lore. In her 2014 article "Congruence and Concatenation in Jewish Mystical Literature, American Freemasonry, and Mormon Enoch Writings," Cheryl L. Bruno pursues an even closer nexus between Masonry, Enoch and Mormonism:

> In light of the probable interface between Mormonism, Freemasonry, and ancient sources, it is unsurprising that many similarities would exist among the three traditions, but the types of parallels seen in the Enoch stories are instructive. The similarities reinforce the idea that Freemasonry influenced Mormonism earlier and more deeply than generally appreciated. They also highlight the thread of a mystical tradition that sheds light on human spiritual yearnings.[17]

The LDS Church openly explains, "Soon after he became a Mason, Joseph introduced the temple endowment."[18] It is not a secret that some of the signs, tokens and symbols of Freemasonry influenced the endowment ordinance. As with Freemasonry, those introduced to the endowment were put under oath never to reveal certain signs, tokens and secret names. Apostle Heber C. Kimball, among the nine men who received his endowment ordinance in Nauvoo, wrote fellow apostle Parley P. Pratt, who was out of town, in a letter dated June 17, 1842,

> I wish you was here so as to feel and hear fore your self. we have received some pressious things through the Prophet on the preast hood that would caus your Soul to rejoice *I can not give them to you on paper fore they are not to be riten.* So you must come and get them fore your self.—We have organised a Lodge here. of Masons. since we obtained a charter. that was in March since that thare has near two hundred been made masons[.] Br Joseph and Sidny was the first that was Recieved in to the Lodg. all of the twelve have become members Except Orson P. he Hangs back. he will wake

up soon, thare is a similarity.of preast Hood in masonry. Br Joseph ses masonary was taken from preast Hood but has become degennated. but menny things are perfect.[19]

Many of the symbols, signs and rites of the endowment ceremony have remained the same since Joseph's time, but the way the ordinance is administered has changed a few times since it was first performed. Originally, the endowment ceremony lasted the better part of a day. Unlike in the modernized world of video-recorded temple sessions scheduled on the half hour for days on end, the first endowment ceremony was intended to be a singular mystical experience, considering cosmic questions and transcending the limits of human understanding.

What Joseph introduced as the temple endowment in Navoo remained preserved only in the memories of those who had received their own endowment. As we have seen, these would include those of Joseph's saints who left Nauvoo following Joseph's martyrdom in 1844, heading west following Brigham Young to settle what is now the Salt Lake Valley in Utah. The LDS Church's endowment ceremony was not recorded until 1877. According to the LDS Church:

> Joseph Smith never described how the endowment came to be, and there is no recorded revelation outlining its content. ... After Joseph Smith introduced the endowment, he directed Brigham Young to "organize and systematize all these ceremonies" so they could be administered within the temple. At first, the endowment ceremony was preserved only in the memory of the participants. In 1877, when the St. George Utah Temple was completed, Brigham Young directed a small group, including the temple's president, Wilford Woodruff of the Quorum of the Twelve Apostles, to write down the ceremony to ensure consistency over time and between temples.[20]

The temple endowment is written as a play. As the Church officials publicly describe, the temple endowment ceremony invites participants to "*reenact* key aspects of the plan of salvation" including the creation, the Garden of Eden, and the expulsion into this mortal world. To imagine how one participates in the temple endowment ceremony today, think of being seated in a small theatre to watch a play, with women seated left of the center aisle, men on the right. Participants are first given instructions before the lights are dimmed and the ceremony begins.

Actors appropriately costumed take on parts portraying God, Jesus, Michael (the archangel), Adam, Eve, Peter, James, John and Lucifer—all appearing in the flesh, their characters played out in live performance in different parts of the ceremony. Where does the story start?

Chapter Ten. The Mormon Temple Endowment

Where all do; *in the beginning*. The ceremony begins with our creation story, and our preexistence before our mortal lives.

The doctrine and symbols of the creation, man and woman's temptation and casting out of the garden, and the redemption of mankind are all played out before the audience of participants, who are there receiving their own endowment and being taught this new light and knowledge through allegories, symbols and mutual promises. Whether there are 2 or 100 participants, each is there participating personally in the ordinance being performed.

The endowment ceremony has changed somewhat over time. An individual's personal endowment experience has been streamlined by later generations of Latter-day church leaders. Some unnecessary parts have been wholly removed, like the Masonic-influenced blood oaths and ghastly gestures depicting the penalties for revealing certain secrets. With advances in technology, the addition of filmed video depicting the cosmos and costumed characters was later adopted in lieu of a cast of live actors reading or reciting lines of script. But temple-recommend-holding members of the LDS Church could still catch a live performance of the endowment ceremony in both the LDS Salt Lake and Manti, Utah, temples up to as recently as 2019.

On July 20, 2020, the LDS Church announced additional changes to the temple endowment ceremony. "Through inspiration, the methods of instruction in the temple experience have changed many times, even in recent history, to help members better understand and live what they learn in the temple," the LDS Church leaders wrote.[21] They also explained,

> Part of the temple experience includes the making of sacred covenants, or promises, to God. Most people are familiar with symbolic actions that accompany the making of religious covenants (such as prayer, immersion of an individual at baptism, or holding hands during a marriage ceremony). Similar simple, symbolic actions accompany the making of temple covenants. With a concern for all and a desire to enhance the temple learning experience, recent changes have been authorized to the temple endowment ceremony.[22]

This endowment of light and knowledge, this secret knowledge veiled by secret names and secret oaths, has long been associated with specific Mormon doctrine, themes, teachings and familiar motifs, narratives and vocabulary that can also be found in the Book of Enoch.[23] LDS scholars recognize clear parallels, similarities and connections between the temple endowment and the Book of Enoch. Jeffrey M.

Bradshaw has outlined "how the Book of Moses reflects elements of temple architecture, furnishings, and ritual in the story of the Creation and the Fall."[24] In his article "The LDS Story of Enoch as the Culminating Episode of a Temple Text," he explains how "the Book of Moses follows a pattern exemplifying faithfulness and unfaithfulness to a specific consequence of covenants that is familiar to members of the LDS Church who have received the temple endowment." He urges "that the story of Enoch and his people provides a vivid demonstration of the final steps on the path that leads back to God and up to exaltation." He continues:

> Thus, we are told that Adam was "after the order of him who was without beginning of days," and that he was "one" in God, "a son of God." Through this same process—having received every priesthood ordinance and covenant and also having successfully completed the probationary tests of earth life—all may become sons of God (Moses 6:67–68).
>
> Within the LDS temple endowment, a narrative relating to selected events of the primeval history provides the context for the presentation of divine laws and the making of covenants that are designed to bring mankind back into the presence of God. Because the Book of Moses, in which the greatest portion of Joseph Smith's revelations on Enoch are found, is the most detailed account of the first chapters of human history found in LDS scripture, it is already obvious to endowed members of the Church that the Book of Moses is a temple text *par excellence*, containing a pattern that interleaves sacred history with covenant-making themes. What may be new to them, however, is that the temple themes in the Book of Moses extend beyond the first part of this story that contains the fall of Adam and Eve. There is a part two of the temple story related in the Book of Moses that culminates with the translation of Enoch and his city.

Mormon Temple Allusions and Book of Enoch Parallels

Recall that Professor Richard Laurence's 1821 Book of Enoch was not just the first English translation of 1 Enoch. It opens with his 48-page "Preliminary Dissertation," which explains the origin of the Enoch texts, a summary of many of its pre–Christian apocalyptic teachings, his methodology for dating the original author's writing, and a description for his translation process for deciphering unknown Ethiopic characters by comparing them with known Greek and Hebrew characters or sounds. Some words and names are left spelled out phonetically, others found to be mistranslated and corrected in later translations of the

Chapter Ten. The Mormon Temple Endowment

same work. Regardless of later or better translations of the Enoch manuscript, the 1821 book benefits from Professor Laurence's introduction, which is rich with deep Mormon doctrinal allusions. The following considers some doctrines peculiar to Joseph's temple theology and literary parallels and themes found in Laurence's Book of Enoch.

Latter-day Saints, Given Secret Names, Clothed in Garments and Anointed as Kings, Queens, Priests and Priestesses

LDS members attending the temple endowment ceremony "receive their endowments," meaning they are personally ordained. A members' personal endowment is required for their personal "exaltation," Mormon lingo for the highest level of immortality and everlasting glory. Initially, all endowment ceremonies performed by the early saints were personal endowments for each of the participants. Later developments allowed for members to return and reexperience the endowment ceremony, standing in proxy in the endowment ceremony on behalf of a deceased member. Participants are endowed after completing a series of ordinances in which they are washed and anointed and clothed in the "Garment of the Holy Priesthood" during the temple endowment ceremony.

In the endowment ordinance, a lecturer instructs participants that a garment is placed upon them, representing the garments given to Adam and Eve when they were found naked in the garden. They are instructed that it is called the Garment of the Holy Priesthood and instructed to wear it throughout their life as a shield and a protection as long as they are not defiled. In a letter to the church members, the LDS First Presidency instructs:

> Church members who have been clothed with the garment in the temple have made a covenant to wear it throughout their lives. ... The principles of modesty and keeping the body appropriately covered are implicit in the covenant and should govern the nature of all clothing worn. Endowed members of the Church wear the garment as a reminder of the sacred covenants they have made with the Lord and also as a protection against temptation and evil. How it is worn is an outward expression of an inward commitment to follow the Savior.[25]

All participants are also instructed that each has been given a "new name" in connection with the ordinance, and they must remember it to pass through necessary steps later in the endowment ritual. The lecturer continues instructing those attending that they have been washed and pronounced clean, and promising them "the day will come when you will be chosen, called up, and anointed Kings and Queens, Priests and Priestesses, whereas you are now anointed only to become such" and that "the realization of these blessings depends upon your faithfulness."

We find all these allusions and references in Laurence's Book of Enoch.

Kings, Princes and Priests

Enoch LXI.
1. Thus the Lord commanded the kings, the princes, the exalted, and those who dwell on earth, saying; Open your eyes, and lift up your horns, if you are capable of comprehending the Elect one.
5. In that day shall all the kings, the princes, the, exalted, and those who possess the earth, stand up, behold, and perceive, that he is sitting on the throne of his glory; that before him the saints shall be judged in righteousness;
10. Then shall the kings, the princes, and all who possess the earth, glorify him who has dominion over all things, him who was concealed; for from the beginning the Son of man existed in secret whom the Most High preserved in the presence of his power, and revealed to the elect.
11. He shall sow the congregation of the saints, and of the elect; and all the elect shall stand before him in that day.
12. All the kings, the princes, the exalted, and those who rule over the earth, shall fall down on their faces before him, and shall worship him.

Queens and Priestesses

The divinity of women, even a "Mother in Heaven," is another peculiar LDS doctrine that Joseph Smith taught personally in more detail with close companions, in perhaps more spiritually intimate moments. A gifted and renowned Mormon poet, Eliza R. Snow, wrote after the prophet's death about the things Joseph taught her personally about this doctrine.[26] Eliza was the second General President of the Relief Society (following Emma's presidency), and was one of Joseph Smith's plural wives.

The LDS Church teaches that all God's children, sons and daughters, are children of beloved heavenly parents, a Heavenly Father and

Chapter Ten. The Mormon Temple Endowment

Heavenly Mother. This doctrine is "rooted in scriptural and prophetic teachings about the nature of God, our relationship to Deity, and the godly potential of men and women."[27] It is considered "a cherished and distinctive belief among Latter-day Saints."[28]

In the LDS Church's study guide *Gospel Topics Essays,* we find a chapter on "Mother in Heaven," in which the Church explains Joseph Smith's early teachings on this point of doctrine:

> While there is no record of a formal revelation to Joseph Smith on this doctrine, some early Latter-day Saint women recalled that he personally taught them about a Mother in Heaven. The earliest published references to the doctrine appeared shortly after Joseph Smith's death in 1844, in documents written by his close associates. The most notable expression of the idea is found in a poem by Eliza R. Snow, entitled "My Father in Heaven" and now known as the hymn "O My Father." This text declares: "In the heav'ns are parents single? / No, the thought makes reason stare; / Truth is reason— truth eternal / Tells me I've a mother there."[29]

In comparison, consider the divinity of woman (and gnostic undertones) found among verses in 1 Enoch,

Enoch XLII
1. Wisdom found not a place on earth where she could inhabit; her dwelling therefore is in heaven.
2. Wisdom went forth to dwell among the sons of men, but she obtained not an habitation. Wisdom returned to her place, and seated herself in the midst of the angels.

Enoch LXI.
8. One portion of them shall look upon another. They shall be astonished, and shall humble their countenance;
9. And trouble shall seize them, when they shall behold the Son of woman sitting upon the throne of his glory.

Clothed in Garments

The apocryphal Book of Jasher includes a connection between Adam and his posterity, specifically including Enoch, and the "garments of skin" that God placed upon them in the garden. In Jasher 7:24–26 we read:

> 24. And the garments of skin which God made for Adam and his wife, when they went out of the garden, were given to Cush.
> 25. For after the death of Adam and his wife, the garments were given to Enoch, the son of Jared, and when Enoch was taken up to God, he gave them to Methuselah, his son.
> 26. And at the death of Methuselah, Noah took them and

brought them to the ark, and they were with him until he went out of the ark.

The Book of Enoch also alludes to garments and white robes:

> There I beheld the fathers of the first men, and the saints, who dwell in that place for ever. ... I beheld the sons of the holy angels treading on flaming fire, whose garments and robes were white[.][30]

And

> The saints and the elect have arisen from the earth, have left off to depress their countenances, and have been clothed with the garment of life. That garment of life is with the Lord of spirits, in whose presence your garment shall not wax old, nor shall your glory diminish.[31]

Secret Names

As part of the temple endowment ceremony, each participant is given a new name, which they are instructed that they should never forget, keep sacred, and never reveal except at a certain place they are shown within the temple nearing the end of the ceremony. According to Mormon doctrine, the practice is restored from the lost doctrines of early Christianity, as obscurely recorded in Revelation 2:17:

> He that hath an ear, let him hear what the Spirit saith unto the churches; To him that overcometh will I give to eat of *the hidden manna,* and will give him a white stone, and in the stone *a new name written,* which no man knoweth saving he that receiveth it.

In 1843, Joseph Smith recorded a revelation found in today's Doctrine & Covenants Section 130, verses 10–11, expounding on St. John's revelation in the New Testament scripture:

> Then the white stone mentioned in Revelation 2:17, will become a Urim and Thummim to each individual who receives one, whereby things pertaining to a higher order of kingdoms will be made known;
> And a white stone is given to each of those who come into the celestial kingdom, whereupon a new name is written, which no man knoweth save he that receivith it. The new name is the key word.

We also find allusions to secret names given under oath in Enoch LXVIII:

> 7. He seduced Eve; and discovered to the children of men the instruments of death, the coat of mail, the shield, and the sword for slaughter; every instrument of death to the children of men.

Chapter Ten. The Mormon Temple Endowment

19. This is the number of the Kesbel: the principal part of the oath which the Most High, dwelling in glory, revealed to the holy ones.
20. Its name is Beka. He spoke to holy Michael to discover to them the secret name, that they might understand that secret name, and thus remember the oath; and that those who pointed out every secret thing to the children of men might tremble at that name and oath.
21. This is the power of that oath; for powerful it is, and strong.
22. And he established this oath of Akae by the instrumentality of the holy Michael.
23. These are the secrets of this oath, and by it were they confirmed.
24. Heaven was suspended by it before the world was made, for ever.

Latter-day Saints

Eight years after Joseph established his church, he revealed what has become the official name of the Mormon church as recorded in April 1838, now found in D&C 115:4–5:

> For thus shall my church be called in the last days, even The Church of Jesus Christ of Latter-day Saints.
> Verily I say unto you all: Arise and shine forth, that thy light may be a standard for the nations.

Similar literary echoes are found in *1 Enoch*:

> **Enoch XXVI**
> 3. *In the latter days* an example of judgment shall be made of them in righteousness before *the saints*; while those who have received mercy shall for ever, all their days, bless God, the everlasting King.
> **Enoch LXIV. SECT. XI.**
> 11. *He, the holy One, will establish thy name in the midst of the saints*, and will preserve thee from those who dwell upon the earth. He will establish thy seed in righteousness, with dominion and great glory; and from thy seed shall spring forth righteous and holy men without number for ever.

The Archangel Michael/Adam Creator Doctrine

LDS teachings about who Adam really was (is) in the eternities are unique to Mormonism. According to LDS orthodoxy, Adam is that same archangel Michael who fought against Lucifer and his armies in the war in heaven before this mortal life.[32] Brigham Young University professor of ancient scripture Robert L. Millet instructs:

> As Michael, the archangel, Adam led the forces of God against the armies of Lucifer in the War in Heaven. Under the direction of Elohim and Jehovah, he assisted in the Creation of the earth. Adam and Eve brought mortality into being through partaking of the fruit of the tree of knowledge of good and evil. With the Fall of our first parents came blood and posterity and probation and death, as well as the need for redemption through a Savior, a "last Adam."[33]

This is peculiar because Michael is not identified as Adam anywhere in the KJV Bible. The Epistle of Jude, by the same writer, recall, who quoted from the writings of Enoch, speaks of "Michael the archangel" and the devil in a struggle over the body of Moses:

> Yet Michael the archangel, when contending with the devil he disputed about the body of Moses, durst not bring against him a railing accusation, but said, The Lord rebuke thee. (Jude 1:9)

Jude's verse reminds us of the only dispute we know about Moses's body found in Deuteronomy 34:6, which tells us Moses was buried in the land of Moab, "but no man knoweth of his sepulchre unto this day." Aside from that, there is no other dispute over the body of Moses, let alone between Moses and Satan. More curiously, Jude's is the only direct reference to Michael as an "archangel." The Book of Revelation in the New Testament refers to "Michael and his angels" fighting against the dragon, which also derives from the Enoch prophecies, but Jude's is the only reference to Michael as an archangel in the entire Bible.

Joseph Smith's understanding of Adam was expounded in a blessing administered to his father, Joseph Smith, Sr., on December 18, 1833, in which Joseph likened his father to Adam and being "blessed of the Lord ... for he shall stand in the midst of his posterity ... and shall be called a prince over them, and shall be numbered among those who hold the right of Patriarchal Priesthood, even the keys of that ministry: for he shall assemble together his posterity like unto Adam."[34] The blessing mentions the first High Priests called, including Enoch by name, and refers to Adam as "Michael, the Prince, the Archangel."

Michael the archangel and the Ancient of Days are found throughout the Book of Enoch. Joseph's blessing of his Father appears to incorporate terms, phrases and titles found in the Book of Enoch:

Chapter Ten. The Mormon Temple Endowment

Joseph's blessing to his father:	Enoch XLVI:1–2
Three years previous to the death of Adam, he called Seth, Enos, Cainan, Mahalaleel, Jared, Enoch and Methuselah, *who were High Priests, with the residue of his posterity, who were righteous*, into the valley of Adam-ondi-Ahman, and there bestowed upon them his last blessing. *And the Lord appeared unto them, and they rose up and blessed Adam, and called him Michael, the Prince, the Archangel*. And *the Lord administered comfort unto Adam*, and said unto him, I have set thee to be at the head: a multitude of nations shall come of thee, and thou art a Prince over them forever. So shall it be with my father: he shall be called a prince over his posterity, holding the keys of the patriarchal Priesthood over the kingdom of God on earth, even the Church of the Latter-day Saints, and he *shall sit in the general assembly* of Patriarchs, even *in council with the Ancient of Days* when he shall sit and all the Patriarchs with him and shall *enjoy his right and authority* under the direction of *the Ancient of Days*.[35]	There I beheld *the Ancient of days*, whose head was like white wool, *and with him another, whose countenance resembled that of man.* His countenance was full of grace, *like that of one of the holy angels.* Then I inquired of one of the angels who went with me, and who shewed me every secret thing, concerning this Son of Man, who he was; whence he was; and *why he accompanied the Ancient of days.* He answered and said to me; This is the Son of man, to whom righteousness belongs; with whom righteousness has dwelt; and who will reveal all the treasures of that which is concealed; *for the Lord of spirits has chosen him; and his portion has surpassed all before the Lord* of spirits in everlasting uprightness. **Enoch XL. SECT. VII** 2. In that day shall *the holy ones assemble, who dwell above the heavens*, and with united voice petition, supplicate, praise, laud, and bless the name of the Lord of spirits.... 3. At that time I beheld *the Ancient of days*, while he sat upon the throne of his glory, while the book of the living was opened in his presence, and while *all the powers which were above the heavens stood around and before him.* 4. Then were the hearts of the saints full of joy, because the consummation of righteousness was arrived, the supplication of the saints heard[.]

The "Ancient of Days" in Enoch refers to God, not Adam or Michael. However, the allusions and parallel literary references within a similar context are worth considering. Other allusions to the Ancient of days and

Michael the archangel together in the same verses are found several places throughout the Book of Enoch. In one example, Enoch, in a vision, saw "the *heaven of heavens* shook," and shook so violently that "the powers of the Most High, and the angels, thousands of thousands, and myriads of myriads, were agitated with great agitation."[36] In the vision, Enoch beheld the Ancient of Days who "was sitting on the throne of his glory, while the angels and saints were standing around him." Terrified, Enoch fell to his face, fearful of his own demise. Then, "the holy Michael, another holy angel, one of the holy ones, was sent, who raised me up," and asked Enoch, "Wherefore art thou disturbed at this vision?"[37] Michael the angel then explains the vision, comforting Enoch and assuring, "That day has been prepared for the elect as a day of covenant." This accompanying angel motif for temple patrons is also found in the LDS temple endowment.

The "Adam the Archangel" doctrine was explained by Mark E. Peterson, as a member of the Quorum of the Twelve Apostles of the LDS Church, speaking from the pulpit at the LDS general conference in October 1980:

> Indeed, Adam was very special and very important. Before coming into mortality, he was known as Michael. The Prophet Joseph Smith clearly identifies both Adam and Michael as one and the same person, an angel, the chief angel, or archangel, of heaven, the special servant of God and Christ.
>
> When Michael came into mortality he was known as Adam, the first man, but he was still his own self. Although he was given another name, that of Adam, he did not change his identity.[38]
>
> After his mortal death he resumed his position as an angel in the heavens, once again serving as the chief angel, or archangel, and took again his former name of Michael.
>
> In his capacity as archangel, Adam, or Michael, will yet perform a mighty mission in the coming years, both before and after the Millennium. This is startling, but the scriptures declare it.
>
> One important assignment that awaits him is to be the angel to sound the trumpet heralding the resurrection of the dead. The scripture reads, "Behold, verily I say unto you, before the earth shall pass away, *Michael, mine archangel,* shall sound his trump, and then shall all the dead awake, for their graves shall be opened, and they shall come forth" (D&C 29:26). What a marvelous calling for Adam, or Michael.[39]

The scriptures that declare this to us are Joseph Smith's own revelations, not in the KJV Bible. Michael the archangel is a prominent figure in Mormon temple liturgy, and we find Michael in an assisting-by-the-hand role similar to that paralleled in the Enoch parables. Michael, in the Book of Enoch, is "one of the archangels, ... [who]

brought me out to where was every secret of mercy and secret of righteousness" (Enoch LXX:4). It was Michael the archangel that "shewed [Enoch] all the hidden things of the extremities of heaven, all the receptacles of the stars, and the splendors of all, from whence they went forth before the face of the holy," just as LDS temple participants are instructed regarding the cosmos and its splendors as each is guided through the reenactment (Enoch LXX:5).

ACT I: The Cosmos and Creation

The endowment ceremony begins with participants taking their seats left and right of center aisle, as noted. A soft-spoken ordinance worker reverently welcomes those to the temple endowment ceremony and offers additional instructions before the video presentation begins (in lieu of the live performance). The lights are dimmed and attendees hear the voices of persons representing Elohim (God), Jehovah (Jesus), and Michael. With the lights still down, the voice of Elohim commands Jehovah and the archangel Michael to go down and organize a world. Six creative periods are represented, and their creative process, starting with the expanse of the cosmos, dividing the light from the darkness, the land from the sea, then fishes and fowls and all creepy-crawly things, and eventually they organize man "in their own likeness and image, male and female." The voice of Elohim instructs Jehovah and Michael to "see, yonder is matter unorganized," and tells them to go create a world like unto other worlds they have formed. In repeating fashion, Jehovah and Michael go down, each day to do their daily creation work, and each day returning and reporting their work to Elohim, demonstrating the pattern of divine order.

The LDS temple creation story leaves no room for ambiguity. The creation is performed by the hands of multiple "Gods" (deities), including Michael, who in Mormon doctrine is revealed also to be Adam when incarnated in this mortal probation. The idea of multiple gods, or a council or assembly of creators, also comes into Mormon scripture in yet another creation story translated by Joseph in the Book of Abraham, Chapter 4:

> 1. And then the Lord said: Let us go down. *And they went down at the beginning, and they, that is the Gods*, organized and formed the heavens and the earth.
> 2. And the earth, after it was formed, was empty and desolate, because they had not formed anything but the earth; and darkness reigned upon the face of the deep, and the Spirit of the Gods was brooding upon the face of the waters.

> 3. *And they (the Gods) said: Let there be light; and there was light.*
> 4. And they *(the Gods)* comprehended the light, for it was bright; and they divided the light, or caused it to be divided, from the darkness.
> 5. *And the Gods called the light Day, and the darkness they called Night.* And it came to pass that from the evening until morning they called night; and from the morning until the evening they called day; and this was the first, or the beginning, of that which they called day and night.

Again, the Adam/God/co-creator is unique to Mormon doctrine. The LDS Church explained the doctrine in the article in its periodical the *Ensign* titled "The Man Adam":

> Adam's role in the eternal plan of God began in our premortal first estate. There he was known as Michael, literally one "who is like God." Indeed, "by his diligence and obedience there, as one of the spirit sons of God, he attained a stature and power second only to that of Christ, the Firstborn. None of all our Father's children equalled him in intelligence and might, save Jesus only." He was "called and prepared from the foundation of the world according to the foreknowledge of God" (Alma 13:3) to perform his labors on earth. Michael stood with Jehovah in defense of the plan of the Father, the plan of salvation, this in opposition to the amendatory offering of Lucifer, a "son of the morning."....
>
> Michael was directly involved in the preparation of the physical world in which he and his posterity would undergo a mortal probation. Elder Bruce R. McConkie of the Quorum of the Twelve wrote: "Christ and Mary, Adam and Eve, Abraham and Sarah, and a host of mighty men and equally glorious women comprised that group of 'the noble and great ones,' to whom the Lord Jesus said: '*We* will go down, for there is space there, and *we* will take of these materials, and *we* will make an earth whereon these may dwell.' (Abr. 3:22–24; emphasis added.) This we know: Christ, under the Father, is the Creator; Michael, his companion and associate, presided over much of the creative work; and with them, as Abraham saw, were many of the noble and great ones." The Prophet Joseph Smith thus taught that "the Priesthood was first given to Adam; he obtained the First Presidency, and held the keys of it from generation to generation. He obtained it in the Creation, before the world was formed, as in Gen. 1:26, 27, 28."[40]

Earth: A Footstool of God, for the Dominion of the Sons of Man

Mormon temple attendants also learn that the Gods (Elohim, Jehovah and Michael) form man and woman in their image to have dominion

Chapter Ten. The Mormon Temple Endowment

over all things on the face of the earth. In the prologue to the creation story in Joseph Smith's Moses 1:33, we are told,

> And worlds without number have I created; and *I also created them for mine own purpose*; and by the Son I created them, which is mine Only Begotten.

In Joseph's Abraham 4:26 we again learn of the creation's purpose for mankind:

> And the Gods took counsel among themselves and said: Let us go down and form man in our image, after our likeness; *and we will give them dominion* over the fish of the sea, and over the fowl of the air, and over the cattle, and over all the earth, and over every creeping thing that creepeth upon the earth.

In the Book of Enoch, the patriarch has a vision of creation and "inquired of the angel who went with me," asking about the purpose of creation, "What are these things, which in secret I behold?"[41] The angel answered,

> He said; All things which thou beholdest shall be for the dominion of the Messiah, that he may command, and be powerful upon earth.

This same doctrine is revealed in Joseph's Book of Abraham 2:7, with notable themes and vocabulary from the Book of Enoch:

Abraham 2:7	Enoch LXXXIII:2–4
For I am the Lord thy God; I dwell in heaven; *the earth is my footstool*; I stretch my hand over the sea, and it obeys my voice; I cause the wind and the fire to be my chariot; I say to the mountains—Depart hence—and behold, they are taken away by a whirlwind, in an instant, suddenly. *Cf.*, Isaiah 66:1 "Thus saith the Lord, the heaven is my throne, and the earth is my footstool; where is the house that ye built unto me? And where is the place of thy rest?"	Blessed art thou, O Lord, the King, great and powerful in thy greatness. Lord of all the creatures of heaven. King of kings, God of the whole world, whose reign, whose kingdom, and whose majesty endure for ever and ever. From generation to generation shall thy dominion exist. All the heavens are thy throne for ever, and *all the earth thy footstool* for ever and for ever.

ACT II: The Garden

Transitioning from the creation scene of the cosmos, temple participants are metaphorically transferred to the garden of Eden, at the time man was created. Attendees in the endowment ceremony are instructed to close their eyes, as if they were asleep. A voice then calls out, as if heard coming out of a deep sleep, prompting Adam to "awake and arise." Adam is then shown the garden before being introduced to the character, Eve, who Elohim instructs has been "formed and whom we give unto you to be a companion and help meet."[42] She is referred to as the "mother of all living." They are informed that there has been planted a garden, eastward in Eden, and commanded that they there shall multiply and replenish the earth.

Enoch likewise has a creation story and Eden, which mirrors stories also found in Genesis. Enoch also has a vision of the garden of Eden in XXXI:2–5. In this garden

> I beheld, among other trees, some which were numerous and large, and which flourished there.
> Their fragrance was agreeable and powerful, and their appearance both varied and elegant. The tree of knowledge also was there, of which if any one eats, he becomes endowed with great wisdom.
> It was like a species of the tamarind tree, bearing fruit which resembled grapes extremely fine; and its fragrance extended to a considerable distance. I exclaimed; How beautiful is this tree, and how delightful is its appearance!
> Then holy Raphael, an angel who was with me, answered and said; This is the tree of knowledge, of which thy ancient father and thy widowed mother eat, who were before thee; and who, obtaining knowledge, their eyes being opened, and knowing themselves to be naked, were expelled from the garden.

And a similar expulsion from a spiritual life to mortality is also found in Enoch. Referring to those same "giants" we read of in Genesis 6:4, Enoch prophesies,

> **Enoch XV:5–8**
> Therefore have I given to them wives, that they might cohabit with them; that sons might be born of them; and that this might be transacted upon earth.
> But you from the beginning were made spiritual, possessing a life which is eternal, and not subject to death for ever.
> Therefore I made not wives for you, because being spiritual, your dwelling is in heaven.

Chapter Ten. The Mormon Temple Endowment

Now the giants, who have been born of spirit and of flesh, shall be called upon earth evil spirits, and on earth shall be their habitation. Evil spirits shall proceed from their flesh, because they were created from above; from the holy Watchers was their beginning and primary foundation. Evil spirits shall they be upon earth, and the spirits of the wicked shall they be called. The habitation of the spirits of heaven shall be in heaven; but upon earth shall be the habitation of terrestrial spirits, who are born on earth.

A "New World" and Renewed Awakening

As Adam and Eve are portrayed perusing the garden, Lucifer enters stage left, dressed in ominously dark and gaudy robes. Introducing himself he says, "Well, Adam, you have a new world here ... patterned after the old one where you used to live." Adam retorts quizzically, "A *new* world?" Lucifer then explains that Adam's "eyes are not yet opened," and persuades him to eat some of the fruit of the Tree of Knowledge, "so that your eyes may be opened."

In Enoch we find several allusions to a "new world," both for the earth itself and its inhabitants, where the saints undergo a change and are "made to see" that they must repent and forsake material and carnal temptations of the world:

Enoch CV:13
Then I, Enoch, answered and said; *The Lord will effect a new thing upon the earth*. This have I explained, and seen in a vision.
Enoch XLIX:1 & 3
In those days *the saints and the chosen shall undergo a change*. The light of day shall rest upon them; and the splendor and glory of the saints shall be changed.
Others shall be made to see, that they must repent, and forsake the works of their hands; and that glory awaits them not in the presence of the Lord of spirits; yet that by his name they may be saved.
Enoch L:1 & 5
In those days shall *the earth deliver up from her womb*, and hell deliver up from hers, that which it has received, and destruction shall restore that which it owes.
Their countenance shall be bright with joy; for in those days shall the Elect one be exalted. *The earth shall rejoice*; the righteous shall inhabit it, *and the elect possess it*
Enoch XLV:5
I will also *change the face of the earth*; will bless it; and cause those whom I have elected to dwell upon it. But those who

have committed sin and iniquity shall not inhabit it; for I have marked their proceedings. My righteous ones will I satisfy with peace, placing them before me; but the condemnation of sinners shall draw near, that I may destroy them from the face of the earth.
Enoch XCII:15 & 17
Every work of the ungodly shall disappear from the whole earth; *the world shall be marked for destruction*; and all men shall be on the look out for the path of integrity.

The *former heaven* shall depart and pass away; *a new heaven* shall appear; and *all the celestial powers shine* with sevenfold splendor for ever.

"The tree of knowledge also was there"

The scene continues with Adam rejecting Lucifer's offer to eat the fruit of the tree. Lucifer then approaches Eve to beguile her to partake of the fruit. She does, and then goes to Adam, insisting that he now must partake, or he'll be left alone after she is cast out. Having partaken, her reasoning quickened, Eve then turns to Lucifer, saying, "I know thee now." Lucifer replies, "Yes, you are beginning to see already."

The Book of Enoch similarly invites those seeking knowledge to open their eyes. Regarding the "tree of knowledge," Enoch relates in his visions:

Enoch XXI:3–5
Their fragrance was agreeable and powerful, and their appearance both varied and elegant. *The tree of knowledge also was there*, of which if any one eats, *he becomes endowed with great wisdom*.

... I exclaimed; How beautiful is this tree, and how delightful is its appearance!

Then holy Raphael, an angel who was with me, answered and said; This is the tree of knowledge, of which thy ancient father and thy widowed mother eat, who were before thee; and who, *obtaining knowledge, their eyes being opened*, and knowing themselves to be naked, were expelled from the garden.

Adam and Enoch Are Ashamed, Naked and Wear Veils

Because Adam and Eve have their eyes opened, they discover they are naked. They then hear the voices of Elohim and Jehovah coming, who had promised to visit and give Adam and Eve further instructions.

Chapter Ten. The Mormon Temple Endowment

Adam exclaims to Eve, "I hear their voices, they are coming." Lucifer interjects, "See you are naked. Take some fig leaves and make you aprons. Father will see your nakedness. Quick! Hide!" Adam and Eve ashamedly hide themselves and the lights dim.

Soft but bellowing voices are heard as if approaching, and Elohim is heard calling out, "Adam? Adam? Where art thou?" Adam sheepishly emerges, saying, "I heard thy voice and hid myself, because I was naked."

Enoch XXXI describes Enoch's vision in which he sees Adam ashamed for being naked:

> 5. ... and who, obtaining knowledge, their eyes being opened, and knowing themselves to be naked, were expelled from the garden

Enoch XIV similarly depicts a timid Enoch, afraid or ashamed to look upon God when called for by name:

> 24. ... I also was so far advanced, with a veil on my face, and trembling. Then the Lord with his own mouth called me, saying; Approach hither, Enoch, at my holy word.
> 25. And he raised me up, making me draw near even to the entrance. My eye was directed to the ground.

Casting Out and Condemning Lucifer

After figuring out that Lucifer must have been up to his same no-good persuasions regarding that most forbidden of all fruits—carnal reality—Elohim wants an explanation. Turning to Lucifer, Elohim demands, "[W]hat has thou been doing here?" After Lucifer explains he is doing the same thing he's done over and over in other worlds by giving fruit of the Tree of Knowledge to make men fallen, cast out, sensual and devilish children, Elohim has had enough. He casts Lucifer out, exclaiming, "Lucifer, because thou hast done this, thou shalt be cursed above all the beasts of the field. Upon thy belly shalt thou go, and dust thou shalt eat all the days of thy life."

The story of the devil, the fallen star and the other fallen stars that follow him, is found in the Book of Enoch also. Enoch saw yet another vision in which he "looked attentively, while sleeping, and surveyed heaven above,"

> And behold a single star fell from heaven. ... Again I looked in my vision and surveyed heaven; when behold I say many stars which descended, and projected themselves from heaven to where the first star was [Enoch LXXXV:1–2, 4].

Joseph Smith and the Book of Enoch

The devil and first fallen star are similarly scorned as the source of all evil and rebuked therefore in Enoch:

Enoch IX:5 & 9
Thou hast seen what Azazyel has done, how he has taught every species of iniquity upon earth, and has disclosed to the world all the secret things which are done in the heavens. Thus has the whole earth been filled with blood and with iniquity.
Enoch X:12
All the earth has been corrupted by the effects of the doctrine of Azazyel. To him therefore ascribe the whole crime.
Enoch XIII:1–4 & 6
Then Enoch passing on said to Azazyel; Thou shalt not obtain peace. A great sentence has gone forth against thee. He shall bind thee; Neither shall relief, mercy, and supplication be thine, on account of the oppression which thou hast taught; And on account of every act of blasphemy, tyranny, and sin, which thou hast discovered to the children of men.

In the endowment dialogue, Lucifer doesn't take this casting out very lightly. He wells in a fury; lashing back before leaving, he threatens to "take the spirits that follow me, and they shall possess the bodies thou createst for Adam and Eve!" Elohim then places enmity between Lucifer and "the seed of the woman." Lucifer isn't done, finally retorting,

"Then with that enmity I will take the treasure of the earth, and with gold and silver I will buy up armies and navies, false priests who oppress, and tyrants who destroy, and reign with blood and horror on the earth!"

Fallen angels inhabiting the bodies of the sons and daughters of Adam and Eve is a direct story line in the Book of Enoch. The threats of carnal influence, worldly treasures, corrupt powers and principalities are also echoed in passages from the Book of Enoch:

Enoch XV:8–9
Now the giants, who have been born of spirit and of flesh, shall be called upon earth evil spirits, and on earth shall be their habitation. Evil spirits shall proceed from their flesh, because they were created from above; from the holy Watchers was their beginning and primary foundation. Evil spirits shall they be upon earth, and the spirits of the wicked shall they be called. The habitation of the spirits of heaven shall be in heaven; but upon earth shall be the habitation of terrestrial spirits, who are born on earth.
The spirits of the giants shall be like clouds, which shall oppress, corrupt, fall, contend, and bruise upon earth.

Enoch LXII:1

In those days the kings who possess the earth shall be punished by the angels of his wrath, wheresoever they shall be delivered up, that he may give rest for a short period; and that they may fall down and worship before the Lord of spirits, confessing their sins before him.

Enoch XLVI:2–3

He answered and said to me; This is the Son of man, to whom righteousness belongs; with whom righteousness has dwelt; and who will reveal all the treasures of that which is concealed; for the Lord of spirits has chosen him; and his portion has surpassed all before the Lord of spirits in everlasting uprightness.

This Son of man, whom thou beholdest, shall raise up kings and the mighty from their couches, and the powerful from their thrones; shall loosen the bridles of the powerful, and break in pieces the teeth of sinners.

Defeated, Satan Departs

After threatening to corrupt the children of men with the treasures of the world, Elohim again commands Lucifer, "Depart!" after which he thunders away.

Considering similar literary parallels, after being rebuked by Enoch for his corruption of the world, Azazel trembled and departed in Enoch XIII:1–6, "Then departing from him I spoke to them all together; ... And they all became terrified, and trembled."

ACT III: Knock and It Shall Be Opened Unto You

Following the creation scene, the endowment attendees are then given additional instructions about the priesthood, which are symbolized, remembered and reiterated by the attendees' demonstration of associated symbols and words as instructed in the ceremony. They are promised additional knowledge and further instructions at the veil, a sheer curtain where participants are led to by an accompanying "veil worker" who uses a mallet to knock three times at the doorway of the veil. The veil worker informs another veil worker (out of sight, behind the curtain) that the participant has come to "converse with the Lord through the veil." The participant is then presented at the veil. The accompanying veil worker helps the participant rehearse all the signs and tokens given earlier during the endowment, reminding the participant, if necessary, of the new name he or she has been given. In this role, each participant in the endowment ends the experience there at the veil, with the symbolic opportunity to experience what they had been promised—a personal theophany of some kind. A heavenly experience on earth is enacted. Participants symbolically get to personally commune with and be individually received into God's presence and glory forever.

Seeking Light and Divine Knowledge

Just like LDS temple participants, Enoch was "desirous of instruction," taken to a "lofty tower" and allowed to enter the "house of glory" with accompanying angels eventually leading him into God's "throne room." Enoch's prophecies envision saints in the latter days, dressed in holy garments, and taught about the creation, where there would be an "endowment" of knowledge.

And let's not forget that the characters of Michael the archangel, Adam, and the Ancient of Days all find themselves in both the Book of Enoch and Joseph's temple endowment. Like the performers playing the roles of deities and guiding angels in the LDS endowment ceremony, in the Book of Enoch it was Michael who described the creation and "shewed [Enoch] all the *hidden things* of the *extremities of heaven,* all the *receptacles of the stars, and the splendors of all,* from whence they went forth before the face of the holy" (Enoch LXX:5). Michael is also the archangel who "took [Enoch] *by my right hand,* raised me up, and *brought me out to where was every secret of mercy and secret of righteousness*" (Enoch LXX:4).

Here are some additional parallels and allusions to the temple ceremony found in Laurence's Book of Enoch:

> **Enoch LXXXVI:2–3**
> Those three, who came forth last, seized me by my hand; and raising me up from the generations of the earth, elevated me to a high station.
> Then they shewed me a lofty tower on the earth,[43]
>
> **Enoch XXIV:3–9**
> Among these there was a tree of an unceasing smell; ... its leaf, its flower, and its bark never withered, and its fruit was beautiful.
> ... I exclaimed; Behold! this tree is goodly in aspect, pleasing in its leaf, and the sight of its fruit is delightful to the eye. Then Michael, one of the holy and glorious angels who were with me, and one who presided over them, answered,
> And said; Enoch, Why dost thou inquire respecting the odour of this tree?
> Why art thou inquisitive to know it?

Chapter Ten. The Mormon Temple Endowment

Then I, Enoch, replied to him, and said; Concerning every
thing I am desirous of instruction, but particularly concerning
this tree.
... The fruit of this tree shall be given to the elect.

Secret Names and Swearing Oaths

Certain rituals in the temple ceremony come directly from the influence of Freemasonry.[44] Joseph's endowment emerged in 1842, just two months after he and other Mormon apostles were inducted into Freemasonry in Nauvoo, Illinois. Notwithstanding the overwhelming Masonic influence in the temple ceremonies, the Book of Enoch, too, has a number of verbal parallels to secret names and oaths—and even secret combinations—worth mentioning:

> **Enoch LXVIII:20–23**
> He spoke to holy Michael to discover to them the secret name, that they might understand that secret name, and thus remember the oath; and that those who pointed out every secret thing to the children of men might tremble at that name and oath.
> This is the power of that oath; for powerful it is, and strong.
> And he established this oath of Akae by the instrumentality of the holy Michael.
> These are the secrets of this oath, and by it were they confirmed.
> **Enoch LIV 9–10:**
> Then shall princes combine together, and conspire. ... They shall rise up to destroy each other; their right hand shall be strengthened; nor shall a man acknowledge his friend or his brother.
> **Enoch XII. SECT. II :5–8**
> But they answered him and said; We all swear; And bind ourselves by mutual execrations, that we will not change our intention, but execute our projected undertaking. Then they swore all together, and all bound themselves by mutual execrations.
> ... That mountain therefore was called Armon, because they had sworn upon it, and bound them themselves by mutual execrations.

After participants are presented at the veil to converse with the Lord through the veil, they are guided through and rehearse each of the symbols and secret names needed to pass through. Only there, at the veil, is where the secret names and tokens may be spoken and displayed, and nowhere else. And participants are sworn to keep them secret earlier in their endowment ceremony.

Joseph Smith and the Book of Enoch

Recall the passage cited in Enoch XIV:24, where God speaks to Enoch by name, inviting him to approach, and Enoch "advanced, *with a veil on my face.*" In XIII:9, Enoch again writes of another vision in which he "fell down, and saw a vision of punishment, that I might relate it to the sons of heaven, and reprove them.... All being collected together ... *with their faces veiled.*" These are interesting parallels to the LDS endowment ceremony, as the word "veil" is used in a completely different way in the KJV Bible. In the Old and New Testaments, the veil is a curtain that divides areas and rooms within the tabernacle or temple. It is a physical symbol for the separation between God and man in this physical world.[45]

Like the verses above in which the angel Michael accompanies Enoch "to discover then the secret name that they might understand that secret name," an even closer parallel to the endowment ceremony is found in Enoch XLIII:2:

> Then I inquired of the angel, who proceeded with me, and explained to me secret things. What their names were. He answered; A similitude of these has the Lord of spirits shewn thee. They are the names of the righteous who dwell upon earth, and who believe in the name of the Lord of spirits for ever and for ever.

Verses throughout the Book of Enoch ring with familiar themes and verbiage that Latter-day Saints familiar with the temple ceremony should readily recognize. Consider, for example, the whisperings of the writings of Enoch, such as in LXXXII:1, "I lifted up my hands in righteousness, and blessed the holy and great One. I spoke with the breath of my mouth...." And Enoch LXIX:35–38:

> They glorify with all their power of praise; and he sustains them in all that act thanksgiving, while they laud, glorify, and exalt the name of the Lord of spirits for ever and ever.
> And with them he establishes this oath, by which they and their paths are preserved; nor does their progress perish.
> Great was their joy.
> They blessed, glorified, and exalted, because the name of the Son of man was revealed to them.

And Enoch LXII:3–5:

> He shall enlighten every secret thing.
> Thy power is from generation to generation; and thy glory for ever and ever.
> Deep are all thy secrets, and numberless.

Chapter Ten. The Mormon Temple Endowment

And going back to LXXXII:3:

> From generation to generation shall thy dominion exist. All the heavens are thy throne for ever, and all the earth thy footstool for ever and for ever.

The Celestial Room; the Throne Room

Professor of New Testament and ancient Judaism studies George W. E. Nickelsburg's[46] article "The Temple According to 1 Enoch" refers to specific language from 1 Enoch and draws parallels with the ancient Jewish temples of King Solomon and Jerusalem.[47] Professor Nickelsburg describes Enoch's narration "how in a dream vision he ascended to heaven and progressed through the heavenly temple to the divine throne room." Nickelsburg summarizes Enoch's heavenly (celestial) description of his tour of the temple:

> Enoch recounts how he moves through the temple in a vision. ... The vision is similar to all three biblical accounts in that it describes the architectural components of the temple. But here the similarities end, and not surprisingly. Heaven is not the place for stone and metal, wood and goats' hair. Instead, what Enoch sees and experiences is unimaginable for the earthbound.

Mormon temples also have different rooms that participants are led through before reaching the holiest of holies for participants, the Celestial room. There are different rooms for different purposes throughout LDS temples. Different rooms have varying levels of accessibility. Endowment participants might be gathered first in a waiting or instruction room. They will begin (typically) the endowment in the Endowment Room, where most of the ceremony takes place. In early Mormon temples, those participating in live ceremonies at one time were guided from room to room through the temple throughout the endowment ordinance. These rooms include a Creation room, the first of four ordinance rooms once used in the endowment ordinance. In the Salt Lake temple, for example, after gathering and being instructed in the Creation room, participants would then exit and enter the Garden room, which is adjacent to the Creation room, but has rows of seating at an inclined level for a better view as the reenactment of the creation story plays out. Ultimately, participants await their turn to present themselves at the veil, the curtain dividing them from entering the Celestial room.

After temple endowment participants end their experience by

being presented at the veil, the curtain separating them from the presence of God, where they can symbolically commune with God and be personally accepted into his eternal presence with the company of family and friends eagerly awaiting on the other side. "There are no ceremonies performed in this room. Rather, it is a place of quiet peace, prayer, and reflection meant to symbolize heaven."[48]

In LDS theology, the endowment is preparatory for salvation, and each man's potential for godhood of his own world. A popularly debated Mormon doctrinal couplet is "As man is, God once was; as God is, man may become." Whether this is doctrinally concrete or not, it might as well be. These are not secret teachings, and they are peculiarly Joseph Smith's. The individual experience of the endowment is intended as a reflection on incomprehensible eternities, for participants to consider where we fit into this world where spirit and matter collide to animate some kind of order from the chaos. The individual's instruction at the veil and entry into the Celestial room is akin to receiving enlightenment that allows one to transcend the corrupt constructed "world," and accept one's own divine possibility. To recognize the *potential* to become as God is, is mystical and transcendental.

Chapter Eleven

Mormon Cosmology
The Book of Abraham and 1 Enoch

> "Now, for this cause I know that man is nothing, which thing I never had supposed."
>
> —Moses 1:10

Before the Big Bang theory was a theory, was there a beginning to the story of time? Cosmology, the study of our universe (Greek *kosmos*, "world," and *logia*, "study of"), for as long as it has been looking in on itself, is the quest to discover the mystery of infiniteness. The ultimate prize is an understanding, in our finite minds, of never-ending time and the unlimited expanse of space—matters that were never far from the farm boy prophet's ever inquisitive mind.

While incarcerated in the misery of Liberty Jail in the cold winter of 1838, Joseph's contemplations were "of deep import, and time, and experience, and careful and ponderous and solemn thoughts can only find them out." His revelations continued, "Thy mind, O man! if thou wilt lead a soul unto salvation, must stretch as high as the utmost heavens, and search into and contemplate the darkest abyss, and the broad expanse of eternity—thou must commune with God."[1] From the beginning of his calling to the end, his quest was to commune with God and know all that God knows.

Joseph Smith taught that the intelligent part of man has always existed: "The spirit of man is not a created being; it existed from eternity, and will exist to eternity. Anything created cannot be eternal, and earth, water, etc., had their existence in an elementary state, from eternity" (*History of the Church*, 3:387). In D&C 93:29, Joseph taught, "Man was also in the beginning with God. Intelligence, or the light of truth, was not created or made, neither indeed can be." Later, in verse 33, we read, "For man is spirit. The elements are eternal, and spirit and element are inseparably connected." Section 93, verses 35–36 continue, "The elements are the tabernacle of God; yea, man is the tabernacle of God, even temples.... The glory of God is *intelligence,* or, in other words, light and truth."

In Joseph's Book of Abraham, we are introduced to Joseph's understandings of eternal existence, and a glimpse into his understanding of the cosmos. The patriarch Enoch is never referenced by name in the Book of Abraham, and little is written about what potential influence, if any, Enoch had on Joseph's translation of the Book of Abraham. But it appears to have been an influential source for some themes and specific language. Significant themes in the Book of Abraham include our preexistence, the war in heaven, the creation and a reckoning of celestial luminaries and their revolutions. These are all found in the Book of Enoch, and with some surprising vocabulary and usage reflected in Joseph's Abraham.

"An existence previous to the formation of the luminaries of heaven"

The War in Heaven

As far as Christian orthodoxy is concerned, the belief in the premortal existence of the soul was formally excised from the church in AD 553 by an edict declared by the Roman emperor Justinian, known as the *Anathemas against Origen.*[2] The pope is said to have consented under extreme duress. This lost doctrine remained hinted at in scripture, and broached in literary works, such as John Milton's seventeenth-century *Paradise Lost.*

James E. Talmage, as an apostle of the LDS Church, instructs of the doctrinal basis for the Mormon belief in our premortal life:

> John the Revelator beheld in vision some of the scenes that had been enacted in the spirit-world before the beginning of human history. He witnessed strife and contention between loyalty and rebellion, with the hosts defending the former led by Michael the archangel, and the rebellious forces captained by Satan, who is also called the devil, the serpent, and the dragon. We read: "And there was war in heaven: Michael and his angels fought against the dragon; and the dragon fought and his angels."[3]
>
> In this struggle between unembodied hosts the forces were unequally divided; Satan drew to his standard only a third part of the children of God,

who are symbolized as the "stars of heaven"; the majority either fought with Michael, or at least refrained from active opposition, thus accomplishing the purpose of their "first estate"; while the angels who arrayed themselves on the side of Satan "kept not their first estate," and therefore rendered themselves ineligible for the glorious possibilities of an advanced condition or "second estate." The victory was with Michael and his angels; and Satan or Lucifer, theretofore a "son of the morning," was cast out of heaven, yea "he was cast out into the earth, and his angels were cast out with him."[4]

Here again we have echoes of archangels, Michael and the multitudes of "stars in heaven." *These are all from 1 Enoch, right?* Elder Talmage suggests these are from St. John's Book of Revelation in the New Testament. And they are indeed found there. What is generally unknown, however, and thus it is never discussed, is that John's Book of Revelation is an evangelical plagiarism and adaptation of the apocalyptic visions and ancient writings of Enoch, melding it from a piece of ancient Jewish literature into a phantastic work of Christian scripture. St. John borrowed—heavily—from the then extant writings of Enoch; he just didn't mention that fact, unlike Jude, who did when he borrowed from Enoch's ancient works.

Exactly why the book of Revelation made its way into the canonized New Testament remains a debatable question. What is unquestionable, however, is that St. John's "revelation" came (in part) from the ancient apocalyptic writings of Enoch then available as a literary source. The word "revelation" is translated directly from the Greek word *apocalypse*, meaning "an unveiling" (lifting of the veil) or "revealing." Apocalyptic literary works were popular in the Second Temple era (516 BC to AD 70) among Hebrew- and Greek-speaking Jews and early Christians. St. John was writing his own version of unveilings around the year 95 of the first century. The Jewish writings penned under the name of Enoch in St. John's personal possession were written long before John's apocalypse was recorded. The borrowing is clear in considering a few parallel passages from both books:

A Star Fell from Heaven

Revelation 9:1	**Enoch LXXXV:2 & 4**
And the fifth angel sounded, and I saw a star fall from heaven unto the earth: and to him was given the key of the bottomless pit.	And behold a single star fell from heaven. **Enoch LXXXVII:2–3** He seized the first star which fell

down from heaven. And, binding it hand and foot, he cast it into a valley; a valley narrow, deep, stupendous, and gloomy.

Other Stars Also Cast Out from Heaven with the First

Revelation 12:4 & 9
And his tail drew the third part of the stars of heaven, and did cast them to the earth:
And the great dragon was cast out, that old serpent, called the Devil, and Satan, which deceiveth the whole world: he was cast out into the earth, and his angels were cast out with him.

Enoch LXXXV:4
Again I looked in my vision, and surveyed heaven; when behold I saw many stars which descended, and projected themselves from heaven to where the first start was.

Enoch IX:5
Thou has seen what Azazyel has done, how he has taught ever species of iniquity upon earth, and has disclosed to the world all the secret things which are done in the heaven.

He Shall Dwell Among His Elect

Revelation 7:15
He that sitteth on the throne shall dwell among them.

Enoch XLV. SECT. VII:3–4
In that day shall the Elect one sit upon a throne of glory....
In that day I will cause my Elect one to dwell in the midst of them.

The Judgment Throne

Revelation 20:11
And I saw a great white throne, and him that sat on it, from whose face the earth and the heaven fled away; and there was found no place for them.

Enoch XIV:17–20
[I] saw that it contained an exalted throne; The appearance of which was like that of frost; while its circumference resembled the orb of the brilliant sun; ... To look upon It was impossible.

Chapter Eleven. Mormon Cosmology

The Judged Are Cast into a Lake of Fire and Brimstone

Revelation 20:10 & 14	Enoch LXVI:6–8
And the devil that deceived them was cast into the lake of fire and brimstone, where the beast and the false prophet *are*, and shall be tormented day and night for ever and ever. .... And death and hell were cast into the lake of fire. This is the second death.	And when all this was effected, from the fluid mass of fire, and the perturbation which prevailed in that place, there arose a strong smell of sulphur, which became mixed with the waters; and the valley of the angels, who had been guilty of seduction, burned underneath its soil. Through that valley also rivers of fire were flowing, to which those angels shall be condemned, who seduced the inhabitants of the earth.

These are just a few of dozens of incidents of borrowing from Enoch in Revelation, and in many other Christian writings in the New Testament, such as Jude, 2 Peter, 2 Corinthians and the apocalyptic verses and themes throughout the synoptic gospels of Mark, Matthew and Luke. Closer evidence of John the Revelator's literary borrowing from the ancient Enoch writings appears in other verses:

Tens of Thousands of Angels Surrounding God's Throne

Revelation 5:11	Enoch XI:1
I beheld, and I heard the voice of man angels round about the throne ... and the number of them was ten thousand times ten thousand, and thousands and thousands.	After this I beheld thousands of thousand and then thousand time ten thousand, and an infinite number of people standing before the Lord of spirits.

A New Heaven and Earth

Revelation 21:1	Enoch XCII:17:
And I saw a new heaven and a new earth: for the first heaven and the first earth were passed	The former heaven shall depart and pass away, a new heaven shall appear.

away; and there was no more sea;	**Enoch XIV:4** ... I will change the face of the heaven: I will bless it and illuminate it for ever. I will also change the face of the earth:

These parallels are unmistakable. John the Revelator had access to and was influenced by the ancient writings of Enoch then available. The doctrines of preexistence and the war in heaven found in John's Revelation, therefore, are directly influenced by the written prophecies of Enoch, as the extant translations confirm this. We know that some early Christian authors considered the prophecies of Enoch to be inspired scripture. Jude expressly quotes Enoch in Jude 1:14: "Enoch also, the seventh from Adam, prophesied of these, saying, 'Behold, the Lord cometh with then thousands of his saints, to execute judgment upon all." (*Cf.* Enoch II, XXVI: 2: "Behold, he comes with then thousand of his saints, to execute judgment upon them.") The influence of the prophesies of Enoch into the LDS doctrine of preexistence is beyond speculation because the New Testament verses that are foundational for the LDS belief are ultimately premised on ancient writings of Enoch themselves.

Joseph Smith was intimately familiar with the Book of Revelation, and the magical, mystical and mythological story surely captured his attention. If Joseph availed himself of Laurence's Book of Enoch, he would have certainly recognized the parallels in the Revelation story. Some specific Enochic themes and doctrines were taken out of Christian orthodoxy with the exclusion of 1 Enoch as canonized scripture. These have been restored as a part of latter-day teachings, connecting the ancient Jewish and Christian orthodoxies through Joseph Smith's revelations and writings.

The First Estate

Another example of obscure New Testament doctrine directly influenced by Enoch and finding itself restored and clarified in modern-day Mormon orthodoxy is Jude's reference to a "first estate" in Jude 1:6–8:

> And the angels which kept not their *first estate*, but left their own habitation, he hath reserved in everlasting chains under darkness unto the judgment of the great day.
> Even as Sodom and Gomorrha, and the cities about them in

like manner, giving themselves over to fornication, and going after strange flesh, are set forth for an example, suffering the vengeance of eternal fire.

Likewise also these filthy dreamers defile the flesh, despise dominion, and speak evil of dignities.

This motif of spirits falling from their "first estate," or fallen angels leaving their spiritual existence, is a prevailing story line specific to the Book of Enoch. After witnessing one star fall, Enoch witnesses a great perturbation: "Again I looked in my vision, and surveyed heaven; when behold *I saw many stars which descended*, and projected themselves from heaven to where the first star was" (Enoch LXXXV:4).

This same story line emerges in Joseph's Book of Abraham. As with Joseph's other revealed translations, we have the beginnings of another creation story. Better yet, we get another prologue to the beginning. This scripture in Abraham expands on the metaphorical depictions of the heavenly war in St. John's Revelation, wherein the "Son of man" is chosen by God among the angels. Compare these verses from Joseph Smith's Abraham and Enoch stories, in which the preexisting intelligences are introduced more anthropomorphically:

Abraham 3:24–28:	Enoch XLVI:1–3
24. And *there stood one among them that was like unto God*, and he said unto those who were with him: *We will go down, for there is space there, and we will take of these materials, and we will make an earth whereon these may dwell*; 25. And we will prove them herewith, to see if they will do all things whatsoever the Lord their God shall command them; 26. *And they who keep their first estate shall be added upon*; and *they who keep not their first estate shall not have glory* in the same kingdom with those who keep their first estate; *and they who keep their second estate shall have glory added upon their heads for ever and ever*. 27. And the Lord said: Whom shall I send? And one answered like unto *the Son of Man*[5]: Here am I,	1. There I beheld the *Ancient of days*, whose head was like white wool, and *with him another, whose countenance resembled that of man. His countenance was full of grace, like that of one of the holy angels.* Then I inquired of one of the angels, who went with me, and who shewed me every secret thing, concerning this Son of man; who he was; whence he was; and why *he accompanied the Ancient of days*. 2. He answered and said to me; this is the *Son of man*, to whom righteousness belongs; with whom righteousness has dwelt; and who will reveal all the treasures of that which is concealed; for the Lord of spirits has chosen him; and his portion has surpassed all before the Lord of spirits in everlasting uprightness.

> send me. And another answered and said: Here am I, send me. And the Lord said: I will send the first.
> 28. And the second was angry, and kept not his first estate; and, at that day, many followed after him.

The Second Estate

An estate is a place, or state of being. A life or lifetime. If there was a "first," then there must be a second. Recall that St. John in Revelation speaks of death and hell, and of being "cast into the lake of fire" as a "second death" (Rev. 20:14). If the judgment and assignment to our eternal state is the second death, then our mortal life must be the second life, or "second estate."

This mortal existence, being born children of God ("sons of God") (Genesis 6:2) and thus leaving a pre-life estate to inhabit another, comes from the creation story in Genesis 6:1–6:

> And it came to pass, when men began to multiply on the face of the earth, and daughters were born unto them,
> That the sons of God saw the daughters of men that they were fair; and they took them wives of all which they chose.
> And the Lord said, My spirit shall not always strive with man, for that he also is flesh: yet his days shall be an hundred and twenty years.
> There were giants in the earth in those days; and also after that, when the sons of God came in unto the daughters of men, and they bare children to them, the same became mighty men which were of old, men of renown.
> And God saw that the wickedness of man was great in the earth, and that every imagination of the thoughts of his heart was only evil continually.
> And it repented the Lord that he had made man on the earth, and it grieved him at his heart.

These "sons of God" referred to in verse 2 are known as fallen angels, and the "giants" (or Nephilim)[6] are the offspring between the sons of God and daughters of men. (Genesis 6:4). The fallen angels have left their first estate to enter the carnal and corrupt world of mortality. Like the angels who kept not their first estate in Jude 1:6, the Book of Enoch tells of those who have fallen, who become carnal in the material world. This is the second estate, or mortal probation. This ancient

Chapter Eleven. Mormon Cosmology

Jewish story line is right from Genesis. In both Genesis and the Book of Enoch, the fallen angels are called "giants" who lusted after the daughters of men, so they "took them as wives" (stated politely in Genesis) or "defiled yourselves with" (more directly in Enoch). In Enoch, these "giants" are also called "the Watchers." These Watchers are the "giants" we find in Genesis 6:4, which obviously share a similar source and story:

Genesis 6	Enoch XV
1. And it came to pass, when men began to multiply on the face of the earth, and daughters were born unto them,	2. Wherefore have you forsaken the lofty and holy heaven, which endures for ever, and have lain with women; have defiled yourselves with the daughters of men; have taken to yourselves wives; have acted like the sons of the earth, and have begotten an impious offspring?
2. That the sons of God saw the daughters of men that they were fair; and they took them wives of all which they chose.	
3. And the Lord said My spirit shall not always strive with man, for that he also is flesh: yet his days shall be an hundred and twenty years.	3. You being spiritual, holy, and possessing a life which is eternal, have polluted yourselves with women; have begotten in carnal blood; have lusted in the blood of men; and have done as those who are flesh and blood do.
4. There were giants in the earth in those days; and also after that, when the sons of God came in unto the daughters of men, and they bare children to them, the same became mighty men which were of old, men of renown.	5. Therefore have I given to them wives, that they might cohabit with them; that sons might be born of them; and that this might be transacted upon earth. But you from the beginning were made spiritual, possessing a life which is eternal, and not subject to death for ever.
	7. Therefore I made not wives for you, because being spiritual, your dwelling is in heaven.
	8. *Now the giants, who have been born of spirit and of flesh, shall be called upon earth evil spirits, and on earth shall be their habitation.* Evil spirits shall proceed from their flesh, because they were created from above; from the holy Watchers was their beginning and primary foundation. Evil spirits shall they be upon earth, and the spirits of

> the wicked shall they be called. The habitation of the spirits of heaven shall be in heaven; but upon earth shall be the habitation *of terrestrial spirits*, who are born on earth.

The Preexistence

The idea of a preexistence—literally—is found in Professor Richard Laurence's 1821 Book of Enoch. Enoch prophesies of the coming of the Son of man "invoked before the Lord of Spirits, and in his name in the presence of the Ancient of Days," and "Before the Sun and signs were created, before the stars of the heaven were formed, his name was invoked in the presence of the Lord of spirits" (Enoch XLVIII:2–3). This is not exclusive to Enoch. It is reminiscent of the allusion to Christ's preexistence in the opening of the gospel of John 1:1–3:

> In the beginning was the Word, and the Word was with God, and the Word was God. The same was in the beginning with God. All things were made by him; and without him was not anything made that was made. And the Word was made flesh, and dwelt among us, (and we beheld his glory, the glory as of the only begotten of the Father,) full of grace and truth.

To understand Christ's role in the preexistence and creation from these verses takes a little thought process. In the Hebrew creation story in Genesis, God spoke, saying "let there be light," and creation commenced. We understand through John's gospel that Christ is the light of the world, and Christ was the Word spoken by God, made flesh to dwell among us. As you can see, the proof of Jesus's preexistence in the Old and New Testaments is based on an understanding of these words, and their presumed intention and theological explanation. Neither Genesis nor Revelation expressly tells us of Christ's pre-mortal existence. There are allusions to foreordination in the Hebrew bible (Old Testament), but not directly as to Christ. And Joseph Smith understood this theology. In Joseph's Book of Moses, the creation prologue, Joseph reveals: "And *by the word* of my power, have I created them, *which is mine Only Begotten Son*, who is full of grace and truth" (Moses 1:32).

The "Preliminary Dissertation" Laurence included in his published translation of the Book of Enoch addresses the ancient Jewish author's express references to the preexistence of the Son of man, and his part in the creation story:

Chapter Eleven. Mormon Cosmology

In this point of view, at least, his sentiments are of considerable importance; because necessarily uninfluenced by Christian prepossessions. Alluding to the Son of man, he [Enoch] says; "Before the sun and the signs were created, before the stars of heaven were formed, his name was invoked in the presence of the Lord of spirits all, who dwell on earth, shall fall down and worship before him; shall bless and glorify him, and sing praises to him in the name of the Lord of spirits." *Therefore the Elect and the Concealed one existed in his presence before the world was created, and for ever....*

In both these passages the preexistence of the Messiah is asserted in language that admits not the slightest shade of ambiguity. Nor is it such a preexistence as the philosophical Cabbalists attributed to him, their believing that the souls of all men, and consequently that of the Messiah, to have been originally created together, when the world itself was formed. Rather, it is an existence antecedent to all creation; an existence previous to the formation of the luminaries of heaven, an existence prior to all things visible and invisible, "before every thing concealed." It should likewise be remarked, that the preexistence ascribed to him is a divine preexistence; for before all things his name was invoked in the presence of the Lord of spirits—the Elect and the Concealed one existed in his presence—who has dominion over all things, for from the beginning the Son of man existed in secret, whom the Most High preserved in the presence of his power.

....

Here then we have not merely the declaration of a Plurality, but that of a precise and distinct Trinity, of persons, under the supreme appellation of Lords; two of whom, denominated the Elect one and the other (divine) Power, are represented as not less engaged than the Lord of spirits himself in the formation of the world. And it should be added, that upon these, as upon the more immediate agents in the work of creation, a particular class of angels is mentioned as appropriately attendant.

This argument, in proof that the Jews before the birth of Christ believed the doctrine of a Trinity, appears to me much more important and conclusive than that which has been indeed frequently, but to my mind, I confess, not satisfactorily, deduced from the philosophical principles of the ancient Cabbala. Cabbalistical theology, I well know, has its *aziluth* or emanations of Deity; but these, I am convinced, notwithstanding the persuasions of many Christians upon the subject, were at no period ever contemplated by the Jews themselves as distinct persons, but merely as distinct energies, in the Godhead.[7]

A Spirit Prison

In the New Testament we hear allusions to a "spirit paradise" after death, e.g., Christ promising one of the thieves crucified next to him that "today you will be with me in paradise" (Luke 23:42–43). We also have scripture referring to teaching those waiting in a "spirit prison." More specifically, 1 Peter 3:18–20 tells us that there are "spirits in prison," where some who were disobedient are relegated after this mortal life, but before the ultimate day of reckoning:

> For Christ also hath once suffered for sins, the just for the unjust, that he might bring us to God, being put to death in the flesh, but quickened by the Spirit:
> By which also he went and preached unto the spirits in prison;
> Which sometime were disobedient, when once the longsuffering of God waited in the days of Noah, while the ark was a preparing, wherein few, that is, eight souls were saved by water.

The LDS Church offers this version of its orthodoxy of the Postmortal Spirit World, found in its simplest terms of instruction in the *Gospel Principals* manual:

> The Apostle Peter referred to the postmortal spirit world as a prison, which it is for some (*see* 1 Peter 3:18–20). In the spirit prison are the spirits of those who have not yet received the gospel of Jesus Christ. These spirits have agency and may be enticed by both good and evil. If they accept the gospel and the ordinances performed for them in the temples, they may leave the spirit prison and dwell in paradise.
> Also in the spirit prison are those who rejected the gospel after it was preached to them either on earth or in the spirit prison. These spirits suffer in a condition known as hell. They have removed themselves from the mercy of Jesus Christ, who said, "Behold, I, God, have suffered these things for all, that they might not suffer if they would repent; but if they would not repent they must suffer even as I; which suffering caused myself, even God, the greatest of all, to tremble because of pain, and to bleed at every pore, and to suffer both body and spirit" (D&C 19:16–18). After suffering for their sins, they will be allowed, through the Atonement of Jesus Christ, to inherit the lowest degree of glory, which is the telestial kingdom.[8]

The spirit prison motif is expounded by Joseph's revealed prophecies of Enoch found in Chapter 6 of the Book of Moses. Consider first these parallels:

Moses 6:38 & 57	Enoch XVIII:15; XIX:2
38. But behold, these which thine eyes are upon *shall perish in the floods*; and behold, *I will shut them up; a prison have I prepared for them.*	15. Then the angel said; This place, *until the consummation of heaven and earth, will be the prison of the stars, and of the host of heaven.*

57. And *as many of the spirits as were in prison* came forth, and stood on the right hand of God; and the *remainder were reserved in chains of darkness until the judgment of the great day.*	2. And being numerous in appearance made men profane, and caused them to err; so that they sacrificed to devils as to gods. *For in the great day there shall be a judgment, with which they shall be judged, until they are consumed*; and their wives also shall be judged, who led astray the angels of heaven without resistance

We share a more explicit view of this heavenly holding cell through Enoch's eyes in his guided vision in Enoch XXII, Section V:

> 3. Then Raphael, one of the holy angels who were with me, answered and said; These are the delightful places where the spirits, the souls of the dead, will be collected; for them were they formed; and here will be collected all the souls of the sons of men.
> 4. These places, in which they dwell, shall they occupy until the day of judgment, and until their appointed period.
> 5. Their appointed period will be long, even until the great judgment. And I saw the spirits of the sons of men who were dead; and their voices reached to heaven, while they were accusing.
> 6. Then I inquired of Raphael, an angel who was with me, and said; Whose spirit is that, the voice of which reaches to heaven, and accuses?
> 7. He answered, saying; This is the spirit of Abel, who was slain by Cain his brother; and who will accuse that brother, until his seed be destroyed from the face of the earth;
> 8. Until his seed perish from the seed of the human race.
> 9. At that time therefore I inquired respecting him, and respecting the general judgment, saying; Why is one separated from another? He answered; *Three separations have been made between the spirits of the dead, and thus have the spirits of the righteous been separated.*

Multiple Heavens and Celestial and Terrestrial Kingdoms

> In my Father's house are many mansions.
> —John 14:2

It was Joseph's wonderment of the cosmos that brought him to his understanding of God and the eternities. "The mind or the intelligence

Joseph Smith and the Book of Enoch

which man possesses is co-equal with God himself," Joseph professed in what would be one of his last doctrinal discourses on the subject before his martyrdom in 1844.[9] We can't help but see the similarities between Joseph's and Enoch's appreciation for the expanse of space:

Joseph Wonders at the Luminaries Joseph Smith's *History*:	**Enoch Wonders at the Luminaries** Enoch XCII:20–24
... for I looked upon the sun *the glorious luminary* of the earth and also the moon rolling in their magesty through the heavens and also the stars shining in their courses and the earth also upon which I stood and the beast of the field and the fowls of heaven and the fish of the waters and also man walking forth upon the face of the earth in magesty and in the strength of beauty whose power and intiligence in governing the things which are so exceding great and marvilous even in the likeness of him who created ~~him~~<them> and when I considered upon these things my heart exclaimed well hath the wise man said ~~the~~<it is a> fool<that> saith in his heart there is no God my heart exclaimed all marvelous these bear testimony and bespeak an omnipotant and omnipreasant power a being who makith Laws and decreeeth and bindeth all things in their bounds who filleth Eternity who was and is and will be from all Eternity to Eternity.	Who [is] capable of contemplating all the workmanship of heaven? Who of comprehending the deeds of heaven? He may behold its animation, but not its spirit. He may be capable of conversing respecting it, but not of ascending to it. He may see all the boundaries of these things, and meditate upon them; but he can make nothing like them. Who of all men is able to understand the breadth and length of the earth? By whom has been seen the dimensions of all these things? Is it every man who is capable of comprehending the extent of heaven; what its elevation is, and by what it is supported? How many are the numbers of the stars; and where *all the luminaries* remain at rest?

In the Book of Enoch, the patriarch is shown "all the repositories of the superior and inferior kingdom" of heaven, and a vision of a "tree of life."[10] In his "Preliminary Dissertation," Laurence expounds, invoking many words and ideas that found their way into Joseph's doctrines and teachings,

> These allusions of the Zohar to the *repositories of the celestial and terrestrial kingdoms*, and to the tree of knowledge in the garden of Eden, shewn

Chapter Eleven. Mormon Cosmology

to Enoch after his ascent into heaven, are distinctly stated to have been taken from a book, entitled the Book of Enoch; and the very same allusions will be found minutely detailed between the sixteenth and thirty-seventh chapters of the present version. The reference to the tree of knowledge in the garden of Eden occurs in the thirty-first chapter. *Now the authors of the Cabalistical remains wrote or conveyed down their recondite doctrines in Chaldee.* Scarcely therefore, I apprehend, will it be questioned, that the copy of the Book of Enoch which they cited was written either in that language or in Hebrew. For they appear to have regarded it as the genuine work of him whose name it bore, and not as the spurious production of a later age. Presuming therefore that the book before us was the composition of some unknown Jew, under the borrowed name of Enoch, I shall next consider what criteria are afforded us to determine the period at which it may have been written.[11]

Another peculiar piece of information that we can extract from this excerpt is the explanation that "authors of the Cabalistical remains wrote or conveyed down their recondite doctrines in Chaldee." This is interesting on several levels, but most relevant to the present inquiry is that we find the word "Chaldee" used in Joseph's Book of Abraham. Abraham opens his revealed scripture narrative, "In the land of the Chaldeans, at the residence of my fathers," and then explains that he "left the land of Ur, *and the Chaldees*, to go into the land of Cannan" (Abraham 1:1; 2:1 & 4). While Joseph's revelations may have been influenced by scholarly bible commentaries he had access to at the time, the word "Chaldee" in that spelling does not appear anywhere in the KJV Bible or the Apocrypha.

Professor Laurence explains the apocalyptic visions where Enoch is also hoisted into a heavenly vision, where his "eyes are opened" and shown "all the repositories of the superior and inferior kingdom" of heaven, and a vision of a "tree of life."[12] Laurence explains that "these allusions ... to the repositories of the celestial and terrestrial kingdoms, and to the tree of knowledge in the garden of Eden, shewn to Enoch after his ascent into heaven" are "distinctly stated to have been taken from a book, entitled the Book of Enoch." These are unmistakable connections with Joseph's restored doctrines and teachings.

The Book of Enoch alludes to multiple "heavens" and varying degrees of torment or glory assigned according to our righteousness, likened to celestial bodies. In a similar sounding way, Joseph Smith and Sidney Rigdon were caught up in a heavenly vision in February 1832, while working on the New Testament. They were transformed and perceived with their spiritual eyes "the Vision," which is now recorded in

Joseph Smith and the Book of Enoch

D&C Section 76 and reveals Mormon doctrine concerning varying degrees of heavenly potential in the afterlife.

Joseph's revealed "degrees of glory" are likened unto "celestial and terrestrial kingdoms," and related to the respective glories of the sun, moon and stars—just as we find in the Book of Enoch:

D&C 76	Enoch XCIX:8
70. These are they whose bodies are celestial, whose glory is that of the sun, even the glory of God, the highest of all, whose glory the sun of the firmament is written of as being typical.	And now know ye, that the angels shall inquire into your conduct in heaven; of the sun, the moon, and the stars, shall they inquire respecting your sins; for upon earth you exercise jurisdiction over the righteous.
71. And again, we saw the terrestrial world, and behold and lo, these are they who are of the terrestrial, whose glory differs from that of the church of the Firstborn who have received the fulness of the Father, even as that of the moon differs from the sun in the firmament.	**Enoch XLI:4** I beheld also the receptacles of the moon, whence the moons came, whither they proceeded, their glorious return, and how one became more splendid than another. I marked their rich progress, their unchangeable progress, their disunited and undiminished progress; their observance of a mutual fidelity by a stable oath; their proceeding forth before the sun, and their adherence to the path allotted them, in obedience to the command of the Lord of spirits. Potent is his name for ever and for ever.
78. Wherefore, they are bodies terrestrial, and not bodies celestial, and differ in glory as the moon differs from the sun.....	
80. And now this is the end of the vision which we saw of the terrestrial, that the Lord commanded us to write while we were yet in the Spirit.	**Enoch XLI:1** After this I beheld the secrets of the heavens and of paradise, according to its divisions; and of human action, as they weight it there in balances. I saw the habitations of the elect, and the habitations of the holy.
81. And again, we saw the glory of the telestial, which glory is that of the lesser, even as the glory of the stars differs from that of the glory of the moon in the firmament.	
91. And thus we saw the glory of the terrestrial which excels in all things the glory of the telestial, even in glory, and in power, and in might, and in dominion.	**Enoch LVIII:1–6** 1. Then another angel, who proceeded with me, spoke to me; 2. And shewed me the first and last secrets in heaven above, and in the depths of the earth. 3. In the extremities of heaven,
92. And thus we saw the glory of the celestial, which excels in all things—where God, even the Father, reigns upon his throne forever and ever;	

Chapter Eleven. Mormon Cosmology

96. And the glory of the celestial is one, even as the glory of the sun is one. 97. And the glory of the terrestrial is one, even as the glory of the moon is one. 98. And the glory of the telestial is one, even as the glory of the stars is one; for as one star differs from another star in glory, even so differs one from another in glory in the telestial world; 100. These are they who say there are some of one and some of another—some of Christ and some of John, and some of Moses, and some of Elias, and some of Esaias, and some of Isaiah, and some of Enoch.	and in the foundations of it, and in the receptacle of the winds. 4. He shewed me how their spirits were divided, how they were balanced, and how both the springs and the winds were numbered according to the force of their spirit. 5. He shewed me the power of the moon's light, that its power is a just one, as well as the divisions of the stars, according to their respective names; 6. That every division is divided

If we back up just a few verses to D&C 76:67, we read:

> These are they who have come to an innumerable company of angels, to the general assembly and *church of Enoch*, and of the Firstborn.

Echoes of Enoch in the Book of Abraham

This wonderment of the "luminaries" and reckoning of the celestial bodies from the Book of Enoch carries over into Joseph's Book of Abraham. Although neither the patriarch Enoch nor his prophecies are mentioned by name, several correspondences surface between these two texts. Here is just one example of a familiar repeating theme in Joseph's revelations that is also found in the Book of Enoch:

Keeping Records for the Benefit of Future Generations

Abraham 1:31	Enoch LXXX:1 & 9
31. But *the records of the fathers*, even the patriarchs, concerning the right of Priesthood, *the Lord my*	*He said; O Enoch*, look on the book *which heaven has gradually dropped down*; and, reading that

God preserved in mine own hands; therefore a knowledge of the beginning of the creation, and also of the planets, and of the stars, *as they were made known unto the fathers*, have I kept even unto this day, and I *shall endeavor to write some of these things upon this record, for the benefit of my posterity that shall come after me.* (*Cf.* Moses 1:40–41: *And now, Moses, my son,* I will speak unto thee concerning this earth upon which thou standest; and *thou shalt write the things which I shall speak.* And in a day when the children of men shall esteem my words as naught and take many of them from the book which thou shalt write, behold, I will raise up another like unto thee; *and they shall be had again among the children of men—* among as many as shall believe)	which is written in it, understand every part of it. ... *that thou mayest instruct they family, write these things, and explain them to all thy children.* **Enoch LXXXI:1–3** Now, my son Mathusala, all these things I speak unto thee, and write for thee. *To thee I have revealed all, and have given thee books of every thing.* *Preserve, my son Mathusala, the books written by thy father that thou mayest transmit them to future generations.* Wisdom have I given to thee, to thy children, and *thy posterity, that they may transmit to their children, for generations for ever,* this wisdom in their thoughts

Abraham Chapter 3 takes a complete turn from any of Joseph's prior revelations, beginning with Abraham's visions of the stars, moon, sun and planets. Abraham learns of the "eternal nature of spirits" by the gift and power of the "Urim and Thummim," or seer stones (Abraham 3:1). ("And I, Abraham, had the Urim and Thummim, which the Lord my God had given unto me, in Ur of the Chaldees.") Consider the thematic and verbal parallels between the texts:

A Vision of the Celestial Stars, and the Names of the Great Ones

Abraham 3:2–4	**Enoch XLIIL**
2. *And I saw the stars*, that they were very great, and that one of them was nearest unto the throne of God; and *there were many great ones* which were near unto it; 3. *And the Lord said unto me:* These are the governing ones; and	1. *I beheld another splendor, and the stars of heaven.* I observed that he called them all by *their respective names*, and that they heard.

Chapter Eleven. Mormon Cosmology

the name of the great one is Kolob, because it is near unto me, for I am the Lord thy God: I have set this one to govern all those which belong to the same order as that upon which thou standest.

Observing the Times and Seasons and Heavenly Operations

Abraham 3:4	Enoch XXXIII:2–4
And the Lord said unto me, by the Urim and Thummim, that Kolob was after the manner of the Lord, *according to its times and seasons in the revolutions thereof*; that one revolution was a day unto the Lord, after his *manner of reckoning*, it being one thousand years according to the time appointed unto that whereon thou standest. This is the reckoning of the Lord's time, according to the reckoning of Kolob.	The gates of heaven stood open, and *I beheld the celestial stars come forth*. I numbered them as they proceeded out of the gate, and wrote them all down, as they came out one by one according to their number. I wrote down their names altogether, *their times and their seasons*, as the angel Uriel, who was with me, pointed them out to me. **Enoch LXXVIII:1–2** He shewed me every ordinance respecting these [the stars of heaven], which takes place *at all times and in all seasons* under every influence, in all years, at the arrival and under the rule of each, during every month and every week.

A Reckoning of a Day on Earth in the Lord's Time

Abraham 3:4	Book of Enoch: Laurence's Remarks in Comments to Ch. LXXII
And the Lord said unto me, by the Urim and Thummim, that Kolob was after the manner of the Lord, according to its times and seasons in the revolutions thereof; *that one revolution was a day unto the Lord, after his manner of reckoning, it*	Ver. 4. *I have been born the seventh in the first week. In the mode of reckoning here adopted, it is evident, that a day stands for a hundred years*; so that consequently a

Joseph Smith and the Book of Enoch

being one thousand years according to the time appointed unto that whereon thou standest. *This is the reckoning of the Lord's time, according to the reckoning of Kolob.* (*Cf.*, 2 Peter 3:8: "But, beloved, be not ignorant of this one thing, that one day is with the Lord as a thousand years, and a thousand years as one day.")	week is made to express a period of seven hundred years. The chronology however thus established, does not always accord with that which has been deduced from the Bible, in consequence of the necessity of computing from the uncertain era of creation. This is the case when we attempt to assign dates to the different events alluded to in the first six weeks. But at the latter end of the sixth week an event is recorded, the precise date of which can be ascertained.

A Book of the Revolutions of the Luminaries

Abraham 3:4	Enoch LXXI. SECT. XIII
And the Lord said unto me, by the Urim and Thummim, that Kolob was after the manner of the Lord, according to its times and seasons in *the revolutions thereof; that one revolution was a day unto the Lord,* after his manner of reckoning, it being one thousand years according to the time appointed unto that whereon thou standest. *This is the reckoning of the Lord's time, according to the reckoning of Kolob.*	1. *The book of the revolutions of the luminaries of heaven,* according to their respective classes, their respective powers, their respective periods, their respective names, the places where they commence their progress, and their respective months, which Uriel, the holy angel who was with me, explained to me; he who conducts them. The whole account of them, according to every year of the world for ever, until a new work shall be effected, which will be eternal.

Inferior and Superior Luminaries of the Night and Day

Abraham 3:5	Enoch LXXII. SECT. XIV.
And the Lord said unto me: The planet which is *the lesser light, lesser than that which is to rule the day,* even the night, is above or greater	1. After this law I beheld another law of *an inferior luminary, the name of which is the moon,* and the orb of which is as the orb of heaven.

Chapter Eleven. Mormon Cosmology

than that upon which thou standest in point of reckoning, for it moveth in order more slow; this is in order because it standeth above the earth upon which thou standest, therefore the reckoning of its time is not so many as to its number of days, and of months, and of years.

6. And the Lord said unto me: Now, Abraham, these two facts exist, behold thine eyes see it; *it is given unto thee to know the times of reckoning*, and the set time, yea, the set time of the earth upon which thou standest, *and the set time of the greater light which is set to rule the day, and the set time of the lesser light which is set to rule the night.*

7. Now the set time of the lesser light is a longer time as to its reckoning than the reckoning of the time of the earth upon which thou standest.

8. *And where these two facts exist, there shall be another fact above them, that is, there shall be another planet whose reckoning of time shall be longer still;*

9. And thus there shall be the reckoning of the time of one planet above another, until thou come nigh unto Kolob, which Kolob is after the reckoning of the Lord's time; which Kolob is set nigh unto the throne of God, to govern all those planets which belong to the same order as that upon which thou standest.

2. Its chariot, which it secretly ascends, the wind blows; and light is given to it by measure.

LXII. SECT. XIV

3. Every month at its exit and entrance it becomes changed; and *its periods are as the periods of the sun. And when in like manner its light is to exist,* its light is a seventh portion from the light of the sun.

4. Thus it rises, and at its commencement towards the east goes forth for thirty days.

5. At that time it appears, and becomes to you the beginning of the month. Thirty days it is with the sun in the gate from which the sun goes forth.

....

12. When the sun rises in heaven, it goes forth through this fourth gate thirty days, and by the fourth gate in the west of heaven on a level with it descends.

13. During that period the day is lengthened from the day, and the night curtailed from the night for thirty days. And then the day is longer by two parts than the night.

It is here, too, in Joseph's Book of Abraham, that we are introduced to *a council of Gods,* even an assembly of great ones—a puzzling part of Joseph Smith's developing theology and an example of his weaving metaphorical bases from revealed scripture into standard works to offer a foundational basis for his doctrine.

Chapter Twelve

Gods of Our Own Worlds

"As man is, God once was; as God is, man may become."
—Lorenzo Snow[1]

"Here is the question that will, peradventure, from this time henceforth occupy your attention."
—Joseph Smith[2]

Consoling a crowd of mourning saints at a funeral service for Brother King Follett in Nauvoo, Illinois, in April 1844, Joseph Smith publicly introduced his evolving understanding of a peculiar piece of Mormon theology: the idea of a *plurality* of Gods, each of which reigns over innumerable other inhabited worlds throughout our physical universe. Recorded in what is known as Joseph's "King Follett Discourse," Joseph opened his instruction to his congregation where he often began—in the very beginning:

> In the first place, I wish to go back to the beginning—to the morn of creation. There is the starting point for us to look to, in order to understand and be fully acquainted with the mind, purposes and decrees of the Great Eloheim, who sits in yonder heavens as he did at the creation of this world. It is necessary for us to have an understanding of God himself in the beginning.

All of Joseph's translation projects (i.e., the Book of Mormon, Book of Moses and Book of Abraham) include their own expansions of the biblical creation story with Adam and Eve. Each of them differs in developing theology, as Joseph's personal understandings and theologies evolved over time. This ubiquitous creation story line invokes the potential to reset, start anew and create one's own trajectory. It was Joseph's way of teaching others to recognize the divine within, by giving them a starting point in the incomprehensible context of the eternities.

Joseph's first translation project following the Book of Mormon

Chapter Twelve. Gods of Our Own Worlds

was the Bible, starting with the Book of Moses. Moses includes an expanded version of creation mirroring the Genesis story, wherein we find only *one* God who created the cosmos and the earth:

> And the earth was without form, and void; and I caused darkness to come upon the face of the deep; and my Spirit moved upon the face of the water; for I am God. *And I, God, said:* Let there be light; and there was light.[3]

This monotheistic creation story later changes when weaved into Joseph's last translation project, the Book of Abraham. Here, we are introduced to a plurality of Gods involved, not in creating, but in organizing and forming the Earth:

> And then the Lord said: *Let us go down.* And they went down at the beginning, and they, *that is the Gods,* organized and formed the heavens and the earth.
> And the earth, after it was formed, was empty and desolate, because they had not formed anything but the earth; and darkness reigned upon the face of the deep, and *the Spirit of the Gods* was brooding upon the face of the waters.
> *And they (the Gods) said*: Let there be light; and there was light.[4]

Following the creative periods mirroring those in Genesis, the Gods in Abraham rested on the seventh:

> And the Gods concluded upon the seventh time, because that on the seventh time they would rest from all their works which they *(the Gods) counseled among themselves* to form; and sanctified it. And thus were their decisions at the time that they counseled among themselves to form the heavens and the earth.
> And the Gods came down and formed these the generations of the heavens and of the earth, when they were formed in the day that the Gods formed the earth and the heavens.[5]

This marked a change of doctrine commensurate with the teachings of the temple endowment and priesthood ordinances revealed to Joseph in Nauvoo. Within this doctrine of a plurality of Gods, Joseph taught that each of us has the potential for eternal exaltation, becoming Gods of our own earthlike worlds, which are our footstools. Notice also the change from "creating" the world (in Moses) to "organizing" and forming existing matter (Abraham). This reflects Joseph's continued education in an attempt to understand the laws of physics that govern heavenly motions and the perpetual existence of all matter, light and energy—ideas trending more toward natural sciences and Newtonian laws of thermodynamics than metaphysics or magic. Joseph wanted to understand what it meant to be fully crowned with eternal salvation and glory in the afterlife, and how this promise extends to each of God's children. He wanted to understand what ultimate *energy* it is that gives us pause to think. If *everything* is eternal and infinite, what then does it mean to become exalted, and be "even as your Father which is in heaven is" (Matt. 5:48)?

In his article "Joseph Smith's Changing Doctrine of Deity," Luke P. Wilson explains this curious realm of Joseph's doctrine where theology and astrobiology meet:

> Directly related to the doctrine of the plurality of Gods is Joseph's teaching that Heavenly Father is an exalted man who Himself has a Father, and whose Father has a Father, ad infinitum. ... According to Joseph Smith, the Book of Abraham teaches that our Heavenly Father is but one link in this infinite ancestral chain of Gods stretching back through eternity; He is thus only one of innumerable Gods. This, in turn, leads to the Mormon Church's teaching that human beings are the literal offspring of Heavenly Father and one of His celestial wives, and that we are thus "Gods in embryo" who have the potential to achieve exaltation to divine status.[6]

What was Joseph's source for a plurality of Gods? Joseph disclosed his sources in another sermon on the plurality of gods offered just months after his King Follett discourse:

> I want to reason a little on this subject. I learned it by translating the papyrus which is now in my house. I learned a testimony concerning Abraham, and he reasoned concerning the God of heaven. "In order to do that," said he, "suppose we have two facts: that supposes another fact may exist—two men on the earth, one wiser than the other, would logically show that another who is wiser than the wisest may exist. *Intelligences exist one above another*, so that there is no end to them."[7]

"The holy, *holy*, Lord of spirits fills the whole world of spirits"

(Enoch XXXIX:11)

In that same June 16, 1844, "Sermon on the Plurality of Gods" recorded in a meeting in the grove, east of the Nauvoo Temple, Joseph tipped his hand at the source for this doctrine. He opened his sermon reading from the apocalyptic revelator St. John's Book of Revelation 1:6,

> And hath made us kings and priests unto God and his Father; to him be glory and dominion for ever and ever.

Chapter Twelve. Gods of Our Own Worlds

As Joseph continued his teaching, he said he learned about the plurality of Gods during his Abraham translation project. He said, "Wanting to reason a little more on this subject" of plural Gods, "I learned it by translating the papyrus which is now in my house."[8] The papyrus he referred to were the Egyptian funerary scrolls that Joseph believed to contain the millennia-old manuscript writings of the ancient Hebrew father Abraham. Joseph had convinced the beleaguered saints to pool their funds to purchase the funerary scrolls and some mummies from a traveling salesman making his way through town with the last of a truckload of pilfered antiquities in the wake of the Napoleonic conquests.

Within this sermon, therefore, we have the unique scenario where Joseph expressly tells us what specific biblical source he was reading and referring to for inspiration in his Abraham project. Joseph was reading the Book of Revelation, in the New Testament. This is no surprise, as the Book of Revelation is the acknowledged biblical source the LDS Church offers for corresponding scriptural doctrine revealed in Abraham (i.e., the preexistence, the war in heaven and the plurality of Gods). Let's not forget, as discussed in the prior chapter, St. John the Revelator had the written prophecies of Enoch unrolled before him, and was borrowing from his favorite parts in his own evangelical piracy and version of the war-in-heaven story. The author of the Book of Revelation was taking what he respected as a piece of ancient Jewish literature from his scrolls of old Enoch to create a version of epic Christian-era literature (so epic, it almost didn't make it into the canon). It was included among our 27 books in the New Testament, despite many other and much more historically interesting and forgotten contemporary gospels and other proto-Christian literary works (i.e., gnostic) being more enlightening and worthy of serious scripture study.

A reader familiar with 1 Enoch might say that St. John slavishly borrowed with some fantastic artistic license. Specific comparisons of direct borrowing from Enoch incorporated into Revelation are offered in a prior chapter, and Enochic writings as John's source is unquestionable. Whether Joseph Smith was borrowing directly from 1 Enoch or not, the prophecies of old Enoch found influence in his continued revelations and evolving understanding of the nature of God.

Yet another example of echo of 1 Enoch that we find paralleled in St. John's Revelation is in that same verse Joseph Smith opened his "Sermon on the Plurality of Gods" with:

Joseph Smith and the Book of Enoch

Revelation 1:6	Enoch LXI:1–3
And hath made us *kings* and priests unto God and his Father; to him be glory and dominion *for ever and ever*.	Thus the Lord commanded the kings, the princes, the exalted, and those who dwell on earth, ... The Lord of spirits sat upon the throne of his glory.

Joseph Smith's developing theology of multiple gods, and individual potential to be enthroned as Gods, corresponds with his evolving expressions of cosmology that we find in the Book of Abraham. Joseph's Abraham translation incorporated the unique doctrines of preexistence and godliness into expressions of cosmology. As discussed in previous chapters, we find influences of 1 Enoch, both in themes and specific word use, in Joseph's Book of Abraham.

Consider these additional parallels between Abraham's metaphoric and cosmic explanations of those heavenly great ones, as revealed through Joseph Smith, and correspondingly similar passages found in 1 Enoch:

Abraham 3	Enoch XLIIL
2. And I saw the stars, that they were very great, and that *one of them was nearest unto the throne of God*; and *there were many great ones* which were near unto it; 3. And the Lord said unto me: *These* are *the governing ones; and the name of the great one is Kolob*, because it is near unto me, for I am the Lord thy God: I have set this one to govern all those which belong to the same order as that upon which thou standest. [...] 21. I dwell in the midst of them all; *I now, therefore, have come down unto thee to declare unto thee the works which my hands have made*, wherein my wisdom excelleth them all, for *I rule in the heavens above, and in the earth beneath*, in all wisdom and prudence, over all the intelligences thine eyes have seen	1. *I beheld another splendor, and the stars of heaven. I observed that he called them all by their respective names*, and that they heard. **Enoch XXXIX:1, 10–12** In those days shall *the elect and holy race descend from the upper heavens....* That place long did my eyes contemplate. I blessed and said; Blessed be He, blessed from the beginning for ever. *In the beginning, before the world was created, and without end is his knowledge.* *What is this world?* Of every existing generation those shall bless thee who do not sleep in the dust, but stand before thy glory, blessing, glorifying, exalting thee, and saying; *The holy, holy, Lord of spirits* fills the whole world of spirits. There *my eyes beheld all who,*

Chapter Twelve. Gods of Our Own Worlds

from the beginning; *I came down in the beginning in the midst of all the intelligences thou hast seen.*

22. Now the Lord had shown unto me, Abraham, *the intelligences* that were organized before the world was; *and among all these there were many of the noble and great ones*;

23. And God saw these souls that they were good, and *he stood in the midst of them*, and he said: *These I will make my rulers*; for he stood among those that were spirits, and he saw that they were good; and he said unto me: Abraham, thou art one of them; thou wast chosen before thou wast born.

without sleeping, stand before him and bless him, saying; Blessed be thou, and blessed be the name of God for ever and for ever.

Enoch LXIV. SECT. XI.

11. He, the holy One, will establish thy name *in the midst of the saints*, and will preserve thee from those who dwell upon the earth. He will establish thy seed in righteousness, with dominion and great glory; and *from thy seed shall spring forth righteous and holy men without number for ever.*

Counsels of Gods in the Heavens

In his "King Follett Discourse" of April 7, 1844, Joseph more formally pronounced his doctrine regarding the council in heaven:

> I will go back to the beginning before the world was, to show what kind of being God is. What sort of a being was God in the beginning? ... God himself was once as we are now, and is an exalted man, and sits enthroned in yonder heavens! That is the great secret. If the veil were rent today, and the great God who holds this world in its orbit, and who upholds all worlds and all things by his power, was to make himself visible,—I say, if you were to see him today, you would see him like a man in form—like yourselves in all the person, image, and very form as a man;....
>
> ... Thus the head God brought forth the Gods in the grand council. I will transpose and simplify it in the English language. ... The head God called together the Gods and sat in grand council to bring forth the world. The grand councilors sat at the head in yonder heavens and contemplated the creation of the worlds which were created at the time.
>
> ... In the beginning, the head of the Gods called a council of the Gods; and they came together and concocted a plan to create the world and people it. When we begin to learn this way, we begin to learn the only true God, and what kind of a being we have got to worship. Having a knowledge of God, we begin to know how to approach him, and how to ask so as to receive an answer. When we understand the character of God, and how to come to him, he begins to unfold the heavens to us, and to tell us all about it.[9]

Joseph Smith and the Book of Enoch

The source for Joseph's developing doctrine regarding a plurality of Gods and a council in heaven remains a question. Consider, however, the similar themes and language from the Book of Enoch:

> **Enoch IX:3**
> Then they said to their Lord, the King; Thou art Lord of lords, God of gods. King of kings. The throne of thy glory is for ever and ever, and for ever and ever is thy name sanctified and glorified.
>
> **Enoch XV:5, 7–8**
> But you from the beginning were made spiritual, possessing a life which is eternal, and not subject to death for ever ... being spiritual, your dwelling is in heaven.
> ... because they were created from above; *from the holy Watchers was their beginning and primary foundation*. Evil spirits shall they be upon earth, and the spirits of the wicked shall they be called. The habitation of the spirits of heaven shall be in heaven; but upon earth shall be the habitation of terrestrial spirits, who are born on earth.
>
> **Enoch XXXIX:10–12**
> In the beginning, before the world was created, and without end is his knowledge. ... What is this world? Of every existing generation those shall bless thee who do not sleep in the dust, but stand before thy glory, blessing, glorifying, exalting thee, and saying; *The holy, holy, Lord of spirits* fills the whole world of spirits.

Infinite Intelligences

> And in those days shall the Elect one sit upon his throne, while every secret of intellectual wisdom shall proceed from his mouth; for the Lord of spirits has gifted and glorified him. ... Their countenance shall be bright with joy; for in those days shall the Elect one be exalted. The earth shall rejoice; the righteous shall inhabit it, and the elect possess it (Enoch L:3 & 5).

"The mind or the intelligence which man possesses is co-equal with God himself," Joseph taught the mourners at Brother Follett's funeral just months before he was martyred.[10] The subject of intelligences is found in the Book of Abraham, where the prophet is shown "intelligences that were organized before the world was" in Abraham 3:22, "and among all these there were many of the noble and great ones." Verse 23 continues: "And God saw these souls that they were good, and he stood in the midst of them, and he said: These I will make my rulers."

Chapter Twelve. Gods of Our Own Worlds

LDS president Joseph Fielding Smith taught,

> Some of our writers have endeavored to explain what an intelligence is, but to do so is futile, for we have never been given any insight into this matter beyond what the Lord has fragmentarily revealed. We know, however, that there is something called intelligence which always existed. It is the real eternal part of man, which was not created or made. This intelligence combined with the spirit constitutes a spiritual identity or individual.[11]

What philosophers have referred to as the innermost "psyche," "essence of being," "pneuma," "anima," "ego," "id" and "spirit"—the soul—Joseph identified as "intelligence." The idea of intelligences as eternal personages was a latter development in Joseph's theology. In earlier revelations, however, Joseph taught, "Man was also in the beginning with God. Intelligence, or the light of truth, was not created or made, neither indeed can be" (D&C 93:29, revealed in 1833). It is also recorded in the *History of the Church*: "The spirit of man is not a created being; it existed from eternity, and will exist to eternity. Anything created cannot be eternal."[12] Joseph's doctrine equated light and knowledge with existence.

Light of the World

> Before the sun and the signs were created, before the stars of heaven were formed, his name was invoked in the presence of the Lord of spirits. A support shall he be for the righteous and the holy to lean upon, without falling; and *he shall be the light of nations* [Enoch XLVIII:3].
>
> I beheld another splendor, and *the stars of heaven*. I observed that *he called them all by their respective names*, and that they heard. In a righteous balance I saw that he weighed out with their light the amplitude of their places, and the day of their appearance and their conversion. *Splendor produced splendor; and their conversion was into the number of the angels*, and of the faithful [Enoch XLIIL:1].
>
> The saints shall exist in the light of the sun, and the elect in the light of everlasting life, the days of whose life shall never terminate; nor shall the days of the saints be numbered, who seek for light [Enoch LVL. SECT. IX:3].

In May 1833, Joseph Smith revealed what is now recorded in D&C 93, a revelation that teaches that light is a constituent part of glory. In verses 1–2, Joseph began this discourse on light:

Joseph Smith and the Book of Enoch

> Verily, thus saith the Lord: It shall come to pass that every soul ... shall see my face and know that I am; And that I am the true light that lighteth every man that cometh into the world.

Does this sound familiar? Joseph brilliantly demonstrates his understanding of the light motif as it was expressly used by biblical authors in both the New Testament and the Hebrew Bible. To the ancient Hebrews, the children of Israel, God's magnificence and power has always been displayed through *light*. The New Testament authors brought his light into the world, in the flesh. Joseph Smith's D&C 93 opens with familiar "I am" statements that we find throughout the Gospel of John. The author of John's Gospel refers to Jesus using the "I am" statement seven times, including:

> I am the bread of life; whoever comes to me shall not hunger [John 6:35].
>
> I am the true vine, and my Father is the vinedresser [John 15:1].
>
> I am the door. If anyone enters by me, he will be saved and will go in and out and find pasture [John 10:9].
>
> I am the good shepherd. The good shepherd lays down his life for the sheep [John 10:11].
>
> I am the resurrection and the life. Whoever believes in me, though he die, yet shall he live [John 11:25].
>
> I am the way, and the truth, and the life. No one comes to the Father except through me [John 14:6].
>
> I am the light of the world. Whoever follows me will not walk in darkness, but will have the light of life [John 8:12].

John included an additional "I am" reference to Jesus's identity in John 8:58, when Jesus answered his accusers (the religious leaders), saying, "Truly, truly, I say to you, before Abraham was, *I am.*" John is clearly alluding to the ancient Hebrew scripture found in Exodus 3:14: "And God said to Moses, I AM THAT I AM: and he said, Thus shalt thou say unto the children of Israel, I AM has sent me unto you." In Judaism, for the Jews living in Jesus's time, they knew that "I am" was the name of God.

John's Gospel and the references to Jesus as "I am" (or God) is obviously very allegorical and laden with symbolism. It is borrowed and used intentionally. In John's Gospel, what Christ represented to be, he then performed miracles proving as much. Jesus was the bread of life, and he proved it by feeding the multitudes. He was the true vine, so he turned water into wine, symbolically demonstrating that even the simplest can be deemed sacramental. Jesus is the way and the life, and he

Chapter Twelve. Gods of Our Own Worlds

proved it by resurrecting the dead. Jesus is the light of the world, so he healed the blind to see.

John's Gospel is full of allusions to light, right from the start, in Chapter 1:1–4:

> In the beginning was the Word, the Word was with God, and the Word was God. ... all things were made by him, and without him was not anything made that was made.
> In him was life, and *the life was the light of man*.

John was not authoring a fourth Gospel. He was re-writing history, starting over again "in the beginning." This early Christian writer understood his readers would be familiar with the other ancient Jewish writings that tell of our beginnings. Genesis 1:1: "In the beginning God created the heaven and the earth." And in verse 3: "And God said, *Let there be light*, and there was light."

God spoke, and there was light. What *words* did he first speak? As John wrote, "In the beginning the Word was with God, and the Word was God." God's word (the good news) is light—*enlightenment*. Notwithstanding the magical and mystical side of Joseph Smith, he lived in the "Age of Enlightenment," where intelligence and reasoning were likened to measurable light. He knew this, and taught, as he revealed in D&C 88:67,

> And if your eye be single to my glory, your whole bodies shall be filled with light, and there shall be no darkness in you; and that body which is filled with light comprehendeth all things.

In his last discourse, Joseph asked those who were there listening, *what kind of being is God?*

> I want to ask this congregation, every man, woman and child, to answer the question in their own heart, what kind of a being God is? Ask yourselves; turn your thought into your hearts, and say if any of you have seen, heard, or communed with him. This is a question that may occupy your attention for a long time. I again repeat the question—What kind of a being is God? Does any man or woman know? Have any of you seen him, heard him, or communed with him? Here is the question that will, peradventure, from this time henceforth occupy your attention.

In D&C 93, Joseph Smith taught that God's glory is intelligence. In verse 33, he revealed, "For man is spirit. The elements are eternal, and spirit and element, inseparably connected, receive a fulness of joy." In D&C 131:7, he taught, "There is no such thing as immaterial matter. All spirit is matter." These are teachings of an eternal material world, not a metaphysical one. Going back to D&C 93:35, Joseph reminds us, "The elements are the tabernacle of God; yea, man is the tabernacle of God, even temples."

These simple truths echo those taught in the Bible, circling back to our beginnings, in Genesis 2:7, "And the Lord God formed man of the dust of the ground, and breathed into his nostrils the breath of life; and man became a living soul." And in Matthew 5:13, we're reminded that we "are the salt of the earth," and even that at times we "have lost [our] savour," and wonder "wherewith shall it be salted?" But while we may be just shuffling off this mortal coil, even to be cast out and trodden under the foot of men, let's not also forget, "Ye are the light of the world," so "Let *your light* so shine before men, that they may see your good works" (Matt. 5:16).

Contrary to his honorable but misguided Zionistic visions, Joseph Smith's fundamental teachings have nothing to do with the measure of what can be amassed. God's glory is not how much matter you are; rather, God's glory shines through truth and enlightenment, or as Joseph revealed, "The glory of God is intelligence, or, in other words, light and truth" (D&C 93:36).

In 1 Enoch, the prophet records "the third parable concerning the saints and the elect."[13] Compare these prophecies of old Enoch with those revealed through Joseph Smith:

Enoch LVL. SECT. IX: 3	D&C 50:24
The saints shall exist in the light of the sun, and the elect in the light of everlasting life, the days of whose life shall never terminate; nor shall the days of the saints be numbered, who seek for light.	That which is of God is light; and he that receiveth light, and continueth in God, receiveth more light; and that light groweth brighter and brighter until the perfect day.

And echoing Joseph's teaching of our eternal potential, the ever-living prophet Enoch wrote,

> I will bring them into the splendid light of those who love my holy name; *and I will place each of them on a throne of glory, of glory peculiarly his own.*[14]

Chapter Notes

Preface

1. Robert H. Charles, trans., *Apocrypha and Pseudepigrapha of the Old Testament* (Oxford: Clarendon Press, 1913).
2. *Times and Seasons*, February 1, 1843, vol. 482–85.
3. See Cheryl L. Bruno, "Congruence and Concatenation in Jewish Mystical Literature, American Freemasonry, and Mormon Enoch Writings," *Journal of Religion & Society* 16 (2014): 1–19. In her article, Ms. Bruno describes the discovery of this long-lost book of scripture: "After arriving in that country, Bruce wrote that he spent much of his time within the libraries of dilapidated monasteries, fingering through dusty volumes of neglected religious works." Her words, and her description of the Book of Enoch as having been buried in time, found covered and coming out the dust and speaking with a familiar sound and spirit as other revered scripture, are worth repeating. Whether any parallel was intended or not, her words sparked inspiration. (*See also* Isaiah 26:4: "thy speech shall be low out of the dust, and thy voice shall be, as of one that hath a familiar spirit ... and they speech shall whisper out of the dust.")

Introduction

1. Joseph Smith, letter to W.W. Phelps dated November 27, 1832 (www.josephsmithpapers.org).
2. For the purposes of this book, all references to the Bible, including the Old and New Testaments, are to the King James Version (KJV), unless another version is specifically referenced (i.e., the Geneva Bible or Joseph Smith's *Inspired Version*).
3. R. Grant Athay, "Worlds Without Number: The Astronomy of Enoch, Abraham, and Moses," *BYU Studies Quarterly* 8, no. 3 (Spring 1968).
4. Michael Graziano, *Consciousness and the Social Brain* (New York: Oxford University Press, 2013). The attention schema theory (AST) of consciousness is an evolutionary theory of consciousness, proposing that our brains construct subjective awareness as a schematic model of the process of attention.
5. James Gleick, *The Information: A History, a Theory, a Flood* (New York: Knopf Doubleday, 2011), 50.
6. Richard N. Soulen and R. Kendall Soulen, *Handbook of Biblical Criticism*, 3rd ed. (Louisville, KY: Westminster John Knox Press, 2001), 78.
7. "Literary Motifs," Bible.org (https://bible.org/seriespage/2-literary-motifs), *citing* Ross Murfin and Supryia M. Ray, *The Bedford Glossary of Critical and Literary Terms* (Boston: Bedford, 1997), 224.
8. Colby Townsend, "Translation as Expansion: The Method of Joseph Smith's Revision of Genesis in Moses 1 and 7," *Journal of Mormon History* 46, no. 4 (October 2020): 45–59; *and see* Colby Townsend, "Appropriation and Adaption of J Material in the Book of Mormon" (undergraduate thesis, University of Utah, 2016), 3–75.
9. Richard Hays, *Echoes of Scripture in the Letters of Paul* (New Haven: Yale University Press, 1989).
10. Herbert Spencer, *The Principles of Sociology*, vol. 1 (1877), 421.

Notes—Introduction

11. John W. Welch, "Chiasm, Chiasmus: I. Ancient Near and Hebrew Bible/Old Testament," in the *Encyclopedia of the Bible and Its Reception*, ed. Hans-Josef Klauck (Berlin: de Gruyter, 2012), 5:78.

12. This is how it is transcribed in the history books by those who were watching. For Neil's sake, through his Wapakoneta, Ohio, accent, he said: "That's one small step for a man, one giant leap for mankind." The words were *his*, after all, that he prepared for that epic moment when he did it.

13. See John W. Welch, "What Does Chiasmus in the Book of Mormon Prove?" in *Book of Mormon Authorship Revisited: The Evidence for Ancient Origins*, ed. Noel B. Reynolds (Provo: FARMS, 1997).

14. Welch, "Chiasm, Chiasmus," 78.

15. Shakespeare, *Twelfth Night*, Act 1, Scene 1.

16. Ecclesiastes 8:15 and Isaiah 11:13.

17. Robert F. Smith "Evaluating the Sources of 2 Nephi 1:13–15: Shakespeare and the Book of Mormon," *Journal of Book of Mormon Studies* 22, no. 2 (2013): 99.

18. Douglas F. Salmon, "Parallelomania and the Study of Latter-day Scripture: Confirmation, Coincidence, or the Collective Unconscious?" *Dialogue: A Journal of Mormon Thought* 33, no. 2 (Summer 2000): 129.

19. Smith, "Evaluating the Sources of 2 Nephi 1:13–15," 99.

20. Salmon, "Parallelomania," 135; *see also* Kent P. Jackson, review of *Old Testament and Related Studies*, by Hugh Nibley, *BYU Studies* 28, no. 4 (Fall 1988): 115–16.

21. Hugh Nibley, *Enoch the Prophet*, vol. 2 of *The Collected Works of Hugh Nibley* (Provo: Deseret Book and Foundation for Ancient Research and Mormon Studies, 1986).

22. Salmon, "Parallelomania," 131. The term "parallelomania" has been used to describe the overuse or improper use of parallels in the exposition of a text. As the Jewish scholar of the New Testament Samuel Sandmel explains, parallelomania is "that extravagance among scholars which first overdoes the supposed similarity in passages and then proceeds to describe source and derivation as if implying connection flowing in an inevitable or predetermined direction" ("Parallelomania," *Journal of Biblical Literature 31* (1962): 1; reprinted in Samuel Sandmel, *Two Living Traditions: Essays on Religion and the Bible* (Detroit: Wayne State University Press, 1972), 291–304.

23. Richard Lyman Bushman, *Joseph Smith: Rough Stone Rolling* (New York: Alfred A. Knopf, 2005), 138.

24. Jeffrey M. Bradshaw and Ryan Dahle, "Could Joseph Smith Have Drawn on Ancient Manuscripts When He Translated the Story of Enoch?: Recent Updates on a Persistent Question," *Interpreter: A Journal of Latter-day Saint Faith and Scholarship* 33 (2019): 305–74.

25. Jed L. Woodworth, "Extra-Biblical Enoch Texts in Early American Culture," in *Archive of Restoration Culture: Summer Fellows' Papers 1997–1999*, ed. Richard Lyman Bushman (Provo: Joseph Fielding Smith Institute for Latter-day Saint History, 2000), 190–92.

26. This book limits literary comparisons to Richard Laurence's *Book of Enoch*, published in 1821; however, more than 80 sources of extracts or summaries of Enochic literature were published in English before Laurence's 1821 publication. See Colby Townsend, "Revisiting Joseph Smith and the Availability of the Book of Enoch," *Dialogue: A Journal of Mormon Thought* 53, no. 3 (Fall 2020): 41–71.

27. Bushman, *Joseph Smith: Rough Stone Rolling*, 132.

28. Official LDS history records include a number of testimonies and accounts describing the translation process, most of them expressly making a point to disclaim Joseph having any other literature available to him. We can't discount the fact that these same persons were in Joseph's most intimate and private circles of confidentiality and aligned with his perhaps honorable, but often misguided pursuits. Taking them for their word may end the inquiry; yet, the question still remains. It's a delicate balance between questions of credibility and incredible claims.

Notes—Chapter One

29. Thomas A. Wayment, "Joseph Smith, Adam Clarke, and the Making of a Bible Revision," *Journal of Mormon History* 46, no. 3 (July 2020):1–22; *see also* Townsend, "Sources: Integrating Textual Criticism in the Study of Early Mormon Texts and History," 56; and Colby, *Translation as Expansion*, pp. 45–59.
30. Bushman, *Joseph Smith: Rough Stone Rolling*, 58.
31. Bart D. Ehrman, *Jesus Apocalyptic Prophet of the New Millennium* (New York: Oxford University Press, 1999), 77.
32. D. Michael Quinn, *Early Mormonism and the Magic World View* (Salt Lake City: Signature, 1998), 193.
33. Thomas A. Wayment, "Joseph Smith's Developing Relationship with the Apocrypha," in *Approaching Antiquity: Joseph Smith and the Ancient World*, ed. Lincoln H. Blumell, Matthew J. Grey, and Andrew H. Hedges (Provo: Religious Studies Center; Salt Lake City: Deseret Book, 2015), 331–55.
34. Colby Townsend, "Rewriting Eden with the Book of Mormon: Joseph Smith and the Reception of Genesis 1–6 in Early America" (MA thesis, Utah State University, 2019), 78.
35. Salmon, "Parallelomania," 130.

Chapter One

1. Richard Lyman Bushman, *Joseph Smith: Rough Stone Rolling* (New York: Alfred A. Knopf, 2005), 58.
2. Ibid.
3. Ibid., 41–42.
4. Mark E. Peterson, "It Was a Miracle!" *Ensign* (October 1977).
5. Harold Bloom, *The American Religion: The Emergence of the Post-Christian Nation* (New York: Simon & Schuster, 1992), 96–97.
6. Robert F. Smith, "Evaluating the Sources of 2 Nephi 1:13–15: Shakespeare and the Book of Mormon," *Journal of Book of Mormon Studies* 22, no. 2 (2013).
7. Joseph Smith, Jr., *History of the Church of Jesus Christ of Latter-day Saints*, ed. B. H. Roberts, 2d ed., 7 vols. (Salt Lake City: Deseret Book, 1971), 1:43–45 (hereafter cited as *History of the Church*).
8. Joseph Smith, letter to W. W. Phelps, November 27, 1832 (www.josephsmithpapers.org).
9. Nick Newman, *Deseret News*, January 26, 2010 (www.deseret.com/2010/1/26/20374629/scribes-recorded-prophet-s-crooked-broken-language).
10. Joseph Smith, *History*, 1:11–12.
11. Lucy Mack Smith, *Lucy's Book: A Critical Edition of Lucy Mack Smith's Family Memoir*, ed. Lavina Fielding Anderson (Salt Lake City: Signature, 2001), 344.
12. Ibid.
13. Ibid., 357; *and see* Lucy Mack Smith, *Biographical Sketches of Joseph Smith the Prophet, and His Progenitors for Many Generations* (1853), 90.
14. Smith, *Biographical Sketches*, 59–60.
15. www.churchofjesuschrist.org/study/history/topics/hyrum-smith?lang=eng.
16. Jeffrey S. O'Driscoll, *Hyrum Smith: A Life of Integrity* (Salt Lake City: Deseret Book, 2003).
17. Richard K. Behrens, "Dreams, Visions, and Visitations: The Genesis of Mormonism," *The John Whitmer Historical Association Journal* 27 (2007): 170–83.
18. Bushman, *John Smith: Rough Stone Rolling*, 14, 15, 21.
19. Richard K. Behrens, "Dartmouth Arminianism and Its Impact on Hyrum Smith and the Smith Family," *John Whitmer Historical Association Journal* 26 (2006): 172–77.
20. David Persuitte, *Joseph Smith and the Origins of the Book of Mormon* (Jefferson, NC: McFarland, 1985).
21. Behrens, "Dartmouth Arminianism," 171.
22. Ibid., 179.
23. Kent P. Jackson, "Joseph Smith's Cooperstown Bible: The Historical Context of the Bible Used in the Joseph Smith Translation," *BYU Studies Quarterly* 40, no. 1(2001): 56–57.
24. Ibid.
25. Smith, *History of the Church*, 6:74.
26. *Deseret News*, July 30, 1884, 435.
27. *Deseret News*, January 21, 1885, 2.
28. Colby Townsend, "Revisiting Joseph Smith and the Availability of the

Book of Enoch," *Dialogue: A Journal of Mormon Thought* 53, no. 3 (Fall 2020): 41–71.

Chapter Two

1. Harold Bloom, *The American Religion* (New York: Simon & Schuster, 1992), 99.
2. Genesis 4:17.
3. Genesis 5:19.
4. www.biblegateway.com/resources/all-men-bible/Enos-Enosh.
5. J.J. Steward, ed., *Cambridge Bible for Schools and Colleges* (Cambridge: Cambridge University Press, 1904).
6. *Times and Seasons* 1, no. 8 (June 1840), 127.
7. For additional discussion regarding Joseph Smith's reliance on Adam Clark's biblical commentary in his translation projects, *see* Thomas A. Wayment, "Joseph Smith, Adam Clarke, and the Making of a Bible Revision," *Journal of Mormon History* 46, no. 3 (July 2020): 1–22; *see also* Thomas A. Wayment and Haley Wilson-Lemmon, "A Recovered Resource: The Use of Adam Clarke's Bible Commentary in Joseph Smith's Bible Translation," in *Producing Ancient Scripture: Joseph Smith's Translation Projects in the Development of Mormon Christianity*, ed. Michael Hubbard MacKay, Mark Ashurst-McGee, and Brian M. Hauglid (Salt Lake City: University of Utah Press, 2020).
8. *Book of Jasher Referred to in Joshua and Second Samuel. Faithfully Translated (1840) from the Original Hebrew into English* (Salt Lake City: J.H. Parry & Co., 1887).
9. Edward J. Brandt, "The Book of Jasher and the Latter-day Saints," in *Apocryphal Writings and the Latter-day Saints*, ed. C. Wilfred Griggs (Provo: Religious Studies Center, Brigham Young University, 1986), 297–318.
10. Ibid.
11. Quotations from George H. Schodde, *Book of Jubilees Translated from the Ethiopic* (Oberlin, OH: E.J. Goodrich, 1888).
12. Bruce R. McConkie, *Mormon Doctrine* (Salt Lake City: Deseret Book Co., 1958), 726–27.

Chapter Three

1. Professor Black made the comment to BYU professor Hugh W. Nibley following Professor Black's lectures "The Enoch Legend and the Dead Sea Scrolls" and "The Parables of Enoch" over a two-day period on BYU's campus by invitation on June 30 and July 1, 1977. See Hugh W. Nibley's *Teachings of the Pearl of Great Price*, 267–69. Professor Black also authored of *The Book of Enoch or 1 Enoch, Studia in Veteris Testamenti Pseudepigrapha* (Leiden: Brill, 1985).
2. Laurence's 1821 publication and all translations from that same Bodleian manuscript are considered 1 Enoch. Unless specifically referenced, all quotes in this book are from Laurence's 1821 edition, which is sometimes referred to simply as Enoch.
3. www.babel.hathitrust.org.
4. Laurence, "Preliminary Dissertation," *Book of Enoch* (1821), x–xi.
5. Laurence, "Preliminary Dissertation," xxii.
6. Ibid.
7. George W.E. Nickelsburg, "The Temple According to 1 Enoch," *BYU Studies Quarterly* 53, no. 1 (2014).
8. Laurence, "Preliminary Dissertation," x–xi.
9. Ibid., xxiii–iv.

Chapter Four

1. 863 F.2d 1061 (1988).
2. Thomas A. Wayment, "Joseph Smith's Developing Relationship with the Apocrypha," in *Approaching Antiquity: Joseph Smith and the Ancient World*, ed. Lincoln H. Blumell, Matthew J. Grey, and Andrew H. Hedges (Provo: Religious Studies Center; Salt Lake City: Deseret Book, 2015), 331–55.
3. E.g., Hugh W. Nibley, *Teachings of the Pearl of Great Price*, pp. 267–69; *and see* Jeffrey M. Bradshaw and Ryan Dahle, "Could Joseph Smith Have Drawn on Ancient Manuscripts When He Translated

the Story of Enoch?: Recent Updates on a Persistent Question," *Interpreter: A Journal of Latter-day Saint Faith and Scholarship* 33 (2019): 305–74.

4. Jeffrey M. Bradshaw, "The LDS Story of Enoch as the Culminating Episode of a Temple Text," *BYU Studies Quarterly* 53, no. 1 (2014).

5. Roger A. Stritmatter, *The Marginalia of Edward de Vere's Geneva Bible: Providential Discovery, Literary Reasoning, and Historical Consequence* (PhD diss., University of Massachusetts Amherst, 2001).

6. Bradshaw and Dahle, "Could Joseph Smith Have Drawn on Ancient Manuscripts When He Translated the Story of Enoch?": "Commonalities of equal or perhaps greater interest are also to be found in 2 *Enoch* and 3 *Enoch* ... as well as the Aramaic *Book of Giants*.... In addition, scattered passages in late Jewish and Islamic documents provide unique correspondences and sometimes corroborate earlier Enoch sources."

7. Bradshaw, "The LDS Story of Enoch as the Culminating Episode of a Temple Text," 1.

8. Ibid.

9. *See* Colby Townsend, "Revisiting Joseph Smith and the Availability of the Book of Enoch," *Dialogue: A Journal of Mormon Thought* 53, no. 3 (Fall 2020): 41–71.

10. The discovery of chiasmus in the Book of Mormon is said to have first occurred in Germany in August 1967. See John W. Welch, "Chiasmus in the Book of Mormon," *Brigham Young University Studies* 10, no. 1 (1969): 69–84.

11. Wayment, "Joseph Smith's Developing Relationship with the Apocrypha," in *Approaching Antiquity: Joseph Smith and the Ancient World*, ed. Lincoln H. Blumell, Matthew J. Grey, and Andrew H. Hedges (Provo: Religious Studies Center; Salt Lake City: Deseret Book, 2015), 332.

Chapter Five

1. *Novelty Textile Mills, Inc. v. Joan Fabrics Corp.*, 558 F.2d 1090, 1093 (2d Cir.1977).

2. Herbert Lockwood Willett, *The Popular and Critical Bible Encyclopedia and Scriptural Dictionary: Fully Defining and Explaining All Religious Terms, Including Biographical, Geographical, Historical, Archeological and Doctrinal Themes, Superbly Illustrated with Over 600 Maps and Engravings* (Chicago: Howard-Severance Company, 1910).

3. Kent P. Jackson, "Joseph Smith's Cooperstown Bible: The Historical Context of the Bible Used in the Joseph Smith Translation," *BYU Studies Quarterly* 40, no. 1 (2001).

4. Thomas A. Wayment, "Joseph Smith's Developing Relationship with the Apocrypha," in *Approaching Antiquity: Joseph Smith and the Ancient World*, ed. Lincoln H. Blumell, Matthew J. Grey, and Andrew H. Hedges (Provo: Religious Studies Center; Salt Lake City: Deseret Book, 2015), 331–55.

5. Salvatore Cirillo, *"Joseph Smith, Mormonism and Enochic Tradition"* (master's thesis, Durham University, 2010); D. Michael Quinn, *Early Mormonism and the Magic World View* (Salt Lake City: Signature, 1998); Colby Townsend, "Revisiting Joseph Smith and the Availability of the Book of Enoch," *Dialogue: A Journal of Mormon Thought* 53, no. 3 (Fall 2020): 41–71.

6. Wayment, "Joseph Smith's Developing Relationship with the Apocrypha," 337.

7. Ibid.; Terryl L. Givens and Matthew J. Grow, *Parley P. Pratt: The Apostle Paul of Mormonism* (New York: Oxford University Press, 2011).

8. *History of the Church* 1:131–33.

9. Terryl Givens, *The Prophecy of Enoch as Restoration Blueprint* (Logan: Utah State University Press, 2013), 3.

10. Ibid., 4.

Chapter Six

1. Jed L. Woodworth, "Extra-Biblical Enoch Texts in Early American Culture," in *Archive of Restoration Culture: Summer Fellows' Papers 1997–1999*, ed. Richard Lyman Bushman (Provo: Joseph

Fielding Smith Institute for Latter-day Saint History, 2000), 190–92.

2. *History, circa Summer 1832*, 2, The Joseph Smith Papers (josephsmithpapers.org).

3. Joseph Smith, Jr., "Letterbook 1, 1–3" (1832) (josephsmithpapers.org).

4. *History, circa June 1839–circa 1841 [Draft 2]*, 2, The Joseph Smith Papers.

Chapter Seven

1. Richard Lyman Bushman, *Joseph Smith: Rough Stone Rolling* (New York: Alfred A. Knopf, 2005), 134.

2. Terryl Givens, *The Prophecy of Enoch as Restoration Blueprint* (Provo: Utah State University Press, 2013).

3. Ibid., p. 3.

4. Book of Mormon, 1 Nephi 13:26; *see also* 1 Nephi 13:39–40.

5. For an excellent example of work, see Paul A. Wellington's *Joseph Smith's New Translation of the Bible* (Independence, MO: Herald, 1970).

6. Joseph's *Inspired Version* begins with Genesis 1:1: "And it came to pass, that the Lord spake unto Moses, saying, Behold, I reveal unto you concerning this heaven and this earth; write the words which I speak."

7. E. Douglas Clark, "A Prologue to Genesis: Moses 1 in Light of Jewish Traditions," *BYU Studies Quarterly* 45, no. 1 (2006); *see also* Hugh W. Nibley, *Teachings of the Pearl of Great Price*: Transcripts of Lectures Presented to an Honors Book of Mormon Class at Brigham Young University, Winter Semester 1986 (Provo: Foundation for Ancient Research and Mormon Studies, 2004), 205. (As Clark points out in his article, Nibley described the relationship of Moses 1:2–8 to the rest of the chapter as a "Prologue in Heaven.")

8. Ibid.

9. Ibid.

10. Quotations from the *Book of Jubilees Translated from the Ethiopic*, by Rev. George H. Schodde, PhD, Professor at Capital University, Columbus, Ohio (Oberlin, OH: E.J. Goodrich, 1888).

11. Clark, "A Prologue to Genesis."

12. Moses 5:48–59; 6: 1–2; Genesis 4:24–25.

13. See Cheryl L. Bruno, "Congruence and Concatenation in Jewish Mystical Literature, American Freemasonry, and Mormon Enoch Writings," *Journal of Religion & Society* 16 (2014).

14. Jeffrey M. Bradshaw, "Were Ancient Enoch Manuscripts the Inspiration for Moses 6–7?," The Interpreter Foundation, Essay #5: Enoch's Preaching Mission (May 30, 2020).

15. William Morgan, *Illustrations of Masonry by One of the Fraternity Who has Devoted Thirty Years to the Subject: "God said, Let There be Light, and There was light"* (Batavia, NY: David C. Miller, 1827).

Chapter Eight

1. Richard Lyman Bushman, *Joseph Smith: Rough Stone Rolling* (New York: Alfred A. Knopf, 2005), 132.

2. www.josephsmithpapers.org.

3. *Old Testament Revision 1*, The Joseph Smith Papers (josephsmithpapers.org).

4. Ibid.

5. Ibid., 10.

6. Ibid.

7. *Old Testament Revision 2*, The Joseph Smith Papers (josephsmithpapers.org).

8. *Old Testament Revision 1*, 13.

9. Hugh Nibley, "Enoch the Prophet," in *The Collected Works of Hugh Nibley*, vol. 2 (Salt Lake City: Deseret Book and The Foundation for Ancient Research and Mormon Studies, 1986), 277–81.

10. Concerning the handwriting and editing of Emma Smith in contributing to these transcriptions, see Colby Townsend, "Sources: Integrating Textual Criticism in the Study of Early Mormon Texts and History," *Intermountain West Journal of Religious Studies* 10, no. 1 (2019): 56. In this article, Townsend "invites historians to return to the sources and further analyze what we know about Mormon history."

11. Colby Townsend, "Translation as Expansion: The Method of Joseph

Notes—Chapter Nine

Smith's Revision of Genesis in Moses 1 and 7," *Journal of Mormon History* 46, no. 4 (October 2020): 45–59.

12. *See*, e.g., Hugh W. Nibley's "Teachings of the Pearl of Great Price," in his *Enoch the Prophet*, 277-79.

13. Townsend, "Sources: Integrating Textual Criticism in the Study of Early Mormon Texts and History," *Intermountain West Journal of Religious Studies* 10, no. 1 (2019): 58–85; *see also* Adam Clarke, *The Holy Bible, Containing the Old and New Testaments* (New York: N. Bangs and J. Emory, 1825), 151.

14. *See* D. Michael Quinn, *Early Mormonism and the Magic World View* (Salt Lake City: Signature, 1998).

15. Robert C. Fuller, *Spiritual, but Not Religious: Understanding Unchurched America* (New York: Oxford University Press, 2001), 15, 17; *see also* Mark Ashurst-McGee, "A Pathway to Prophethood: Joseph Smith Junior as Rodsman, Village Seer, and Judeo-Christian Prophet" (master's thesis, Utah State University, 2000), 126–48.

16. *Revelation, April 1829–B* [D&C 8], in Revelation 1:13, josephsmithpapers.org.

17. *Revelation, April 1829–D [D&C 9]*, in Book of Commandments, 20–21, josephsmithpapers.org; *see also* Doctrine and Covenants 9:3, 7–8.

18. Thomas A. Wayment, "Joseph Smith's Developing Relationship with the Apocrypha," in *Approaching Antiquity: Joseph Smith and the Ancient World*, ed. Lincoln H. Blumell, Matthew J. Grey, and Andrew H. Hedges (Provo: Religious Studies Center; Salt Lake City: Deseret Book, 2015), 331–55.

19. Joseph Smith, Jr., March 10, 1844. See *History of the Church*, 6:249–54.

20. For additional discussion on the Spirit World and correlating verses found in the Book of Enoch, explore later chapters discussing Mormon cosmology.

21. Van Wagoner, *Sidney Rigdon: A Portrait of Religious Excess* (Salt Lake City: Signature, 1994), 60–61.

22. Eran Shalev, *American Zion: The Old Testament as a Political Text from the Revolution to the Civil War* (New Haven: Yale University Press, 2013),

84–117. Shalev identified pseudobiblical literature as a literary genre of the eighteenth and nineteenth centuries; *see also* Townsend, *Translation as Expansion*, 45–59.

23. Thomas A. Wayment and Haley Wilson-Lemmon, "A Recovered Resource: The Use of Adam Clarke's Bible Commentary in Joseph Smith's Bible Translation," in *Producing Ancient Scripture: Joseph Smith's Translation Projects in the Development of Mormon Christianity*, ed. Michael Hubbard MacKay, Mark Ashurst-McGee, and Brian M. Hauglid (Salt Lake City: University of Utah Press, 2020), 262–84. Wayment and Wilson-Lemmon argue that "by means of Sidney Rigdon, Smith likely became familiar with [Adam Clarke's] commentary and utilized it at varying levels of engagement throughout the 'translation' process."

24. For an excellent discussion on Joseph's literacy and literary sources in composing his works, *see* Colby Townsend, "Rewriting Eden with the Book of Mormon: Joseph Smith and the Reception of Genesis 1–6 in Early America" (MA thesis, University of Utah, 2019), https://digitalcommons.usu.edu/etd/7681.

25. D&C 35:18–20.

Chapter Nine

1. Richard Lyman Bushman, *Joseph Smith: Rough Stone Rolling* (New York: Alfred A. Knopf, 2005), pg. 138.

2. www.biblicalarchaeology.org/daily/news/canaanite-fortress-discovered-in-the-city-of-david/; *see also* 2 Samuel 5:7 ("Nevertheless David took the stronghold of Zion; the same is the city of David").

3. *Teachings of the Prophet Joseph Smith*, Deseret Book, 2006, pp. 84–86.

4. Bushman, *Rough Stone Rolling*, p. 138.

5. Interestingly, in Joseph's explanation, above, he quotes John's "according to the vision of John upon the isle of Patmos" (St. John's "Revelation") as having been seen also by Enoch ("which Enoch saw"). Nothing in the Book of Revelation admits to John's use of any Enoch writings

Notes—Chapter Ten

or borrowing from Enoch stories. But it appears that he did, and Joseph Smith's comment seems to demonstrate this same understanding. (*See also* Chapter 11).

6. Joseph Smith, *Teachings of the Prophet Joseph Smith*, pp. 84–86 (emphasis added).

7. McConkie, *Mormon Doctrine*, pp. 773–774.

8. Book of Moses 7:62–64.

Chapter Ten

1. "Biographical Note," David J. Buerger papers, 1842–1988, available at Archives West: David J. Buerger Papers, 1842–1988 (orbiscascade.org) (last retrieved October 7, 2021).

2. David John Buerger, "The Development of the Mormon Temple Endowment Ceremony," *Dialogue: A Journal of Mormon Thought* 20, no. 4 (Winter 1987): 33–76.

3. Specifics of the temple ceremonies and summaries of the temple covenants are available as offered by LDS General Authorities, see James E. Faust, "Who Shall Ascend into the Hill of the Lord?," *Ensign* (August 2001); Bruce R. McConkie, "Obedience, Consecration, and Sacrifice," *Ensign* 5, no. 5 (May 1975); Gordon B. Hinckley, *Teachings of Gordon B. Hinckley* (Salt Lake City: Deseret Book, 1997), 147; James E. Talmage, *House of the Lord*, 84; Boyd K. Packer, *The Holy Temple* (Salt Lake City: Bookcraft, 1980), 163; Robert D. Hales, *Return: Four Phases of Our Mortal Journey Home* (Salt Lake City: Deseret Book, 2010), 4–5.

4. D&C 124:31 & 34.

5. Cf., Book of Enoch XCII:9 ("... the house of glory and of dominion shall be erected for ever").

6. Russell M. Nelson, "Closing Remarks," October General Conference, *Liahona* (November 2019).

7. Bruce R. McConkie, *Mormon Doctrine*, 2nd ed. (Salt Lake City: Bookcraft, 1966), 226–27.

8. Buerger, "The Development of the Mormon Temple Endowment Ceremony," 35.

9. *History of the Church*, 2:287.

10. Enoch XXXIX:4–10; Enoch XXXI:3.

11. churchofjesuschrist.org/study/history/topics/temple-endowment.

12. Ibid.

13. John W. Welch, "The Temple, the Sermon on the Mount, and the Gospel of Matthew," in *Mormonism and the Temple: Examining an Ancient Religious Tradition*, ed. Gary N. Anderson (Logan, UT: Academy for Temple Studies, 2013), 63.

14. churchofjesuschrist.org (temple endowment).

15. Ibid.

16. William Morgan, *Illustrations of Masonry by One of the Fraternity Who has Devoted Thirty Years to the Subject: "God said, Let There be Light, and There was light"* (Batavia, NY: David C. Miller, 1827).

17. Cheryl L. Bruno, "Congruence and Concatenation in Jewish Mystical Literature, American Freemasonry, and Mormon Enoch Writings," *Journal of Religion & Society* 16 (2014).

18. churchofjesuschrist.org (masonry).

19. Heber C. Kimball letter to Parley P. Pratt, June 17, 1842; *see also* Parley P. Pratt correspondence, 1842–1855, Church History Library.

20. churchofjesuschrist.org (temple endowment).

21. "A Message from the First Presidency on Changes to the Temple Endowment," July 20, 2020, Official Statement of The Church of Jesus Christ of Latter-day Saints, Salt Lake City, UT.

22. Ibid.

23. Buerger, "The Development of the Mormon Temple Endowment Ceremony"; *see also* George W.E. Nickelsburg, "The Temple According to 1 Enoch," *BYU Studies Quarterly* 53, no. 1 (2014).

24. Jeffrey M. Bradshaw, "The LDS Story of Enoch as the Culminating Episode of a Temple Text," *BYU Studies Quarterly* 53, no. 15 (2014).

25. First Presidency letter, October 10, 1988.

26. "My Father in Heaven," in "Poetry, for the Times and Seasons," *Times and Seasons* 6 (November 15, 1845): 1039; *O My Father*, Hymns, no. 292; *see also* Jill Mulvay Derr, "The Significance of 'O My

Father' in the Personal Journey of Eliza R. Snow," *BYU Studies* 36, no. 1 (1996–97): 84–126.
27. churchofjesuschrist.org (mother in heaven).
28. See Elaine Anderson Cannon, *Mother in Heaven*, ed. Daniel H. Ludlow, 5 vols. (New York: Macmillan, 1992), 2:961. For an extensive survey of these teachings, *see* David L. Paulsen and Martin Pulido, "'A Mother There': A Survey of Historical Teachings about Mother in Heaven," *BYU Studies* 50, no. 1 (2011): 70–97.
29. LDS Church *Gospel Topics* Study Manual, "Mother in Heaven."
30. Enoch LXIX. SECT. XII:4 and LXX:1.
31. Enoch LXI:18.
32. Robert L. Millet, "The Man Adam," *Liahona* (February 1998): 14; Bruce R. McConkie, "Christ and the Creation," *Tambuli* (September 1983), 22; Ezra Taft Benson, "What I Hope You Would Teach Your Children about the Temple," *Tambuli* (April 1986): 1.
33. Millet, "The Man Adam."
34. Joseph Fielding Smith, *Scriptural Teachings of the Prophet Joseph Smith*, ed. Richard C. Galbraith (Salt Lake City: Deseret Book, 1993).
35. Ibid., 38–39.
36. Enoch LIX. SECT. X:1.
37. Enoch LIX. SECT. X:3
38. Mark E. Petersen, "Adam, the Archangel," *Ensign* (November 1980): 16.
39. Ibid.
40. Millet, "The Man Adam," 8–15.
41. Enoch LI:3.
42. Book of Abraham 5:14–17.
43. See George W.E. Nickelsburg, "The Temple According to 1 Enoch," *BYU Studies Quarterly* 53, no. 1 (2014).
44. Morgan, *Illustrations on Masonry*.
45. Exodus 26:33; Matt. 27:51; Mark 15:38; Luke 23:45.
46. George W.E. Nickelsburg, a graduate of Concordia Seminary, in St. Louis, and Harvard Divinity School, is professor emeritus at the University of Iowa, where he taught New Testament and ancient Judaism for thirty-one years. Professor Nickelsburg is a preeminent Enoch scholar.
47. Nickelsburg, "The Temple According to 1 Enoch."
48. churchofjesuschrist.org (temples).

Chapter Eleven

1. *Teachings of Presidents of the Church: Joseph Smith* (Salt Lake City: The Church of Jesus Christ of Latter-day Saints, 2007), 267.
2. Philip Schaff and Henry Wace, eds., *Nicene and Post-Nicene Fathers*, second series, vol. 14 (Grand Rapids: Eerdmans, 1956), 320; cf., *New Catholic Encyclopedia*, 17 vols. (New York: McGraw-Hill, 1967), 8:96–101; 10:771–73; 14:145.
3. *Citing* Revelation 12:7.
4. James E. Talmage, *Jesus the Christ, A Study of the Messiah and His Mission according to Holy Scriptures both Ancient and Modern* (Salt Lake City: Church of Jesus Christ of Latter-day Saints, 2006) (Chapter 2: Preexistence and Foreordination of the Christ).
5. The Son of man motif is abundant throughout the Book of Enoch. It is found in certain ancient Jewish scripture (i.e., Psalms, Isaiah, Ezekiel and Daniel) and apocalyptic writings telling of the imminent coming of a cosmic reversal of powers, where the first will be last and the last will be first. The authors of the synoptic gospels carried over these apocalyptic traditions in their similarly incorporated references.
6. "The Hebrew word *nefilim* is sometimes directly translated as 'giants' or taken to mean 'the fallen ones' (from the Hebrew *naphal*, 'to fall'), but the identity of Nephilim is debated by scholars." "Nephilim," *Encyclopedia Britannica* (www.britannica.com/topic/Nephilim).
7. Richard Laurence, "Preliminary Dissertation," *Book of Enoch*, xli; xliv.
8. *Gospel Principles*, Chapter 41, "The Postmortal Spirit World"; churchofjesuschrist.org (postmortal spirit world).
9. Joseph Smith, Jr., "The King Follett Discourse" (April 7, 1844), *History of the Church*, 6:302–17.
10. Laurence, "Preliminary Dissertation," xxii.
11. Ibid.
12. Ibid.

Notes—Chapter Twelve

Chapter Twelve

1. Fifth President of the Church of Jesus Christ of Latter-day Saints, June 1840. See Eliza R. Snow, *Biography and Family Record of Lorenzo Snow* (Salt Lake City: Deseret News Co., 1884), 46–47. President Snow's son, LeRoi Snow, wrote that after his father returned from a mission in England in January 1843, he shared his "extraordinary manifestation" to the prophet Joseph Smith, who replied, "Brother Snow, that is a true gospel doctrine, and it is a revelation from God to you." LeRoi C. Snow, "Devotion to a Divine Inspiration," *Improvement Era* (June 1919): 656.

2. "King Follett Discourse," in *History of the Church*, 2nd ed., 7 vols. (Salt Lake City: Deseret News, 1950), 6:302–17.

3. Moses 2:2–3.

4. Abraham 4:1–3.

5. Abraham 5:3–4.

6. Luke P. Wilson, "Joseph Smith's Changing Doctrine of Deity," Institute for Religious Research, August 11, 2011, (retrieved 11/19/2021), https://mit.irr.org/joseph-smiths-changing-doctrine-of-deity.

7. "Sermon on the Plurality of Gods," June 16, 1844, *History of the Church*, 6:473–79.

8. Ibid.

9. "King Follett Discourse."

10. Ibid.

11. Joseph Fielding Smith, *The Progress of Man* (Salt Lake City: Genealogical Society of Utah, 1936), 11.

12. *History of the Church*, 3:387.

13. Enoch LVL. SECT. IX:1

14. Enoch CV:26.

Bibliography

Books

Albanese, Catherin L. *America Religions and Religion,* 3rd ed. Wadsworth, 1999.

Alter, Robert. *The Art of Biblical Narrative.* Basic, 1981.

Anderson, Mark. *Shakespeare by Another Name: The Life of Edward de Vere, Earl of Oxford, the Man Who Was Shakespeare.* Gotham, 2005.

Archer, Jeffrey. *Paths of Glory.* St. Martin's Press, 2009.

Archer, Jeffrey. *A Prisoner of Birth.* St. Martin's Press, 2008.

Bloom, Harold. *The American Religion: The Emergence of the Post-Christian Nation.* Simon & Schuster, 1992.

Book of Jasher Referred to in Joshua and Second Samuel. Faithfully translated (1840) from the Original Hebrew into English. J.H. Parry & Co., 1887.

Bowman, Matthew. *The Mormon People: The Making of an American Faith.* Random House, 2012.

Brandt, Edward J. *The Book* of Jasher and the Latter-day Saints." In *Apocryphal Writings and the Latter-day Saints,* ed. C. Wilfred Griggs. Religious Studies Center, Brigham Young University, 1986.

Brodie, Fawn M. *The Devil Drives: A Life of Sir Richard Burton.* W.W. Norton, 1984.

Brodie, Fawn M. *No Man Knows My History: The Life of Joseph Smith.* Vintage, 1995.

Burton, Richard Francis. *The City of the Saints,* ed. Fawn Brodie. Alfred A. Knopf, 1964.

Burton, Richard Francis. *The Kasidah of Haji Abdu El-Yezdi.* 1880.

Burton, Richard Francis. *Pilgrimage to Meccah.* Amberley, 2015.

Bushman, Richard L. *Joseph Smith and the Beginnings of Mormonism.* University of Illinois Press, 1988.

Bushman, Richard L. *Joseph Smith: Rough Stone Rolling.* Vintage, 2005.

Cambridge Bible for Schools and Colleges. Edited by J. J. Steward. Cambridge University Press, 1904.

Cannon, Elaine Anderson. *Mother in Heaven.* Edited by Daniel H. Ludlow. 5 vols. Macmillan, 1992.

Charles, Robert H., trans. *1 Enoch.* In *Apocrypha and Pseudepigrapha of the Old Testament.* Clarendon Press, 1913.

Coelho, Paulo. *The Alchemist.* HarperOne, 2014.

Ehrman, Bart D. *Did Jesus Exist?: The Historical Argument for Jesus of Nazareth.* HarperCollins, 2012.

Ehrman, Bart D. *Forged: Writing in the Name of God.* HarperOne, 2011.

Ehrman, Bart D. *From Jesus to Constantine: A History of Early Christianity.* The Teaching Company, 2004.

Ehrman, Bart D. *Heaven and Hell: A History of the Afterlife.* Simon & Schuster, 2020.

Ehrman, Bart D. *The Historical Jesus of Nazareth? What Was He Like?* The Teaching Company, 2000.

Ehrman, Bart D. *The History of the Bible: The Making of the New Testament Canon.* The Great Courses (Audible Audio). The Teaching Company, 2005.

Ehrman, Bart D. *How Jesus Became God.* The Great Courses (Audible Audio), The Teaching Company, 2005.

Ehrman, Bart D. *How Jesus Became God:*

Bibliography

The Exaltation of a Jewish Preacher from Galilee. HarperOne, 2014.

Ehrman, Bart D. *Jesus Apocalyptic Prophet of the New Millennium.* Oxford University Press, 1999.

Ehrman, Bart D. *Jesus Before the Gospels: How the Earliest Christians Remembered, Changed, and Invented Their Stories of the Savior.* HarperOne, 2016.

Ehrman, Bart D. *Jesus, Interrupted: Revealing the Hidden Contradictions in the Bible & Why We Don't Know About Them.* HarperCollins, 2009.

Ehrman, Bart D. *Lost Christianities: The Battles for Scripture and the Faiths We Never Knew.* Oxford University Press, 2005.

Ehrman, Bart D. *Lost Scriptures: Books That Did Not Make It into the New Testament.* Oxford University Press, 2005.

Ehrman, Bart D. *Misquoting Jesus: The Story Behind Who Changed the Bible and Why.* HarperOne, 2007.

Ehrman, Bart D. *The Triumph of Christianity: How a Small Band of Outcasts Conquered an Empire.* Simon Schuster, 2017.

Euseebius. *The History of the Church from Christ to Constantine.* Translated by G.A. Williamson. Revised and edited by Andrew Louth. Penguin, 1989.

Fitzgerald, David. *The Mormons (The Complete Heretic's Guide to Western Religion #1).* CreateSpace, 2013.

Fuller, Robert C. *Spiritual, but Not Religious: Understanding Unchurched America.* Oxford University Press, 2001.

Givens, Terryl L. *By the Hand of Mormon: The American Scripture That Launched a New World Religion.* Oxford University Press, 2002.

Givens, Terryl L. *Parley P. Pratt: The Apostle Paul of Mormonism.* Oxford University Press, 2011.

Givens, Terryl L. *The Prophecy of Enoch as Restoration Blueprint.* Utah State University Press, 2013.

Gleick, James. *Chaos: Making a New Science.* Penguin Group, 1988.

Gleick, James. *The Information: A History, a Theory, a Flood.* Knopf Doubleday Publishing Group, 2011.

Gleick, James. *Isaac Newton.* Vintage, 2004.

Gonzales, Laurence. *Deep Survival: Who Lives, Who Dies and Why.* W.W. Norton, 1998.

Graziano, Michael S. A. *Consciousness and the Social Brain.* Oxford University Press, 2013.

Green, Brian. *The Fabric of the Cosmos: Space, Time, and the Texture of Reality.* Alfred Knopf, 2004.

Green, Brian. *Until the End of Time: Mind, Matter, and Our Search for Meaning in an Evolving Universe.* Allen Lane, 2020.

Haidt, Jonathan. *The Happiness Hypotheses: Finding Modern Truth in Ancient Wisdom.* Basic Books, 2006.

Hales, Robert D. *Return: Four Phases of Our Mortal Journey Home.* Deseret Book, 2010.

Hall, Manly P., et al. *A Collection of Writings Related to Occult, Esoteric, Rosicrucian and Hermetic Literature, Including Freemasonry, the Kabbalah, the Tarot, Alchemy and Theosophy.* Volume 1, *Lamp of Trismegistus* (Audible Audio), 2017.

Hancock, Graham. *America Before: The Key to Earth's Lost Civilization.* Coronet, 2019.

Harari, Yuval Noah. *Homo Deus: A History of Tomorrow.* Harper, 2017.

Harari, Yuval Noah. *Sapiens: A Brief History of Humankind.* Vintage, 2011.

Hays, Richard. *Echoes of Scripture in the Letters of Paul.* Yale University Press, 1989.

Hinckley, Gordon B. *Teachings of Gordon B. Hinckley.* Deseret Book, 1997.

Hymns, The Church of Jesus Christ of Latter-day Saints, 1985.

Josephus, Flavius. *The Jewish War.* Translated by G.A. Williamson. Penguin Classic, 1981.

Krakauer, Jon. *Under the Banner of Heaven: A Story of Violent Faith.* Pan Macmillian, 2004.

The Kybalion by Three Initiates. Yogi Publication Society, 1908.

Landsing, Alfred. *Endurance: Shackleton's Incredible Voyage.* Carroll & Graf, 1999.

Laurence, Richard. *The book of Enoch the*

Bibliography

prophet: an apocryphal production, supposed to have been lost for ages, but discovered at the close of the last century in Abyssinia: now first translated from an Ethiopic ms. in the Bodleian Library. 1821.

Lewis, Jon E. *Mammon Books Presents Religious Cabals*. Robinson, 2012.

Lewis, Meriwether, & William Clark. *The Journals of Lewis and Clark*. Edited by Bernard DeVoto. Mariner Books, 1997.

Lindsey, Robert. *A Gathering of Saints: A True Story of Money, Murder and Deceit*. Simon & Schuster, 1988.

The Lost Books of the Bible. Bell, 1979.

Lozano, Gustavo Vazquez. *The Apocryphal Gospels: The History of the New Testament Apocrypha Not Included in the Bible*. Charles River Editors, 2016.

Lozano, Gustavo Vazquez. *The Lost Books of the Old Testament: The History of Ancient Jewish Apocrypha Not Included in the Bible*. Charles River Editors, 2018.

Mann, Charles C. *1491: New Revelations of the Americas Before Columbus*. Vintage, 2005.

Matthews, Robert, J. *A Plainer Translation: Joseph Smith's Translation of the Bible: A History and Commentary*. Brigham Young University Press, 1975.

McConkie, Bruce R. *Mormon Doctrine*. Deseret Book Co., 1958.

McConkie, Bruce R. *Mormon Doctrine*. Rev. ed. Bookcraft, 1966.

McGinn, Bernard, ed. *The Essential Writings of Christian Mysticism*. Modern Library, 2006.

Meyer, Marvin W. *The Nag Hamadi Scriptures*. HarperOne, 2009.

Morgan, William. *Illustrations of Masonry by One of the Fraternity Who has Devoted Thirty Years to the Subject: "God said, Let There be Light, and There was light."* David C. Miller, 1827.

Murfin, Ross, and Supryia M. Ray. *The Bedford Glossary of Critical and Literary Terms*. Bedford, 1997.

Murray, Charles, and Catherine Bly Cox. *Apollo: The Race to the Moon*. South Mountain Books, 2004.

New Catholic Encyclopedia, 17 vols. McGraw-Hill, 1967.

Newcomb, Jason Augustus. *The Gospel of Thomas (A New Translation, Commentary and Comparison with the Synoptic Gospels)*. New Hermetics Press, 2014.

Nibley, Hugh. *Enoch the Prophet (The Collected Works of Hugh Nibley)*, volume 2. Edited by Stephen D. Ricks. Shadow Mountain, 1986.

Nibley, Hugh W. 2013. *Teachings of the Pearl of Great Price*. Maxwell Institute, 2013.

Nicene and Post-Nicene Fathers. Edited By Philip Schaff and Henry Wace. Second Series, vol. 14. Eerdmans, 1956.

Nichols, James Hastings. *History of Christianity (1650–1950)*. The Ronald Press Company, 1956.

Nickelsburg, George W.E., and James C. VanderKam. *1 Enoch 1: A Commentary on the Book of 1 Enoch, Chapters 1–36*. Fortress Press, 2011.

Nickelsburg, George E., and James C. VanderKam. *1 Enoch 2: A Commentary on the Book of 1 Enoch, Chapters 37–82*. Fortress Press, 2011.

O'Driscoll, Jeffrey S. *Hyrum Smith: a Life of Integrity*. Deseret Book, 2003.

Packer, Boyd K. *The Holy Temple*. Bookcraft, 1980.

Pagels, Elaine. *The Gnostic Gospels*. Random House, 1979.

Park, Benjamin E. 2020. *Kingdom of Nauvoo: The Rise and Fall of a Religious Empire on the American Frontier*. Liveright, 2020.

Persuitte, David. 1985. *Joseph Smith and the Origins of the Book of Mormon*. McFarland, 1985.

Quinn, D. Michael. 1998. *Early Mormonism and the Magic World View*. Signature, 1998.

Remini, Robert V. 2002. *Joseph Smith*. Viking, 2002.

Riess, Jana. 2019. *The Next Mormons: How Millennials Are Changing the LDS Church*. Oxford University Press, 2019.

Rovelli, Carlo. 2018. *The Order of Time*. Riverhead, 2018.

Saints: The Story of the Church of Jesus Christ in the Latter Days, volume 1, *The Standard of Truth, 1815–1846*. 2018. The Church of Jesus Christ of Latter-day Saints, 2018.

Saints: The Story of the Church of Jesus Christ in the Latter Days, volume 2,

Bibliography

No Unhallowed Hand 1846–1893. 2018. The Church of Jesus Christ of Latter-day Saints, 2018.

Schodde, George H. 1888. *Book of Jubilees Translated from the Ethiopic.* E.J. Goodrich, 1888.

Seuss, Dr. 1997. *Seuss-isms: Wise and Witty Prescriptions for Living from the Good Doctor.* Random House, 1997.

Shalev, Eran. 2013. *American Zion: The Old Testament as a Political Text from the Revolution to the Civil War.* Yale University Press, 2013.

Shipps, Jan. 1987. *Mormonism: The Story of a New Religious Tradition.* University of Illinois Press, 1987.

Sloane, Eric. 1962. *Diary of an Early American Boy: Noah Blake 1805.* Wilfred Funk, 1962.

Smith, Joseph Fielding. *The Progress of Man.* Genealogical Society of Utah, 1936.

Smith, Joseph Fielding. *Scriptural Teachings of the Prophet Joseph Smith,* ed. Richard C. Galbraith. Deseret Book, 1993.

Smith, Joseph, Jr., *History of the Church of Jesus Christ of Latter-day Saints,* ed. B.H. Roberts, 2d ed., rev., 7 vols. Deseret Book, 1971.

Smith, Joseph, Jr. *The Holy Scriptures: Inspired Version.* Herald House (first published 1867).

Smith, Joseph, Jr., *Joseph Smith History* 1:11–12 (Pearl of Great Price).

Smith, Joseph, Jr. *Sermons of Joseph Smith as Included in the Journal of Discourses.* Independently published, 2018 (Audible Audio, LDS Audiobook Foundation).

Smith, Lucy Mack. *Biographical Sketches of Joseph Smith the Prophet, and His Progenitors for Many Generations.* Grandin, 1853.

Smith, Lucy Mack. *The History of Joseph Smith, by His Mother.* Covenant Communications, 2000.

Smith, Lucy Mack. *Lucy's Book: A Critical Edition of Lucy Mack Smith's Family Memoir.* Edited by Lavina Fielding Anderson. Signature, 2001.

Snow, Eliza R. *Biography and Family Record of Lorenzo Snow.* Deseret News Co., 1884.

Soulen Richard N., & R. Kendall Soulen. *Handbook of Biblical Criticism,* 3rd ed. Westminster John Knox Press, 2001.

Spencer, Herbert. *The Principles of Sociology,* vol. 1. Routledge, 2001 (first published 1876).

Talmage, James E. *House of the Lord: A Study of Holy Sanctuaries Ancient and Modern.* Signature, 1998.

Talmage, James E. *Jesus the Christ: A Study of the Messiah and His Mission According to Holy Scriptures Both Ancient and Modern.* The Church of Jesus Christ of Latter-day Saints, 2006.

Teachings of Presidents of the Church: Joseph Smith. The Church of Jesus Christ of Latter-day Saints, 2007.

Tegmark, Max. *Our Mathematical Universe: My Quest for the Ultimate Nature of Reality.* Allen Lane, 2014.

Townsend, Colby. "Translation as Expansion: The Method of Joseph Smith's Revision of Genesis in Moses 1 and 7." *Journal of Mormon History* 46, no. 4. 2020.

Van Wagoner, Richard S. *Sidney Rigdon, A Portrait of Religious Excess.* Signature, 1994.

Von Harrison, Grant. *Drawing on the Powers of Heaven.* PBS, 1979.

Waite, Arthur Edward. *The Holy Kabbalah.* Dover, 2003.

Wayment, Thomas A. *The Complete Joseph Smith Translation of the New Testament: A Side-by-Side Comparison with the King James Version.* Deseret Book, 2005.

Wayment, Thomas A. *Joseph Smith's Developing Relationship with the Apocrypha, Approaching Antiquity: Joseph Smith and the Ancient World,* edited by Lincoln H. Blumell, Matthew J. Grey, and Andrew H. Hedges. Deseret Book, 2015.

Wayment, Thomas A., and Haley Wilson-Lemmon. *A Recovered Resource: The Use of Adam Clarke's Bible Commentary in Joseph Smith's Bible Translation,* in *Producing Ancient Scripture: Joseph Smith's Translation Projects in the Development of Mormon Christianity.* Edited by Michael Hubbard MacKay, Mark Ashurst-McGee, and Brian M. Hauglid. University of Utah Press, 2020.

Bibliography

Welch, John W. *Chiasm, Chiasmus: I. Ancient Near and Hebrew Bible/Old Testament.* In *Encyclopedia of the Bible and Its Reception,* ed. Hans-Josef Klauck, 30 vols. Berlin: De Gruyter, 2012.

Welch, John W. *The Temple, the Sermon on the Mount, and the Gospel of Matthew,* in *Mormonism and the Temple: Examining an Ancient Religious Tradition,* ed. Gary N. Anderson. Academy for Temple Studies, 2013. 30 vols. Vol. 5 cited

Welch, John W. *What Does Chiasmus in the Book of Mormon Prove?* In *Book of Mormon Authorship Revisited: The Evidence for Ancient Origins,* edited by Noel B. Reynolds. Maxwell Institute, 1997.

Wellington, Paul A. *Joseph Smith's New Translation of the Bible.* Herald, 1970.

Willett, Herbert Lockwood. *The Popular and Critical Bible Encyclopedia and Scriptural Dictionary: Fully Defining and Explaining All Religious Terms, Including Biographical, Geographical, Historical, Archeological and Doctrinal Themes, Superbly Illustrated with Over 600 Maps and Engravings.* Howard-Severance Company, 1910.

Woodworth, Jed L. *Extra-biblical Enoch Texts in Early American culture,* Archive of Restoration Culture: Summer Fellows' Papers 1997–1999, ed. Richard Lyman Bushman. Provo, UT: Joseph Fielding Smith Institute for Latter-day Saint History, 2000.

Articles and Periodicals

Ashurst-McGee, Mark. *A Pathway to Prophethood: Joseph Smith Junior as rodsman, village seer, and Judeo-Christian prophet.* Master's thesis, Utah State University, 2000.

Behrens, Richard K. "Dartmouth Arminianism and Its Impact on Hyrum Smith and the Smith Family." *John Whitmer Historical Association Journal* 26 (2006).

Behrens, Richard K. "Dreams, Visions, and Visitations: The Genesis of Mormonism." *The John Whitmer Historical Association Journal* 27 (2007).

Benson, Ezra Taft. "What I Hope You Would Teach Your Children about the Temple." *Tambuli* (April 1986).

Bradshaw, Jeffrey M. "The LDS Story of Enoch as the Culminating Episode of a Temple Text." *BYU Studies Quarterly* 53, no. 1 (2014).

Bradshaw, Jeffrey M. *Were Ancient Enoch Manuscripts the Inspiration for Moses 6–7?,* The Interpreter Foundation, Essay #5: Enoch's Preaching Mission (May 30, 2020).

Bradshaw, Jeffrey M., and Ryan Dahle. "Could Joseph Smith Have Drawn on Ancient Manuscripts When He Translated the Story of Enoch?: Recent Updates on a Persistent Question." *Interpreter: A Journal of Latter-day Saint Faith and Scholarship* 33 (2019): 305–74.

Bruno, Cheryl L. "Congruence and Concatenation in Jewish Mystical Literature, American Freemasonry, and Mormon Enoch Writings." *Journal of Religion & Society* 16 (2014): 1–19.

Buerger, David John. "The Development of the Mormon Temple Endowment Ceremony." *Dialogue: A Journal of Mormon Thought* 20, no. 4 (Winter 1987): 33–76.

Clark, E. Douglas. "A Prologue to Genesis: Moses 1 in Light of Jewish Traditions." *BYU Studies Quarterly* 45, no. 1 (2006).

Derr, Jill Mulvay. "The Significance of 'O My Father' in the Personal Journey of Eliza R. Snow." *BYU Studies* 36, no. 1 (1996): 84–126.

Faust, James E. "Who Shall Ascend into the Hill of the Lord?" *Ensign* (August 2001).

Grant, Athay R. "Worlds without Number: The Astronomy of Enoch, Abraham, and Moses." *BYU Studies Quarterly* 8, no. 3 (Spring 1968).

Jackson, Kent P. "Joseph Smith's Cooperstown Bible: The Historical Context of the Bible Used in the Article 3." 2001.

Kimball, Heber C. Letter to Parley P. Pratt, 17 June 1842 (pratt-family.org) (original spelling retained); *see also* Parley P. Pratt correspondence, 1842–1855, Church History Library.

McConkie, Bruce R. "Christ and the Creation." *Tambuli* (September 1983).

McConkie, Bruce R. "Obedience,

Bibliography

Consecration, and Sacrifice." *Ensign* 5, no. 5 (May 1975).

Millet, Robert L. "The Man Adam." *Liahona* (February 1998).

Nelson, Russell M. "Closing Remarks, October General Conference." *Liahona* (November 2019).

Newman, Nick. "Scribes Recorded Prophet's 'Crooked Broken Language.'" *Desert News,* January 26, 2010.www.deseret.com/2010/1/26/20374629/scribes-recorded-prophet-s-crooked-broken-language.

Nickelsburg, George W.E. "The Temple According to 1 Enoch." *BYU Studies Quarterly* 53, no. 1 (2014).

Old Testament Revision 1. The Joseph Smith Papers. josephsmithpapers.org.

Old Testament Revision 2. The Joseph Smith Papers. josephsmithpapers.org.

Paulsen David L., and Martin Pulido. "'A Mother There': A Survey of Historical Teachings about Mother in Heaven." *BYU Studies* 50, no. 1 (2011): 70–97.

Petersen, Mark E. "Adam, the Archangel." *Ensign* (November 1980): 16.

Peterson, Mark E. *"It Was a Miracle!" Ensign* (October 1977).

Salmon, Douglas F. "Parallelomania and the Study of Latter-day Scripture: Confirmation, Coincidence, or the Collective Unconscious?" *Dialogue: A Journal of Mormon Though* 33, no. 2 (Summer 2000).

Smith, Joseph, Jr. Letter to W.W. Phelps, November 27, 1832. www.josephsmithpapers.org.

Smith, Joseph, Jr. "The King Follett Discourse." Nauvoo, IL: April 7, 1844.

Smith, Robert F. "Evaluating the Sources of 2 Nephi 1:13–15: Shakespeare and the Book of Mormon." *Journal of Book of Mormon Studies* 22, no. 2 (2013).

Stritmatter, Roger A. *The Marginalia of Edward de Vere's Geneva Bible: Providential Discovery, Literary Reasoning, and Historical Consequence.* PhD diss., University of Massachusetts Amherst, 2001.

Times and Seasons. V. 4 (February 1, 1843): 82–85.

Times and Seasons My Father in Heaven in *Poetry, for the Times and Seasons* 6 (November 15, 1845): 1039

Townsend, Colby. *Appropriation and Adaption of J Material in the Book of Mormon.* Undergraduate thesis, University of Utah, 2016.

Townsend, Colby. "Returning to the Sources: Integrating Textual Criticism in the Study of Early Mormon Texts and History." *Intermountain West Journal of Religious Studies* 10, no. 1 (2019).

Townsend, Colby. "Revisiting Joseph Smith and the Availability of the Book of Enoch." *Dialogue: A Journal of Mormon Thought* 53, no. 3 (Fall 2020): 41–71.

Townsend, Colby. *Rewriting Eden with the Book of Mormon: Joseph Smith and the Reception of Genesis 1–6 in Early America.* MA thesis, Utah State University2019.

Townsend, Colby. "Translation as Expansion: The Method of Joseph Smith's Revision of Genesis in Moses 1 and 7." *Journal of Mormon History* 46, no. 4 (October 2020): 45–59.

Wayment, Thomas A. "Joseph Smith, Adam Clarke, and the Making of a Bible Revision." *Journal of Mormon History* 46, no. 3 (July 2020).

Wayment, Thomas A., and Haley Wilson-Lemmon. 2020. *A Recovered Resource: The Use of Adam Clarke's Bible Commentary in Joseph Smith's Bible Translation.* In *Producing Ancient Scripture: Joseph Smith's Translation Projects in the Development of Mormon Christianity,* edited by Michael Hubbard MacKay, Mark Ashurst-McGee, and Brian M. Hauglid, 262–84. Salt Lake City: University of Utah Press) (2020).

Welch, John W. "Chiasmus in the Book of Mormon." *Brigham Young University Studies* 10, no. 1 (1969): 69–84.

Wilson, Luke P. "Joseph Smith's Changing Doctrine of Deity." Institute for Religious Research, August 11, 2011.

Woodworth, Jed L. *Extra-biblical Enoch Texts in Early American Culture.* Archive of Restoration Culture: Summer Fellows' Papers 1997–1999, edited by Richard Lyman. Bushman. Provo, UT: Joseph Fielding Smith Institute for Latter-day Saint History, 2000.

Index

Numbers in **_bold italics_** refer to pages with illustrations

Abel 34, 35, 89, 90, 91, 175
Abraham 8, 10, 11, 19, 46, 94, 103, 108, 124, 126, 150, 180, 186, 187, 189, 192; *see also* Book of Abraham
Abyssinia 47, 49, 51, 99, 207
Adam 31, 34, 35, 36, 40, 44, 46, 50, 53, 61, 89, 90–92, 94, 98, 99, 101–104, 111, 114, 138, 140, 143, 145–158, 168, 184, 203; *see also* Michael
Africa 47, 49, 50
Alexander the Great 11
Alexandria 37
Alma 14, 150
Ancient of Days 4, 53, 66, 120–122, 146, 147, 148, 158, 169, 172
apocalyptic 2, 3, 4, 18, 19, 43, 49, 50, 51, 78, 112, 119–121, 131, 140, 165, 167, 177, 186, 197
Apocrypha 21, 37, 49, 53–55, 57, 59–62, 102, 109, 177, 195, 197–199, 201, 205, 207, 208
apologists 17, 56, 90, 96
archangel 84, 103, 138, 145–149, 158, 164, 165, 203; *see also* Michael
Argos (King) 11
Armstrong, Neil 13, 196
Assyria 12, 125
Athay, R. Grant 8, 195, 209
Azazyel 71, 85, 156, 166

Babylon 12, 53, 125
Behrens, Richard K. 29, 197, 209
Black, Matthew 47, 198
Blake, William **_33_**
Bloom, Harold 23, 33, 197, 198, 205
Bodleian Library 47, 49, 50, 99, 207
Book of Abraham 19, 37, 52, 81, 94, 112, 149, 151, 162–190, 203, 204
Book of Commandments 100, 201

Book of Daniel 43, 49, 53, 120, 203
Book of Jasher 37–43, 61, 143, 198, 205
Book of Jubilees 43–45, 74–79, 81, 82, 198, 200, 208
"Book of Lehi" 3
Book of Mormon 2, 3, 8, 13, 14, 15, 19, 24, 28, 29, 57, 58, 60–62, 90, 93, 98, 99, 113, 124, 126, 128, 129, 184, 195–197, 199–201, 207, 209, 210
Book of Revelation 15, 43, 50, 121, 126, 128, 129, 144, 146, 165–170, 186, 187, 188, 201, 203; *see also* John the Revelator
Bowdoin College 28
Bradshaw, Jeffrey M. 17, 56, 140, 196, 198–200, 202, 209
Brandt, Edward J. 42, 198, 205
Brigham Young University (BYU) 12, 16, 20, 30, 54, 60, 96, 136, 146
Brodie, Fawn M. 205
Bruce, James **_49_**, 50, 99
Bruno, Cheryl L. 137, 195, 200, 202, 209
Buddhism 12
Buerger, David John 132, 202, 209
Burton, Richard Francis 205
Bushman, Richard Lyman 17, 19, 20, 23, 94, 98, 124, 128, 196, 197, 199, 200, 201, 205, 209, 210

Cabbala (cabbalistic) 51, 52, 173, 177
Cain 34, 35, 44, 89–91, 94, 98, 175
Campbell, Alexander 112
Campbellite 113
Cannon, George Q. 31
celestial kingdom 1, 2, 144, 175–179
Celestial room 161, 162
Chaldee 51, 177, 180
Champollion, Jean-Francois 38
chaos 8, 162, 206

211

Index

Charles, Robert H. 49, 195, 205
chiasmus 12, 13, 14, 196, 199, 209, 210
Christianity 125, 144, 198, 201, 205–208, 210
Church of Jesus Christ of Latter-day Saints (LDS Church) 1, 52, 73, 137, 138, 150, 164
Cirillo, Salvatore 199
City of Enoch 43, 45, 46, 128, 131
City of Zion 45, 128, 130, 131, 135, 201; *see also* New Jerusalem
Clark, E. Douglas 74, 75, 78, 200
Clarke, Adam 98, 197, 198, 201, 208, 210
Community of Christ 73, 95; *see also* Reorganized Church of Jesus Christ of Latter-day Saints
consciousness 195, 206
Cooperstown Bible 29, 37, 60, 102, 197, 199, 209
cosmology 4, 5, 19, 20, 29, 163, 188, 201
cosmos 139, 149, 152, 164, 175, 185, 206
Cowdery, Oliver 24, 28, 29, 60, 93, 95, 96–100, 112
creation 8, 19, 34, 44, 45, 53, 56, 74, 77, 81, 86, 94, 98, 114, 122, 138, 139, 140, 146, 149–152, 157, 158, 161, 164, 169, 170, 172, 173, 180, 182, 184, 185, 189

Dahle, Ryan 17, 196, 198, 199, 209
Dartmouth 27–29, 197, 209
David (King) 11, 13, 103, 125, 201
Dead Sea Scrolls 44, 47, 97, 198
Dr. Seuss 14, 208
Doctrine and Covenants (D&C) 1, 15, 25, 31, 60, 62, 98–101, 113, 114, 128, 130, 133, 134, 135, 145, 148, 163, 174, 178, 179, 191, 192, 193, 194, 201, 202

Ecclesiasticus 37, 59, 196
Egbert B. Grandin Book Store 29, 60
Egypt 12, 19, 38, 76, 106, 124, 125, 129, 187
"Egyptomania" 38
Ehrman, Bart. D. 20, 197, 205, 206
Elias 101, 103–108, 111, 179
Elijah 103, 104
Elizabeth 11
endowment 2, 5, 56, 132–145, 148, 149, 152, 156–162, 185, 202, 209; *see also* temple endowment
enlightenment 26, 38, 132, 162, 193, 194
Enos 31, 34, 35, 147, 198
Ensign 16, 96, 150, 197, 202, 203, 209, 210

Erie Canal 29–30
Esdras 37, 59
Ether 128–129
Ethiopia 4, 44, 49, 50
Euseebius 206
Eve 34, 89, 98, 138, 140, 141, 146, 150, 153, 154, 155, 156, 184
Ezekiel 43, 120, 203

First Estate 168
First Vision 2, 63, 69
flood 3, 29, 46, 53, 110, 117, 119, 127, 130, 174, 195
Follett, King 184, 190
Freemasonry 89–91, 137, 159, 195, 200, 202, 206, 209; *see also* Masonic

Garden of Eden 45, 51, 52, 137, 138, 152–157, 176, 177
garments 120, 129, 141, 143–144, 158
Geneva Bible 55, 195, 199, 210
giants 51, 56, 97, 118, 119, 152, 153, 156, 170–172, 203
Givens, Terryl 61, 72, 199, 200, 206
Gleick, James 9, 195, 206
gnostic 143, 187, 207
gospels 13, 14, 18, 20, 21, 36, 49, 50, 71, 90, 103, 104, 119, 120, 167, 172, 187, 192, 193, 203, 206
Graziano, Michael 195, 206
Grease (film) 9
Greek 11, 12, 34, 37, 140, 163, 165
Gregorian calendar 53

Hamlet (play) 57–58
Harris, Martin 3, 29
Hays, Richard 10, 195, 206
Hebrew 34, 35, 37, 38, 42, 44, 47, 50, 51, 97, 98, 103, 125, 140, 165, 172, 177, 187
Hebrew Bible 11, 20, 36, 59, 126, 192, 196, 203
Hebrews 37, 108
Hinduism 12
historical criticism 10, 16
History of the Church 30, 61, 163, 191, 197, 199, 201–204, 206, 208
Hoet, Gerard 36

Illinois, Nauvoo 1, **24**, 38, 63, 73, 96, 131, **133**, 135–138, 159, 184–186, 207
Illustrations of Masonry 91, 200, 202, 203, 207
Inspired Version (Bible) 46, 73, 74, 89, 128, 195, 200, 208

Index

intelligence 18, 19, 21, 27, 30, 68, 150, 163, 164, 169, 186, 175, 188–191, 193, 194
Isaac 10, 38, 46, 103, 108, 124
Isaiah 8, 15, 23, 101, 106, 107, 126, 179, 195, 203
Islam 12, 199
Israel 11, 76, 77, 103, 124, 125, 126, 129, 130, 192

Jackson, Kent P. 30, 196, 197, 199, 209
Jacob 10, 46, 77, 103, 108, 124–126, 128
Jared 31, 34, 35, 44, 78, 102, 119, 143, 147
Jerusalem 3, 19, 38, 49, 77, 125, 126, 129, 130, 161
Jesus 2, 11, 20, 63, 83, 103, 104, 105, 114, 120, 131, 138, 149, 150, 172, 174, 192, 193, 197, 205
John (Gospel) 107, 120, 172, 175, 192–193
John the Baptist 11, 103, 104, 106, 125
John the Revelator 43, 126, 128, 129, 164, 167, 169, 168, 186, 187, 201
Joel 15
Joseph Smith Papers Project 95
Joshua 38, 42, 61, 106, 125, 198
Jude 36, 50, 61, 84, 121, 146, 165, 167, 168, 170
Judea 44
judgment 1, 36, 41, 44, 45, 50, 51, 53, 56, 77, 78, 110, 116, 120, 128, 145, 166, 168, 170, 175
Justinian (Roman emperor) 164

Kennedy, John F. 13
Kimball, Heber C. 137, 202, 209
King Follett Discourse 184, 186, 189, 204
Kingdom of Israel 125
Kingdom of Judah 125
Kirtland Temple 134, 136

Laurence, Richard 17, 18, 20, 32, 39, 47–53, 82, 99, 109, 172, 203
Lehi 3, 4, 126, 129, 130
Liberty Jail 163
light 2, 7–9, 21, 25, 26, 28, 52, 61, 65, 66, 67, 69, 71, 74, 87, 118, 123, 137–139, 145, 149, 150, 152, 153, 155, 158, 163, 164, 172, 179, 182, 183, 185, 191–194, 200
lost 116 pages 3
Louis, King XV of France 50
Luke (Gospel) 11, 14, 21, 36, 103–105, 107, 120, 167, 173, 203

luminaries 53, 68, 87, 164, 173, 176, 179, 182
lunar calendar 53
Luther, Martin 59

Mahijah 95–98, 108
Mahujael 95–98
Mahujah 95–98
Manuscript Found 28
Mark (Gospel) 13, 14, 21, 106, 120, 121, 126, 167
Mary 11, 150
Masonic 89, 90, 91, 113, 137–139, 159; *see also* Freemasonry
Massachusetts 28
Matthew (Gospel) 11, 14, 21, 74, 83, 103, 105, 120, 167, 186, 194, 203
McConkie, Bruce R. 46, 130–131, 134, 198, 202, 207, 209
Mehujael 34, 35, 94–98
Messiah 2, 11, 52, 104, 122, 125, 127, 151, 173, 203
Methuselah 34, 35, 36, 46, 117, 143, 147
Michael 84, 92, 121, 138, 145–150, 158–160, 164–165
Millet, Robert L. 146, 203, 210
Milton, John 164
Moor's Indian Charity School 27, 28, 29
Morgan, William 91, 200, 202, 203, 207
Mormon doctrine 5, 20, 29, 46, 112, 128, 130–131, 139, 144, 149, 150, 178, 198
Mormon studies 16, 21, 24
Mormonism 4, 52, 60, 62, 113, 137, 145, 197
Moroni 69–70

Nauvoo, Illinois 1, 38, 63, 96, 133, 135, 159, 184
Nauvoo Temple *133*, 136, 186
Nelson, Russell M. 202, 210
Nephi 2, 3, 8, 57, 58, 126, 128, 196
Nephilum 2, 170, 203
New Hampshire 27
New Jerusalem 43, 45, 56, 124–131, 135
New Testament 11, 18, 20, 36, 37, 46, 49, 50–51, 57, 59, 61, 74, 84, 103, 106, 112, 119, 121, 126, 128, 135, 144, 146, 160–161, 165, 167, 168, 172, 173, 177, 187, 192
New York 28, 29, 50, 60, 91, 111, 113, 134
New York Star 38
Newman, Nick 25, 210

Index

Nibley, Hugh 16, 17, 96, 97, 196, 200, 201, 207
Nickelsburg, George W.E. 161, 202, 203, 207, 210

Obed 11
O'Driscoll, Jeffrey 27, 197, 207
Ohio, Mentor 113
Ohio, Kirtland 134, 136
Old Testament 11, 12, 14, 31, 33–36, 43, 46, 47, 49, 58, 60, 70, 74, 83, 85, 95, 98, 100, 119, 120, 124, 172
Old Testament Revision 1 (OT1) 95–96, 210
Old Testament Revision 2 (OT2) 95–96, 210
The Outsiders (film) 9
Oxford University 47, 50, 99

Palestine 11, 18, 37, 53, 59
Palmyra, New York 29, 30, 50, 60
parallelism 12, 13, 57
"parallelomania" 17, 196
Park, Benjamin E. 207
pattern recognition 10
patternism 16
patternist historian 16, 96
Patmos, isle of 128–129, 201
Paul (the Apostle) 10, 20, 37, 46, 60, 195, 199
Pearl of Great Price 52, 73, 198
Pennsylvania 29
personages 2, 66, 67, 191
Persuitte, David 197, 207
Peterson, Mark E. 23, 148, 197, 203, 210
Phelps, W.W. 1, 25, 195, 210
pillar 2, 3, 65
Pratt, Parley P. 60–61, 113, 137, 199, 202
preexistence 2, 52, 53, 139, 164, 168, 172–173, 187, 188, 203
Priest, Josiah 58
priesthood 46, 62, 81, 133, 134, 140–141, 146, 147, 150, 157, 179, 185
Promised land 124–126
pseudepigrapha 49, 53, 59, 60, 74, 195

Quinn, D. Michael 20, 197, 201, 207
Qumran 44

Rebekah 10
Reorganized Church of Jesus Christ of Latter-day Saints (RLDS) 73, 95; *see also* Community of Christ Church

Rigdon, Sidney 95, 96, 99, 102, 111–114, 134, 177, 201, 208
Romans 11, 12
Romeo and Juliet (play) 9
Roosevelt, Franklin D. 13
Rosetta Stone 38
Rovelli, Carlo 207
Ruth 11

Salmon, Douglas F. 16, 196
Salt Lake Valley 73, 138
Samson 11
Sarah 10, 150
Sariah 3
Satan 83–85, 138, 156, 164
School of the Prophets 31
sealed books 2, 71
Second Estate 170
secret names 2, 91, 137, 139, 141, 144, 159
secret oaths 89, 91, 92, 139, 159
Sefer Hayasher 42
Seth 31, 34, 35, 44, 89, 90, 94, 147
Shakespeare 14, 15, 55, 57, 58, 196, 205, 210
Smith, Emma 73, 96, 101, 102, 112
Smith, Ethan 28, 29
Smith, Hyrum 27, 29
Smith, Jesse 28
Smith, Joseph Fielding 191
Smith, Joseph III 73
Smith, Lucy Mack 26, 27, 208
Smith, Nathan 28
Smith, Robert F. 24, 196, 197
Snow, Eliza R. 142, 143, 203, 204, 208, 209
Snow, Lorenzo 184, 204, 208
Son of man 1, 2, 49, 52, 53, 56, 66, 83, 119–123, 125, 127, 142, 147, 157, 160, 169, 172, 173, 203
Spain 42
Spaulding, Solomon 28, 29
Spencer, Herbert 195
spirit of Elias 103–104
spirit prison 1, 110, 173–175
stones 2, 42, 43, 71, 85, 144, 180
Stritmatter, Roger A. 199, 210
synoptic gospels 49, 120, 167, 203, 207

Talmage, James E. 164, 165, 203
Taylor, John 30
temple 3, 5, 20, 44, 49, 52, 56, 74, 125, 132–162, 164, 165, 174, 185, 186, 194, 198, 199, 202

Index

temple endowment 5, 132–162, 202, 209
terrestrial kingdom 1, 51, 52, 135, 153, 172, 175–179
theology 4, 14, 19, 20, 29, 136, 141, 162, 172, 183, 184, 186, 188, 191
theophany 74, 79, 134, 158
Times and Seasons 1, 38, 39, 63, 181, 182, 195, 198, 210
Tobit 106–108
Townsend, Colby 97–98, 195, 196, 197, 200, 201, 208, 210
translation projects 19, 20, 29, 31, 32, 93, 126, 184–185, 187, 198
tree of knowledge 2, 40, 51, 132, 135, 146, 152–155, 176, 177
tree of life 2, 51, 52, 176, 177
Twelfth Night (play) 15, 196

University of Vermont 28
Urim and Thummim 71, 144, 180–182

Van Wagoner, Richard S. 201, 208
Vere, Edward de 199, 205, 210
Vermont 28, 29
View of the Hebrews 28, 29
The Vision 1, 2, 177

war in heaven 146, 164, 168, 187
Watchers (Watchmen) 45, 153, 156, 171, 190
Wayment, Thomas A. 54, 57, 60, 197, 201, 208, 210
weeping (wept) 4, 67, 84, 116
Welch, John W. 12, 14, 136, 196, 202, 209, 210
Wellington, Paul A. 200
West Side Story (play) 9
Whitmer, John 95–97, 101, 102, 111, 112, 197, 209
wild man 93, 104–106, 108
Wilson, Luke P. 186, 204, 210
Wilson-Lemmon, Haley 198, 201, 208, 210
Woodworth, Jed L. 17, 63, 196, 199, 209, 210

Yale University 28
Young, Brigham 73, 96, 138

Zeus 11
Zion 19, 31, 43, 45, 46, 62, 77, 114, 115, 122, 124–131, 135, 201
Zionism 19, 112, 113, 135, 194
Zoroaster 12

www.ingramcontent.com/pod-product-compliance
Ingram Content Group UK Ltd.
Pitfield, Milton Keynes, MK11 3LW, UK
UKHW041956140426
5217IPUK00015B/834